THE BIBLICAL MASCULINITY BLUEPRINT

THE BIBLICAL MASCULINITY BLUEPRINT

A CHRISTIAN MAN'S GUIDE TO ATTRACTION, RELATIONSHIPS, AND MARRIAGE IN A MESSED-UP WORLD

Stephen Casper

The Biblical Masculinity Blueprint

Copyright © 2019 by Stephen Casper
All rights reserved.

Published in Houston, Texas by Writer Launch
First Edition

softcover ISBN: 978-1-948252-07-2

RELIGION / Christian Life / Men's Issues

Writer Launch provides assistance to first-time and veteran authors as they navigate the ins and outs of self-publishing. A division of boutique publisher Battle Ground Creative, Writer Launch is based in Space City — Houston, Texas. To learn more about how we partner with authors, please visit www.writerlaunch.today.

Today is the day to leave your mark!

Scripture quotations taken from The New American Standard Bible® (NASB), Copyright © 1960, 1962, 1963, 1968, 1971, 1972, 1973, 1975, 1977, 1996 by The Lockman Foundation. Used by Permission. www.Lockman.org

Concept contributors: Aaron Renn, Dal Rock, Donal Graeme, Henry Stevens, M.N. Fields, Patrick Moore, R.C. McKenzie, Zachary Thomas. Much thanks to these are those who wished to remain anonymous.

Large sections of Chapters 2, 3, and 11 were adapted from an anonymous book and *The Masculinist* with permission.

Managing editor: Jared Stump
Senior editor: Lisa Thompson
Cover design: Corinne Karl
Interior design and typeset: Katherine Lloyd

Printed in the United States of America

CONTENTS

Introduction 1

SECTION 1: THE BIBLE AND CULTURE

Chapter 1: The Bible and Culture 5
    Why the Bible Is in Conflict with Culture 5
    The Battle of Worldviews: Which Frame of Mind Will You Choose? ... 6
    The Cultural Influence on Marriage and the Church 8

Chapter 2: Shifts in Marriage and Society 10
    Shifts in Marriage and Society 10
    Feminism and Women in the Workforce 14
    Top 20 Jobs with the Lowest Percentage of Women 16
    How Men Have Responded to Feminism and Changing Culture ... 19
    Feminism Is the Cause of its Own Problems 22

Chapter 3: The Feminization of the Church 25
    Why Men Hate Going to Church 25
    The Roots of the Feminization of Christianity 26
    The Church Turns Anti-Male Circa 1800 29
    The Church's View of Men Today 30
    Attempted Remedies 33
    Putting It All Together 35

SECTION 2: THE BIBLE ON MARRIAGE

Chapter 4: The Creation of Man, Woman, and Marriage 39
    The Purpose of Marriage: Holiness versus Happiness 39
    Headship Is a Part of God's Design 40
    Authority Is Given to Love 45
    Cultural Blinders on Authority 48

Chapter 5: **Gender Differences and Marital Roles and Responsibilities** 52
   Biblical Marital Roles and Responsibilities 52
   God's Roles and Responsibilities for Marriage are Unconditional 58

Chapter 6: **Marriage is Optional** 60
   Marriage Is Optional per the Bible 60
   Marriage Is the Norm, and the Alternative Is Celibacy 61
   Chastity until Marriage: God's Way Is the Best Way 62
   Avoiding the Pitfalls of Pre-Marital Sexual Temptations 64
   Male and Female Sexual Desire Is not Sinful 66
   Do not Start a Relationship with an Unbeliever 67

SECTION 3: BIBLICAL MASCULINITY

Chapter 7: **What Does it Mean to Be a Man?** 73
   What Does it Mean to Be a Man? 73
   Identity in Christ 75
   Jesus says, "Follow Me" 77
   God and Jesus Lead Perfectly but 80

Chapter 8: **Cultivating Masculine Leadership** 83
   Your New Mission from God 83
   God's Method of Marriage is a Process that Builds on Itself. 84
   You Are the Leader 85
   Understanding leadership 87
   Heart, Soul, and Strength (All-in) 92
   Yes and No (Be Decisive) 94
   You Are not Your Actions, but You Are Your Habits (Be Disciplined) . 95

Chapter 9: **The Orientation of a Man toward a Woman** 97
   Take Women off the Pedestal 97
   Attitudes and Actions. 98
   Suffering Is Normal. 101
   Honor and Love Instead of Respect 105
   Good Intentions Are not Enough for Relationships 107

Chapter 10: **Attraction** 109
   The Bible on Attraction 107

    The Creation of Marriage and its Relation to Attraction 109
    What Men and Women Find Attractive 111
    The Full Context of Attraction and Marriage 115
    Attraction Is a Prerequisite for Romance 117

Chapter 11: **Barriers to Attraction** **122**
    The Infection of Romantic Love via the Paradigm of Godliness
        is Sexy in the Church. 122
    Works and Desire 129
    Soulmates and Infatuation. 131
    The Rise of Obesity 132
    Attractive Jerks versus Unattractive Nice Guys. 133
    The Integration of Your Mission for God and Attraction 136

SECTION 4: THE CULTIVATION PROCESS FROM SINGLENESS TO RELATIONSHIPS TO MARRIAGE

Chapter 12: **A Five-Step Process for Growing in Relationship and Spiritual and Practical Maturity** **145**
    Know what God Says about Relationships: Faith to Moral
        Excellence and Knowledge 146
    Know Your Mission and Goals: Knowledge to Self-Control,
        Perseverance, and Godliness in Your Life. 148
    Know Your Standards for Women: Determine the Self-control,
        Perseverance, and Godliness of the Woman You Want to Marry . . . 149
    Know Your Boundaries in a Relationship: Transform Your Godliness
        into Brotherly Kindness and Love. 152
    Know how to Assertively Communicate: Show You Can Love
        Effectively. 156
    Five Steps: A Summary 158

Chapter 13: **Expectation Pitfalls to Relationships** **160**
    The Church, Marriage, and Social Scripts 160
    It just Happens vs. College Analogy. 162
    Managing Expectations. 164
    Masculine Immaturity Is Placing Responsibilities before Roles. 167
    Christian Values and Selectiveness 168

Chapter 14: **Managing a Healthy Relationship** **170**
    Moneyball for Marriage: Statistics for Vetting to Avoid Divorce 170
    Questions to Ask a Prospective Wife 179
    Standard Christian Questions 179
    Standard Marriage Questions 180
    Questions that Require Deep Thought 182
    Other Personality Questions and Your Preferences 184
    Teachable 184
    Games Don't Matter when You Have the Right Frame 186
    Count the Cost and Do not Fear 187

Chapter 15: **Finding and Choosing a Wife: A Prospective Timeline** **190**
    1. Pre-introductory Phase 190
    2. Introductory Phase (Asking Out) 193
    3. Transitional Phase (Dating) 196
    4. Intentional Relationship Phase (Courtship) 199
    5. Engagement 203
    6. Marriage 204

SECTION 5: LEADING A MARRIAGE

Chapter 16: **Identify and Understand Your Responsibilities** **209**
    Orient Yourself to Always Honor God First 209
    Temptations (Men and Women) 210
    Learn how to Love Yourself 219

Chapter 17: **Understand Dysfunctional Patterns** **222**
    The Five Main Dysfunctional Patterns of Marriage 222
    Other Areas of Dysfunction 228

Chapter 18: **Understanding the Christian Approach to Influence and Solving Marital Issues** **229**
    The First Three Months: Lead by Example 230
    The Next Three Months: Start to Address Scriptural Issues 233
    A Year and Beyond: Continue to Be Persistent and Kind and Stand Strong 237
    Divorce and Separation 240

  Do not Enable and Avoid Manipulation 241
  Duty Sex. 242
Chapter 19: **Common Pitfalls to Marital Headship**. 244
  Master Yourself so that You Aren't Manipulated. 244
  Some Needs Can only Be Met by God. 245
  Attraction and Sex in Marriage 246
  Repentance is Important for Sanctification 251
  Demand Obedience but Accept the Process 252

Chapter 20: **Common Pitfalls to Marital Interactions**. 254
  You're not Responsible for Your Wife's Emotions 254
  Women Think and Feel Differently than Men and Have Different
   Needs than Men Do. 255
  Marriage Counseling Can Work but Can Fail. 257
  Avoid Covert Contracts 259
  Should Wives/Mothers Work Outside the Home? 260
  Do Your Job and Go Above and Beyond 261

Conclusion. 263
Notes 265
About the Author. 273

INTRODUCTION

I wrote this book because I have witnessed a deficiency in the teaching and discipling of men in today's church, especially when it comes to relationships and marriage.

Here are some of the ways this has manifested:

- There has been a lack of teaching passed down from fathers to sons.
- Men are not being discipled, except in small pockets.
- What little teaching we have from the church has assimilated many aspects of the culture
- Culture heavily influences our relationships and marriages when we don't hear from the church on many different topics

This book is written for single and married Christian men to disciple them in godly relationships and marriages. Part of discipling is identifying areas of deficiency, such as cultural and incorrect church influence on our relationships and marriage. Another part of discipling is giving single and married Christian men a biblical blueprint for how to handle conflict and problem scenarios that they might encounter in relationships and marriage. Finally, and most importantly, Christians must stand on God's Word as it is very relevant to our walk with Christ.

The Bible itself is not political in nature. It is about the gospel of Jesus Christ, which tells us we are all sinners in need of a Savior. We acknowledge our sin, repent, follow the teachings of Jesus, and the Holy Spirit begins to transform us from the inside out. This is the Gospel; however, different political stances may aim to implement laws that force people to act in certain ways. Taking different political positions may impair our witness for Christ, as forcing morality on others does not work. Rather, God uses the gospel and our inward-to-outward change to influence the hearts of those around us.

Thus, it is important to understand that this book does not take any "left" or "right" political positions. It is too easy to get caught up into pigeon-holing Christians into certain camps, when our loyalty should be first and foremost to Christ and Christ alone. Rather, this book aims to refute worldly, unbiblical positions. It will critique both conservative and liberal positions that are not of Christ. It will critique Pharisaical positions in the Church, as well as areas in which the Church has fallen to "cheap grace." It will also look at areas where the Church has diverted (either knowingly or unknowingly) away from sound doctrine.

This book is divided into five different sections. The first section highlights many of the problem areas where our culture has influenced the Church. The second section builds a foundation of what the Bible has to say on relationships and marriage, which all Christians, both married and single, should know. It is sad that many Christians enter into marriage without knowing what God has to say about relationships and marriage.

The third section covers material on biblical masculinity, which will destroy many of the cultural and incorrect "Christian" notions of relationship, marriage, and how to be a man. The fourth section speaks to the process of growth required for the single Christian man to progress from singleness to a relationship to marriage. Finally, the fifth section covers leading a marriage according to God's marital guidelines and responsibilities. It elucidates many of the temptations and pitfalls that the husband might encounter with himself as well as with his wife. It also teaches a process to help fix dysfunctional marriage patterns and how to grow in godliness.

SECTION ONE
THE BIBLE AND CULTURE

Chapter 1
THE BIBLE AND CULTURE

WHY THE BIBLE IS IN CONFLICT WITH CULTURE

For any Christian, this is one of the first questions you will have to wrestle with when taking your faith seriously.

As Christians, we live our life with a compilation of scriptures that are thousands of years old as our guide. Some people would (and do) call that crazy. They say the Bible was written for a different people in a different time. They say it's been translated so many times that nobody knows for sure what it even says. They say the Bible is open to individual interpretation and can mean something different to everybody.

Several simple points dismantle these arguments if we believe that the Bible is from God:

- God is eternal. His character and nature do not change. Therefore, His plan for us is unchanging though He has revealed different facets of it through time: from the fall to the old covenant to the new covenant in Jesus. His Word is trustworthy for all peoples and all times.
- If we cannot trust that the Word God sent us to tell us about Him is truth, then why would we live according to what God says? Why shouldn't we just live the way we want?
- If we believe that the Bible is only culturally relevant, then any part of the Bible can be rationalized as only a part of the culture of the time. This is no different than moral relativism.

These questions allude to what is known as cafeteria Christianity. A Christian can go down the cafeteria line and pick and choose—from the

Bible—what they want to eat. Don't like that food? You can ignore it. Like a different food? Pile it up on your plate. Living according to such a morally relative lifestyle is no different than declaring yourself your own god instead of believing in God and following the example of Jesus Christ.

> This is My commandment, that you love one another, just as I have loved you. Greater love has no one than this, that one lay down his life for his friends. You are My friends if you do what I command you. No longer do I call you slaves, for the slave does not know what his master is doing; but I have called you friends, for all things that I have heard from My Father I have made known to you. You did not choose Me but I chose you, and appointed you that you would go and bear fruit, and that your fruit would remain, so that whatever you ask of the Father in My name He may give to you. This I command you, that you love one another (John 15:12–17).

This is Jesus's call to obedience to us as Christians. We lay down our desires to follow Jesus and His commands. We might have to lay down our families and friends to choose Christ. We even lay down what culture tells us. We take up our cross and follow Jesus. This concept is the crux of understanding the rest of this book. If you believe that God's Word is only culturally relevant and not relevant for all time, then you might find the points made in the rest of this book hard to understand.

THE BATTLE OF WORLDVIEWS: WHICH FRAME OF MIND WILL YOU CHOOSE?

Frame of mind refers to God's perspective or the world's perspective. None of us are immune to the culture around us. We were born into it, and we have inherited a fallen nature from original sin. Our thoughts, feelings, and experiences are influenced by our fallen nature and the culture around us, but we have been given free will by God as new creations in Christ. We have the choice to accept the frame of what the world tells us or accept what God and the scriptures tell us. In other words, the question you must always ask yourself is whose world view you will believe.

The Bible is clear that we are not supposed to be conformed to this world but instead to God.

> Therefore I urge you, brethren, by the mercies of God, to present your bodies a living and holy sacrifice, acceptable to God, which is your spiritual service of worship. And do not be conformed to this world, but be transformed by the renewing of your mind, so that you may prove what the will of God is, that which is good and acceptable and perfect (Romans 12:1–2).

Our Creator knows a thing or two about men and women. He made us. He created human nature, and He saw it go astray when Adam and Eve sinned. He also gave us the Bible as a guide to understand His plan and show us how our human nature goes haywire. He knows what works and what doesn't. And He's given us some clear instructions if only we would take them seriously.

We will be approaching scripture with the assumption that it says what it means. That might sound obvious, but you'd be surprised at how our modern discomfort with some passages causes us to try to rationalize them away or simply ignore them altogether. We live in a time in which the highest moral good is equality, non-discrimination, anti-racist, and non-offensiveness. The scriptures highlighted might offend your sensibilities. We only ask that you judge the message on its own merits with a great deal of prayer and Bible study. Don't focus on whether it's offensive to modern sensibilities. Rather ask yourself if it might be *true*.

Compounding this issue is the fact that Christians today aren't reading or understanding the scriptures well, which makes them immature Christians.

> And I, brethren, could not speak to you as to spiritual men, but as to men of flesh, as to infants in Christ. I gave you milk to drink, not solid food; for you were not yet able to receive it. Indeed, even now you are not yet able, for you are still fleshly. For since there is jealousy and strife among you, are you not fleshly, and are you not walking like mere men? (1 Corinthians 3:1–3).

> Concerning him we have much to say, and it is hard to explain, since you have become dull of hearing. For though by this time you ought to be teachers, you have need again for someone to teach you the elementary principles of the oracles of God, and you have come

to need milk and not solid food. For everyone who partakes only of milk is not accustomed to the word of righteousness, for he is an infant. But solid food is for the mature, who because of practice have their senses trained to discern good and evil (Hebrews 5:11–14).

We will examine what the scriptures say about relationships in plain text. This is akin to separating ourselves from all that we think was right and examining the truth of God with a new perspective. This is the milk of the scriptures about male and female interaction and relationships. Such scripture is powerful to equip us to be godly mature Christians.

All Scripture is inspired by God and profitable for teaching, for reproof, for correction, for training in righteousness; so that the man of God may be adequate, equipped for every good work (2 Timothy 3:16–17).

Instead of trusting what the world says about men and women, why not trust our Creator? Our goal as Christians is to always try to set aside our culture and our own biases and understand and follow God.

THE CULTURAL INFLUENCE ON MARRIAGE AND THE CHURCH

According to Gallup polls in 2008 and 2014, 80 percent and 75 percent of those in the United States consider themselves Christians.[1] However, as any Christian living in this nation can tell you, the vast majority of people's lifestyles are inconsistent with their profession of faith.

This is no mistake. Even the early Christian church struggled with this, which was why the New Testament epistles were written. The new Christian converts in Judea, Asia Minor, and the rest of the world were blending their culture with their new-found faith in Christ. The gospels were written so that the new believers would know the gospel of Jesus. Paul, Peter, James, and other disciples wrote letters to the various churches to persuade and correct them from the cultural influences that were negatively influencing their faith. Like the early church, we all have various cultural blinders that influence us away from God and the Bible. Recognizing these blinders can be difficult.

One other common fallacy when it comes to marriage is the concept of so-called progress. This is the notion that what we have learned in the past was old and outdated but what we know now is better. This concept of progressivism is common in the realm of politics and society, and many Christians often do not realize that they have been influenced by it in their Christian walk.

Unfortunately, many of these cultural concepts of progress, such as feminism, equality, and other notions of so-called higher good have crept into the church and marriage in insidious ways. Church services and attendance have become increasingly feminine. Husbands and fathers are held in contempt and disrespecting them is common in the media, the pulpit, and even Christian films. Headship and submission have become taboo topics to discuss or outright rejected. Marriages have become increasingly unhappy, divorces more common, and marital sex has plummeted. Single Christian men and women have difficulty navigating the changing landscape of relationships and marriage.

We will explore these problems, starting with how society has changed and its influence on the church.

Chapter 2
SHIFTS IN MARRIAGE AND SOCIETY

SHIFTS IN MARRIAGE AND SOCIETY

Marriage in civilization (natural marriage) has always been secularized as opposed to sacramental marriage in the church. But in the past hundred years, society has begun to turn its back on marriages that emulate God's design: husband-led marriages. Culture has adopted a progressive ideology that is at odds with God's design. This progressive ideology asserts that there are no fundamental differences between men and women, and therefore gender roles ought to be abolished.

> [Non-gendered socialization] holds that gender has no normative importance of any kind. On this view, the psychological-social aspects of gender are nothing more than arbitrary social constructs, yet they have become infused with normative importance and have been used to promote unjust ends—most tellingly, the subordination of women.
>
> Recognizing this arbitrariness, this view holds that we should do away with the notion that the norms associated with gender generate any demands for maintenance, loyalty, or uptake of any kind. The very notion of gender differences is to be abolished. Some humans have different organs than others, but that is as far as the matter ought to go.[1]

Their goal, whether conscious or subconscious, is complete destruction of God's design for marriage. As the rebellion grows, the brokenness and hurt increases.

Men and women today are constantly bombarded with mixed messages—some from the old order and some from the new. In the case of a military draft, for example, a young man will be expected to enlist while his female peers won't be. Yet he'll be told that holding a door for a woman or offering to carry something heavy for her are sexist actions because they reinforce gender stereotypes that paint women as the weaker sex.

> University of Florida researchers examined benevolent sexism among nearly 400 college-aged men and women. Unlike the kinds of overt gender discrimination most women would blanch at, benevolent sexism can actually seem quite benign. In essence, it's the idea that "women are wonderful, but weak," says lead study author Kathleen Connelly, PhD, a professor in the department of psychology at the University of Florida. "Benevolent sexism shows up all the time, in this attitude that women are warmer and kinder than men, but at the same time weaker and [needing] to be cared for."[2]

Women, on the other hand, are told that they can do anything a man can do. Yet they have their own sports leagues and receive a head start during marathon races because, when they have to compete physically with men on a level playing field, most of them simply can't keep up.[3]

> [In a recent study], the British Defense Ministry conducted an extensive two-year assessment of women and their ability to perform routine ground combat tasks, such as lifting and carrying gear over certain distances . . . The study concluded that only 0.1 percent of female applicants and 1 percent of trained female soldiers "would reach the required standards to meet the demands of these roles. . . . No training system can close this gap," he said. "The reason men and women cannot truly be trained together is not a matter of attitude. It is physical."[4]

These and other contradictions between marriages previously based on God's design and our progressive culture make finding your place in today's world a challenging prospect for both men and women. Some other contradictions that destroy relationships are:

- Love in marriage is based on feelings and romance instead of choosing to act righteously toward your spouse.
- Respect is earned.
- Men and women are the same except for what's between their legs.
- Marriage should not be permanent.
- Divorce is not a big deal.
- Two moms or two fathers are the same as a father and mother.
- Follow your heart.

But the challenges an individual might face in his or her personal life pale in comparison to the larger implications of this tectonic shift in our civilization's foundation. Progressives have ushered in a host of new ideas about how society ought to be structured. Leading this charge against the old social order was the feminist movement. The main thrust of feminism centered on the idea that men and women should be treated as equals in every respect. The Oxford Dictionary defines feminism as " . . . The advocacy of women's rights on the grounds of political, social, and economic equality to men."[5]

This movement has led to a profound disconnect between marriage and society itself. For, it was reasoned, if women and men were indeed interchangeable, then men had nothing to offer women that they didn't already possess. There is no better summary of this mindset than the assertion popularized by feminist Gloria Steinem, that "a woman needs a man like a fish needs a bicycle."

> A societal contract previously existed between the genders that stated that men as a group would always protect women as a group. This premise dictates that a woman without a man of her own, either temporarily or permanently, can procure assistance from a nearby man without any prior relationship existing between them or any expectation of reciprocation. *The Daily Republic* states, "Real men physically protect women. And our society should back them up on it. . . . In a civilized society, men protect and care for women and children. And women should learn to expect that from a good man. When that equation breaks down, trouble ensues."[6]

Society expects every man to be prepared to risk life and limb to protect any woman, even one he doesn't know, at a moment's notice. A man who protects a woman from harm is hailed as a hero while a man who chooses not to get involved is seen as a coward.

A well-worn but fantastic example of this premise in action occurred during the sinking of the Titanic in 1912. The men onboard knew there weren't enough lifeboats for everyone, yet they willingly remained on a sinking ship to allow the women and children a chance to escape an icy death.

> John Jacob Astor, reputedly the richest man of his day, is said to have fought his way to a boat, put his wife in it and then stepped back and waved her goodbye. Benjamin Guggenheim similarly refused to take a seat, saying: "Tell my wife . . . I played the game out straight and to the end. No woman shall be left aboard this ship because Ben Guggenheim was a coward."
>
> In other words, some of the most powerful men in the world adhered to an unwritten code of honor – even though it meant certain death for them.[7]

The actions of these men were considered proper by everyone involved and by society in general. Even the suffragettes, early feminists, believed that men had an obligation to put the safety of women ahead of their own.

> English Suffragettes of prominence, when questioned as to what they thought of the men who died on the Titanic in order that women might be saved, seem to have manifested a disposition, possibly significant, almost to resent the inquirer's obvious belief that the display of chivalry was magnificent.
>
> While the strenuous ladies did not deny that the behavior of the men was rather fine, they hinted that after all it only fulfilled a plain duty and therefore had not earned any particularly enthusiastic praise.[8]

The men on the Titanic did what they did because it was understood that women were weaker than men and were therefore in need of protection. Men, on the other hand, were generally expected to take care of themselves and act according to a code of honor. But if women are to be viewed as equal in every way to men, then this part of the contract no longer applies. To demand total equality is to renounce the clause in the contract that grants special privileges to women based on a presumption of weakness.

Despite our modern society's insistence that women should be treated no differently than men, the notion persists that men should selflessly put women they don't even know ahead of themselves during times of crisis.

> One of the features of the [Costa Concordia, 2012] disaster that has provoked a great deal of comment is the stream of reports from angry survivors of how, in the chaos, men refused to put women and children first, and instead pushed themselves forward to escape.[9]

But you simply can't have it both ways. This is a binary question with only two possible answers: either women are weaker than men and need their protection, or they are equally capable and do not.

The current cultural directive is that women are just as capable as men; therefore men are responding by letting women fend for themselves. To blame men for looking out for their own interests when they have been taught that women don't want or need their help is not only counter-productive, it's unbiblical as well.

To put it plainly, in a world where bicycles are no longer desired, none will be produced. It's simple supply and demand. Women are, by their words and actions, saying that they are fish who no longer need bicycles and are therefore creating for themselves a world without them.

Should a woman ever find herself wishing she had a bicycle, she must keep in mind that the reason she doesn't have one is that women collectively insisted they didn't need one.

FEMINISM AND WOMEN IN THE WORKFORCE

In addition to their role as society's protectors, we've also seen that men have traditionally been expected to be providers. The division of labor baked into the institution of marriage made it possible for men to make the most of this role by allowing them to focus their efforts on building and maintaining an advanced civilization.

But as civilization progressed and many of the jobs became less difficult and more interesting, some women began to envy the male provider role. They considered careers to be exciting and rewarding while they saw housework as nothing more than mindless drudgery.

Feminists began insisting that the role of stay-at-home mom was not noble and fulfilling but rather oppressive and stifling:

> American housewives have not had their brains shot away, nor are they schizophrenic in the clinical sense. But if . . . the fundamental human drive is not the urge for pleasure or the satisfaction of biological needs, but the need to grow and to realize one's full potential, their comfortable, empty, purposeless days are indeed cause for a nameless terror.
> - Betty Friedan[10]

It must be pointed out here that there have always been some women in the workforce. The concept of working women in general didn't come about because of feminism. Rather feminism changed the culture's view of working women by encouraging wives and mothers to seek careers of their own to maximize their autonomy and realize their potential. Ironically, the concept of wives as the main caretakers of the children and the home is invaluable to their husbands and especially to God. By pushing women to pursue careers and ultimately money—which is valuable in the eyes of the world—women have been prostituting themselves for money much like those who trade sex for money.

Prior to feminism, most women who worked outside the home did so only out of necessity or desire. By pushing women into the workforce *en masse*, feminism altered the structure of our civilization in some fundamental ways.

One of the primary effects of this sudden increase in laborers was a shortage of good jobs. These women wanted to join the workforce because they desired respect and fulfillment, but you don't get either of those from being a plumber. On top of that, women simply aren't as good at jobs that require upper body strength or great physical exertion. Therefore we had an influx of women heading straight for the cleanest, most comfortable, and highest paying middle-class jobs on the market.

> Women are beginning to pour into management and professional occupations that require more education and offer higher pay and status. In fact, women are now dominating some of the jobs that used to belong to men, according to the Department of Labor's Women's Bureau.[11]

This has resulted in a large group of men who've lost access to many of the better jobs because there simply aren't enough of them to go around. The only jobs women are leaving many of these men are the dirty, difficult, and low-status jobs that women either can't or don't want to do themselves.

TOP 20 JOBS WITH THE LOWEST PERCENTAGE OF WOMEN[12]

1. Boilermakers
2. Drillers of earth
3. Concrete and cement workers
4. Drillers of oil wells
5. Roofers and slaters
6. Bus, truck and stationary engine mechanics
7. Heating, air conditioning and refrigeration mechanics
8. Heavy equipment and farm equipment mechanics
9. Plumbers, pipe fitters and steamfitters
10. Plasterers
11. Elevator installers and repairers
12. Masons, tilers and carpet installers
13. Operating engineers of construction equipment
14. Automobile mechanics
15. Carpenters
16. Excavating and loading machine operators
17. Forge and hammer operators
18. Other mining occupations
19. Structural metal workers
20. Electric power installers and repairers

Recent analyses show that, in most large cities across the United States, young women are now earning more money than their male peers:

> According to a new analysis of 2,000 communities by a market research company, in 147 out of 150 of the biggest cities in the U.S., the median full-time salaries of young women are 8% higher than those of the guys in their peer group. In two cities, Atlanta and Memphis, those women are making about 20% more. . . . But the new study suggests that the gap is bigger than previously thought, with young women in New York City, Los Angeles and San Diego making 17%, 12% and 15% more than their male peers, respectively. And it also holds true even in reasonably small areas like the Raleigh-Durham region and Charlotte in North Carolina (both 14% more), and Jacksonville, Fla. (6%).[13]

Despite their success in the workforce, women as a group have become less happy than they were before feminism.

> The study, The Paradox of Declining Female Happiness, said the same was true for women of different ages and whether or not they were married or had children. It said the results appeared surprising given that modern women had been liberated from their traditional 1950s role of housewife. Instead, their earning power has soared, women are doing better than men in education and they are in control of decisions over whether to start a family. The findings were released as Sir Stuart Rose, chairman of Marks & Spencer, claimed that women 'have never had it so good.'[14]

Additionally, recent surveys show that the vast majority of working mothers would prefer to be at home raising their children rather than helping support the family financially.

> According to a new partnered survey cosponsored by ForbesWoman and TheBump.com, a growing number of women see staying home to raise children (while a partner provides financial support) to be the ideal circumstances of motherhood. Forget the corporate climb; these young mothers have another definition of success: setting work aside to stay home with the kids. . . .
>
> It's true: according to our survey, 84% of working women told ForbesWoman and TheBump that staying home to raise children is a financial luxury they aspire to. What's more, more than one in three resent their partner for not earning enough to make that dream a reality.[15]

What an appalling indictment of feminism! The very social movement that was supposed to liberate women from oppression has forced most of them to live a lifestyle they wouldn't otherwise have chosen for themselves.

One of the newest and biggest studies in 2018 of women across thirty European countries—in countries where gender equality has supposedly been achieved—demonstrated that homemakers are happier than full-time workers.[16] This was contrary to the expectations of the researchers and was particularly prominent among mothers who had "left high quality employment." The study showed a unanimous positive result for homemaking across all twelve measures of happiness and satisfaction over working full-time.

Sadly these outcomes were not accidental but deliberate. Many radical feminists believe that traditional motherhood should be banned outright for the mothers' own good. For example, Simone de Beauvoir, a prominent French feminist also known for her long-term relationship with philosopher Jean-Paul Sartre, stated, "No woman should be authorized to stay home to raise her children. Society should be totally different. Women should not have that choice precisely because if there is such a choice, too many women would make that one."

Women are pushed to have it all because they thought it would bring them happiness but have found out that having it all does not actually bring happiness. In fact, the slew of responsibilities from trying to have it all burdens women with expectations that they can't meet and stresses and depresses them.

But the disruption to our culture didn't end here. In addition to pushing women into the workforce, feminists also insisted that women should be free and even encouraged to have socially-approved sex outside of marriage. In fact, Gloria Steinem said, "A liberated woman is one who has sex before marriage and a job after."[17]

The sexual revolution ushered in sweeping changes to the way our culture views sex:

> By the 1960s, the conviction that sexual expression was healthy and good—the more of it, the better—and that sexual desire was intrinsic to one's personal identity culminated in the sexual revolution, the animating spirit of which held that freedom and authenticity were to be found not in sexual withholding but in sexual expression and assertion.[18]

This new approach to sex has led more and more empowered young women to choose short-term flings over long-term relationships:

> Single young women in their sexual prime—that is, their 20s and early 30s . . . are for the first time in history more successful, on average, than the single young men around them. They are more likely

to have a college degree and, in aggregate, they make more money. What makes this remarkable development possible is . . . the ability to delay marriage and have temporary relationships that don't derail education or career. To put it crudely, feminist progress right now largely depends on the existence of the hookup culture.

And to a surprising degree, it is women—not men—who are perpetuating the culture, especially in school, cannily manipulating it to make space for their success, always keeping their own ends in mind. For college girls these days, an overly serious suitor fills the same role an accidental pregnancy did in the 19th century: a danger to be avoided at all costs, lest it get in the way of a promising future.[19]

The hook-up culture seems to offer modern women the best of both worlds—casual sex now and marriage later. But these actions rest on the assumption that men will always be standing by, ready to fulfill their traditional roles as male protector and provider when the women decide they are ready for a serious relationship.

HOW MEN HAVE RESPONDED TO FEMINISM AND CHANGING CULTURE

What many of these women are discovering, however, is that a growing number of men are no longer following the script.

We took for granted that we'd spend our 20s finding ourselves, whatever that meant, and save marriage for after we'd finished graduate school and launched our careers, which of course would happen at the magical age of 30. . . . That we would marry, and that there would always be men we wanted to marry, we took on faith. . . .

But what transpired next lay well beyond the powers of everybody's imagination: as women have climbed ever higher, men have been falling behind. We've arrived at the top of the staircase, finally ready to start our lives, only to discover a cavernous room at the tail end of a party, most of the men gone already, some having never shown up.[20]

What nobody stopped to consider was that modifications to our societal contract do not take place in a vacuum. A change that effectively rewards men and women who are seeking casual sex while penalizing men and women who are seeking marriage will produce more men and women who are focused on the short-term rather than the long-term.

To put it bluntly, incentives matter. Author Helen Smith notes many different areas where the incentives are stacked against men:

- You'll lose respect – the media and society consistently present husbands and fathers as buffoons who can't get anything.
- You'll lose out on sex – married men have more sex than singles but less than those who cohabitate.
- You'll lose friends – Both spouses lose friends when married, but it generally affects men's self-esteem more, perhaps because they're less social.
- You'll lose space – the dreaded relegation to the man cave, as your wife takes over the house.
- You could lose your kids and your money – divorce and child support.
- You'll lose in court – men often complain that the court legal system is stacked against them in child support and alimony.
- You'll lose your freedom – if you can't afford child support you'll be jailed.
- Single life is better than ever – singles are no longer passed over for promotions to family men. Sex is available outside of marriage. No conflicting family responsibilities with your own priorities.[21]

By incentivizing men to focus on short-term happiness through easy sexual access, we have unwittingly raised a generation of men who have no reason to work hard in life. As a result, young men seem to have begun to shirk their societal duties. Rather than putting their shoulders to the plow, many men are working just hard enough to get by while filling their free time with pursuits of leisure and fun, which plays into the feminist's thrust to eradicate men from positions of power.

> The statistic . . . that perhaps struck me the most is that teenage boys, ages 12-to-17 years old, actually spend less time playing video games than 18-to-34-year-old men. I can understand the desire to play a video game here and there as a kid, but as an adult? Grow up.

These men should be studying in college, getting a job, and contributing to society through the workforce and family. How in the world do they have time to play video games for hours? The answer is that they just don't ever grow up.²²

Jordan Peterson echoes this in his retelling of Peter Pan in the tragic story of the man-child. Peter has been influenced by his surroundings so that he doesn't want to grow up. Peterson describes the poor adult male role models, such as:

- Captain Hook (disrespected men and lack of father figures).
- Peter's escape of the real world to be king of the lost boys (who won't grow up).
- His interaction with imaginary fairy Tinkerbell (porn).
- Some element of sacrifice that happens as you mature, whether or not you like it.²³

This hits you smack dab in the face by your thirties or forties, if not sooner. Peterson resonates very much with the boys and young men of today because he fills a similar role to that of the father that you've never had who is teaching you about the world and how to mature in it.

It's easy to point the finger at these men and complain that they are just being lazy; however, this will ultimately get us nowhere. Why? Because the societal contract has been breached.

> In contract law, a material breach of contract is a breach (a failure to perform the contract) that strikes so deeply at the heart of the contract that it renders the agreement "irreparably broken" and defeats the purpose of making the contract in the first place. The breach must go to the very root of the agreement between the parties. If there is a material breach (sometimes referred to as a "total" breach), the other party can simply end the agreement.²⁴

The traditional male roles of provider and protector hinged on the idea that women needed to be provided for and protected. Since our modern progressive society insists that women today are perfectly capable of doing both for themselves, the contract is in breach and no longer binding.

In many cases, modern men are still choosing to embrace a traditional masculine identity and the associated responsibilities. In others, however, they are choosing to start to eschew marriage completely because they believe it is a bad deal. Even if they were to get married, a woman can divorce them at any time and take half of everything and the kids. It's not worth it to them.

FEMINISM IS THE CAUSE OF ITS OWN PROBLEMS

One of the main tenets of feminism is that patriarchy and toxic masculinity are to blame for the problems in the culture. Let's follow the logic.

Feminists want to free women and wives from the oppression of men and their husbands under the guise of equality. They introduced many different concepts into culture, such as the following:

- No-fault divorces
- Sexual freedom
- Pushing women into the work force
- Pushing women into education

It should come as no surprise that after the introduction of these things into mainstream culture, divorces increased; sex out of wedlock became much more normalized; and women started pursuing education and careers en masse. This has consequences.[25]

- Divorce rates skyrocketed up to the commonly cited 40-50 percent of marriages today, which leads to increased poverty and single motherhood.[26]
- Abortion, contraceptives, decline of shotgun weddings, and lack of stigma leads to increased single motherhood and a cyclical increase in abortion.[27]
- Marriage rates dropped and have continued to drop, pushing up the age of marriage from the low twenties to close to twenty-eight and thirty for women and men respectively today.[28]

The most common reasons given for abortions are related to money, education, work, and the lack of wanting to care for others.

The reasons patients gave for having an abortion underscored their understanding of the responsibilities of parenthood and family life.

The three most common reasons—each cited by three-fourths of patients—were concern for or responsibility to other individuals; the inability to afford raising a child; and the belief that having a baby would interfere with work, school or the ability to care for dependents. Half said they did not want to be a single parent or were having problems with their husband or partner.[29]

The destruction of marriages and out-of-wedlock birth rates are much more understated since the wife is usually given custody of the children in a divorce. The fatherlessness statistics are quite stark.[30]

- 63 percent of youth suicides are from fatherless homes—five times the average.
- 90 percent of all homeless and runaway children are from fatherless homes—thirty-two times the average.
- 85 percent of all children who show behavioral disorders come from fatherless homes—twenty times the average.
- 80 percent of rapists with anger problems come from fatherless homes—fourteen times the average.
- 71 percent of all high school dropouts come from fatherless homes—nine times the average.
- 75 percent of all adolescent patients in chemical abuse centers come from fatherless homes.
- 85 percent of all youths in prison come from fatherless homes.
- Almost every mass shooter had no father or no parents in their home.[31]

As you can see from these statistics, most of the societal problems with teens today—suicide, homelessness, substance abuse, and more—have been caused by feminism, and in many cases, the church has been complicit with going along with the culture. For instance, the pro-life stance suffers because abortions are mainly occurring to impoverished families, divorced families, single mothers, and women who have had sex out of wedlock. If the church is serious about being pro-life, they might need to take a harder stance against the normalization of divorce, sex out of wedlock, and single motherhood.

Overall, feminism has obtained equality for women but has made them more unhappy because they are pushed away from God's design. Feminism also creates unsafe and toxic men while trying to pass off these toxic men as the fault of the patriarchy. Stable families led by fathers raised responsible, masculine men. Boys without mature masculine direction default to extremely destructive tendencies. What we need isn't less masculinity but more masculinity.

Chapter 3
THE FEMINIZATION OF THE CHURCH

WHY MEN HATE GOING TO CHURCH

Even a cursory look around the sanctuary on Sunday morning will show that far more women attend church than men. In 2004, David Murrow wrote a book about this called *Why Men Hate Going to Church*, in which he surveyed the contemporary scene. His findings made for depressing reading.

> Women comprise more than 60 percent of the typical adult congregation on any given Sunday. At least one-fifth of married women regularly worship without their husbands. There are quite a few single women but hardly any single men in church today. Every day it gets harder for single Christian women to find men for romance or marriage.[1]

Murrow points out that this heavy female skew is unique to Christianity. Other religions, such as Islam and Judaism, do not show this effect. The active practice of Islam and Judaism appear to be primarily male-driven, with many male-only rituals with wide participation. This divide is particularly acute in the black community. Morrow notes, "The African-American community faces the prospect of separate religions for each gender: Christianity for women, Islam for men."[2] Something specific to Christianity or Christian practice today does not attract—or even actively repels—men.

Murrow's thesis is that Christianity became stylistically feminized to cater to a female audience. In effect, it targeted a segment of female customers, then branded and marketed itself accordingly. For example, he cites the love-songs-to-Jesus style—"the greatest of all romance," as one Hillsong tune puts it—that dominates contemporary Christian worship music. But beyond Sunday morning service, the entire infrastructure of Christian culture targets women:

> Women are more likely than men to shop at a Christian bookstore, watch a Christian TV station, or listen to Christian music. Christian retailers and media executives know this. They market and sell their products accordingly. In every Christian bookstore in America the women's section is bigger than the men's section-usually three to four times bigger. . . . Christian AC radio (the format playing on most contemporary Christian music stations today) draws an audience that's 63 percent female and 37 percent male. Christian stations garner, on average, 21 percent more women listeners than mainstream stations. . . . K-Love, America's largest syndicated Christian music radio service, with affiliates in 189 cities and towns, targets its programming at eighteen- to forty-five-year-old women.[3]

Murrow implies this has bled into theology as he created two columns of characteristics and asked people which one best represented Christ. These weren't biblical lists but were instead compilations of masculine and feminine traits taken from the book *Men Are from Mars, Women Are from Venus*.[4] People overwhelmingly said the list of feminine characteristics best described Christ.

THE ROOTS OF THE FEMINIZATION OF CHRISTIANITY

Murrow is writing a typical book geared toward a popular audience that derives most of its thinking from present-day trends in church culture and uses a business-school style of analysis. Leon Podles, who has a PhD, from the University of Virginia, took a more scholarly approach to the question in his 1999 book, *The Church Impotent: The Feminization of Christianity*.

Podles agrees with Murrow on the state of current Christianity but adds some new dimensions. First he argues that this female skew is specific to Western Christianity, saying that it has not affected the Eastern Orthodox Church (which may or may not be true). Second, he points out that this female skew is not new but, in fact, dates back hundreds of years to the High Middle Ages.

Starting in the twelfth and thirteenth century, Podles says Western Christianity underwent a culture change that feminized it. He advances three main key driving causes: the popularization of bridal mysticism by St. Bernard of Clairvaux, a women's movement in the church, and Scholasticism. Bridal mysticism involved the use of highly erotic language to represent the individual believer as the Bride of Christ, inspired by the Song of Solomon:

> The use of erotic language to describe the relation of the believer to God was not unprecedented, but Bernard, for reasons that will become clear, did not choose to acknowledge his intellectual debts. Bernard claimed that "if a love relationship is the special and outstanding characteristic of bride and groom it is not unfitting to call the soul that loves God a bride".... Having established the principle for the use of such language, Bernard then elaborated. He referred to himself as "a woman" and advised his monks to be "mothers"—to "let your bosoms expand with milk, not swell with passion"—to emphasize their paradoxical status and worldly weakness.[5]

The women's movement was a large thirteenth century increase in the number of women flowing into religious orders, possibly resulting from a gender imbalance caused by an unusually high number of male deaths and increasing freedom of travel for women due to widespread peace. The monasteries initially resisted on the instruction of women in religious orders but ultimately capitulated, in part because of papal directives.

Scholasticism was a medieval intellectual movement that merged theology with classical philosophy, especially Aristotle. Thomas Aquinas is the paragon of the Scholastic type. Podles says that prior to Scholasticism, theology was the province of the monastery, where theological study was merged with religious practice as part of masculine daily devotional life. In the university, the home of the Scholastics, theology was a detached, rationalistic endeavor. The Scholastics might have been personally devout or even monks themselves, but their intellectual endeavors were in a scientific mode. Their work also resurrected Aristotelian notions about women that they interpreted as making women superior when it came to grace.

All these threads continued to develop over time in ways that, per Podles, divorced Christianity from masculinity and attached it more and more to femininity and thus drove a female skew in church attendance. Podles also points out that the men Christianity does attract are disproportionately low-masculinity nice-guy types:

> Because Christianity is now seen as a part of the sphere of life proper to women rather than to men, it sometimes attracts men whose own masculinity is somewhat doubtful. By this I do not mean homosexuals, although a certain type of homosexual is included. Rather religion is seen as a safe field, a refuge from the challenges of life, and therefore attracts men who are fearful of making the break with the secure world of childhood dominated by women. These are men who have problems following the path of masculine development.[6]

Those attracted into the ministry were even more feminized with academic research finding both Catholic and Protestant ministers rated as extremely feminine in contrast with other men.

One of the ways that bridal mysticism tends to play out in the modern church is in the corporate worship songs about expressing emotions and feelings of love for Jesus.

> An example of the feminization of the church is its music. Typical praise songs refer to Jesus as a Christian's lover and praise his beauty and tenderness. Rarely do they praise his justice or strength, or refer to him as the head of an army leading his church into spiritual battle, like "Onward Christian Soldiers."
>
> Mike Erre (M.A. '04)—the director of a men's ministry of over 400 men at Rock Harbor Church in Costa Mesa, Calif.—said feminine expressions of spirituality are more validated than masculine expressions. "The classic example is the worship pose of the eyes shut and the arms raised in this tender embrace, singing a song that says, 'I'm desperate for you. You're the air I breathe.' Guys don't talk to guys like that," Erre said.[7]

Many men don't resonate with the worship experience and feel disconnected from the worship of God as a result. While that is not an excuse for men to leave the church, it contributes to men's lack of enthusiasm for attending church.

THE CHURCH TURNS ANTI-MALE CIRCA 1800

A further shift occurred at the dawn of the nineteenth century when the church embraced a worldview that portrayed women as embodying holiness and men as embodying sin. The church increasingly came to have both an extremely negative view of masculinity and men and to uphold women and femininity as, in their natural state, exemplars and bearers of virtue.

This perhaps best illustrated by Callum Brown's 2009 book, *The Death of Christian Britain*. Brown is a professor of history at the University of Strathclyde. His book is about the decline of Christianity in the United Kingdom but is also applicable to America to which Britain was culturally linked. Even secular sources, such as Charles Taylor, the Canadian philosopher who produced the landmark, *A Secular Age*, endorses Brown's take on the sexes.

> Callum Brown here even speaks of a "demonization" of male qualities, and a "feminization of piety". . . . As Callum Brown has shown for the evangelical case, the ethical stance was predicated on the idea of women as wanting a stable family life, which was constantly endangered by male temptation, to drink, to gambling, to infidelity. And we see similar ideas propounded on the Catholic side. . . . It obviously has something to do with the close symbiosis established between Christian faith and the ethic of "family values" and disciplined work, which has downgraded if not been directed against military and combative modes of life, as well as forms of male sociability: drinking, gambling, sport, which took them outside the arenas of both work and home.[8]

It's particularly notable to see Taylor cite Brown in this regard given that these two men have radically different and incompatible takes on secularization.

As Taylor says, Callum Brown documents, through an extensive review of Christian literature, that around 1800, Christianity shifted from viewing piety as a primarily male mode of life to a primarily female one. Men and masculinity came to be perceived as acute threats to holiness. Brown's secularization thesis is that the merger of femininity with Christianity was so complete that when women ceased to unify their Christian and feminine identities around 1960, Christianity suffered a sudden and catastrophic collapse.

> In evangelical stories about piety, women appeared throughout as good but not always converted; men, by contrast, almost always appeared as in a perilous sinful state until near the end. Men were the problem, given manifold temptations: drink (nearly always), gambling (increasingly after 1890), and 'rough' in overall cultural terms. They lived dissipated lives which caused suffering and ruination to mothers, wives, and children. Nowhere did evangelical literature have such a powerful influence in the public domain, including in 'secular' fiction, as in its demonization of men.[9]
>
> A large proportion of evangelical stories of men centered on the destruction of families by male evils.[10]
>
> In the evangelical and temperance movements, women were both the moral guardians and the moral victims of fathers, brothers, husbands, and sons.[11]

To summarize simply: the church came to see women as naturally good and men as naturally evil and the source of most problems in the world. These observations from Brown are based on an extensive examination of evangelical literature itself—not from secular or anti-Christian sources.

Is it any wonder the church skewed so heavily female?

THE CHURCH'S VIEW OF MEN TODAY

How does the church view men and women today? As anyone with even a cursory knowledge of the contemporary church can tell you, it's easy to see that Brown's documentations of the nineteenth century are still in play, updated to modern times.

To pick but one example, consider a recent Christian book by Carolyn Curtis James called *Malestrom: Manhood Swept into the Currents of a*

Changing World. James is a consultant for the major Christian publisher Zondervan and was named a top-fifty evangelical woman to watch by Christianity Today magazine. This book claims most of the tragedies of world history are the fault of men.

> The malestrom is the particular ways in which the fall impacts the male of the human species—causing a man to lose himself, his identity and purpose as a man, and above all to lose sight of God's original vision for his sons. The repercussions of such devastating personal losses are not merely disastrous for the men themselves, but catastrophic globally . . . This is the history of the planet in microcosm—men killing others.[12]

James appears to be a liberal Christian, but conservatives agree with her. A recent "First Things" article by Glenn Stanton of Focus on the Family is illustrative. Titled "Men and Women Are Not Equal," the headline teases us with an expectation of a defense of patriarchy or some such notion. But Stanton is just playing word games. Here's what he really thinks:

> Women create, shape, and maintain human culture. Manners exist because women exist. Worthy men adjust their behavior when a woman enters the room. They become better creatures. Civilization arises and endures because women have expectations of themselves and of those around them. . . . Anthropologists have long recognized that the most fundamental social problem every community must solve is the unattached male. If his sexual, physical, and emotional energies are not governed and directed in a pro-social, domesticated manner, he will become the village's most malignant cancer. Wives and children, in that order, are the only successful remedy ever found . . . . Man and woman are not equal. He owes what he is to her. That is hardly her only power, but it is among her most formidable. Christianity has always known this. The Savior of the world chose to come to us through a wife and mother.[13]

This is identical to what Brown identified as the Christian attitude of the nineteenth century. Women are the natural civilizers, men the great despoilers of society.

Popular conservative pastors sometimes brutalize men from their pulpits. As just one example, consider Matt Chandler, the A-list pastor of the Dallas-area megachurch, the Village Church and head of the Acts 29 network. In one sermon—ostensibly devoted to women's sins, believe it or not—Chandler prays this almost imprecatory prayer:

> Father, for men in this room who prey on insecure women with wounded hearts, Father, I just pray over these men a type of weight on their souls that would be crushing. Father, I thank you that you do not take lightly wolves hunting down your daughters and that there would be a day that these men, hollow-chested boys in grown up bodies, will cry out as you come for mountains to fall and that the mountains will flee before your coming. I thank you that you are a just judge who will not handle lightly boys who can shave who take advantage of your daughters. I pray that there might be repentance for these men for the salvation of their own soul.[14]

There is in stark contrast with Chandler's treatment of male and female sexual sin. In a video clip entitled "Jesus wants the Rose," Chandler is personally babysitting for a single mother who is actively having an affair with a married man. He becomes indignant when another pastor calls out sexual sin in a sermon when he brought her to church—not her specific sin (adultery), mind you, but sexual sin in general as exemplified in the rose being passed around the room and broken.[15]

Chandler's style might be tough on men, but even the most moderate in tone and intellectually sophisticated conservative pastors have a similarly skewed negative few of men. To be clear, many of these men have great ministries—including Chandler. However, numerous books and sermons from various big-name Christian pastors and writers fall into the man-bashing pattern to one degree or another. The female writers and speakers are, if anything, even more extreme as we can see from the quote by James.

Other potential reasons for the gap follow:

- The church has turned into a ladies' club
- Men's ministry is not a priority
- Touchy-feely sermons abound

- Girly-men pastors run the pulpit
- Love songs dominate the worship
- Feminine spirituality has overtaken the Body

The church today is frustrated that it can't seem to get men to "Man up!" and do what they should do, but they fail to see their own role in dis-incentivizing men through vicious negativity and excessive pedestalization of women—unsupported theologically—plays in creating the very conditions they are upset about. Simply look at many Father's Day sermons where husbands are castigated to do better, but on Mother's Day, all the moms are heroes. Father's Day sermons lambast fathers and husbands to do a better job while Mother's Day sermons are all about how mothers are doing a great job with the crappy hand they are dealt with, no thanks to those deadbeat dads. With such attacks against men from the pulpit, is it any wonder Christianity repels men with even a modicum of self-respect?

It's popular today to suggest that churches are misogynistic bastions of patriarchy. But this is hard to square with the messages being delivered. No pastor would ever dare speak to or about a woman the way they speak to men. If one gender was being mistreated or discriminated against, wouldn't we expect that gender to disproportionately abandon the church? Indeed that's exactly what we observe.

ATTEMPTED REMEDIES

This book is hardly the first to point out that the church itself has long been feminized and hostile to men and masculinity. As a recent Wall Street Journal article on "The Messiah of Masculinity" pointed out, concerns about a loss of masculinity are a longstanding feature of our society.[16] This was recognized all along the way, and various strategies have been employed to try to deal with it—obviously, all without success.

One attempt was the muscular Christianity movement of the nineteenth and early twentieth centuries. A great overview of this movement is available from *The Art of Manliness*.[17]

> If the feminization of Christianity was rooted in the faith's lack of physicality, the solution was obvious: to connect the faith to the body. And not just any kind of body—a strong and vigorous one.

> . . . Adherents of the [Muscular Christianity] movement sought to make the Christian faith more muscular both literally and metaphorically—strengthening the physical bodies of the faithful, while pushing the church's culture and ethos in a more vigorous, practical, challenging, and action-oriented direction.[18]

Among the key players here were the YMCA and the Boy Scouts and preachers like Billy Sunday. This effort also included attempts to create a more masculine hymnal and Christian art.

The muscular Christianity movement showed us two things. First, it failed. Second, it inadvertently helped undermine Christianity through the development and promotion of an idea that contributed towards pushing the mainline denominations away from orthodox beliefs, namely the social gospel:

> Muscular Christians were frequently big proponents of embracing what was known as the "Social Gospel." This movement, which emerged at the turn of the 20th century, charged Christians with applying the obligations and ethics found in the gospels to issues related to health, corruption, economic disparities, and social justice, including but not limited to, poverty, alcoholism, crime, unemployment, child labor, unsafe foods/water, and inadequate schools. The Social Gospel movement was considered to be the religious wing of the Progressive movement, which aimed to marshal the tools of science, technology, and economics to alleviate suffering and improve the human condition.[19]

The social gospel, which tended towards a complete immanentization of the kingdom of God, was one of the forces (though certainly not the only one) that fostered the decline of the mainline Protestant denominations.

Another example of this failure is the rise and fall of Mark Driscoll's Mars Hill Church in Seattle.[20] Driscoll's preaching style was very distinctly hyper-masculine to motivate the so-called man-boys present in the culture and church to grow up and be responsible.

For instance, the current Church has is a big problem with missionary dating. Some pastors, like Mark Driscoll, have attacked missionary dating from the pulpit and blamed it on Christian men for various reasons. One such reason is that there aren't enough manly Christian men for Christian women to date, so these men need to step up. Another reason is that the terrible actions of non-Christian men, such as treating women poorly, are touted as examples of what all men do, including Christian men who must be scolded not to do those things.

This type of preaching style is ultimately ineffective because it cuts men off at the knees. Preaching that men need to man up and accept responsibility without distinction for the men who are leading well will undermine men in their own home. The criticism and castigation casts men, husbands, and fathers in a bad light, which encourages disrespect, contentiousness, and bitterness within homes.

PUTTING IT ALL TOGETHER

We should study the history of men, women, and the church and the ways in which the church has tried to respond to gender issues in the past as we try to develop improved approaches going forward.

Today's pastors probably don't realize that they are just reprising two-hundred-year-old talking points. They probably believe their analysis of gender is heavily informed by present events, not recognizing they are drawing from a deep wellspring of anti-male Christian thought. Analysts like Murrow, who simply survey the present-day scene, make a similar mistake. He assumes the present is merely an outcome of modern customer segmentation and marketing techniques. He does call out some of the history but fails to use it to inform his analysis.

As Christians, we can easily fall into a trap and think we are the first people to discover this problem and propose solutions to it. Almost certainly, anything we come up with will have already been tried and been found wanting. We can easily find ourselves actually making the situation worse even with the best of motives. The social-gospel movement, for all its good intent and even accomplishments, helped to undermine the faith in mainline Protestantism. Charles Taylor likewise presents several cautionary tales. He makes it clear that serious Christians themselves were a major component of the development of secularity, often unwittingly.

We can't pretend to have all the answers. What we can say is that the church had and now has a significant tendency to demonize men and put women on pedestals. This view is both false and destructive. We must likewise acknowledge that men are not perfect, and women are not evil. We are all fallen creatures, and a vast potential for sin lies within every human heart. Both men and women have an equally immense capacity to sin.

Finally, if anything, our priority should be to put God's Word ahead of all our preconceived notions of what might work. God's Word does not return to us void, especially when we put it into practice. You can never go wrong by doing what God says, including the following:

- Evangelizing and making disciples (Matthew 28)
- Teaching gender and marriage roles and responsibilities (Ephesians 5)
- Emphasizing the fruit of the Spirit (Galatians 5)
- Using our spiritual gifts in the church to love and serve (1 Corinthians 12)

Any other practical advice or potential wisdom must be tested so that we are sure that it doesn't bear bad fruit.

SECTION TWO
THE BIBLE ON MARRIAGE

Chapter 4
THE CREATION OF MAN, WOMAN, AND MARRIAGE

THE PURPOSE OF MARRIAGE: HOLINESS VERSUS HAPPINESS

Many marriages are you would call happy, and the couple is living the American Dream. They don't divorce; they're still in love with each other; their family gets along well; they have a nice house and cars; their kids go to a nice school; they have enough money to take yearly vacations and retire, and more. But much of this is worldly success, and it doesn't make them godly.

What makes the difference is a Christian husband and a wife following God's model for marriage. You're literally representing Christ and the church to the world. That transforms your marriage so that you make a difference as a witness for eternity. God has reason to be proud and say, "Well done, good and faithful servant." (See Matthew 25.) This is the importance of understanding the various roles and responsibilities for husbands and wives in marriage and of modeling them in your own marriage.

As we see many abuses of authority and disrespect for husbands and fathers in our culture, what an example it would set for Christians and non-Christians to see a husband and wife in perfect headship and submission. What if the husband loved his wife and the wife respected her husband? Following God's marital roles and responsibilities will set you apart from the vast majority of worldly marriages. It is a great witness to show them that you're a Christian living according to God's standards, and it is beautiful.

Sometimes—many times—in a Christian marriage, both holiness and happiness coincide, but this does not always happen. Sometimes we choose a temporary peace or happiness that leads to long-term unhappiness over holiness and godliness. One clear cut example is Adam and Eve. Adam chose to listen to the voice of his wife and eat the fruit instead of obeying the command of God and look where it got him.

One of the big temptations that we see repeatedly is that the husband is called to sacrificially love his wife for the purpose of sanctification and not because it feels good. This is the full context of Christ's love for the church in Ephesians 5. Often husbands can choose or even be counseled into choosing their feelings or their wife over holiness.

You must understand that certain marital roles and responsibilities might create this conflict. You or your wife might be unhappy about you fulfilling your roles and responsibilities in certain circumstances, but the goal is ultimately holiness in the end. Standing on God's commands ultimately brings us the greatest satisfaction and his peace and joy into our lives.

HEADSHIP IS A PART OF GOD'S DESIGN

The influence of culture on Christians is continual and pervasive. We see it in our school system, on TV, on the internet, from our friends and family, and even from those in the church. One of the big ways that culture has continued to attack the Bible and the church is by challenging the notion of headship in the form of husband-led marriages.

You might be thinking to yourself, *No one in popular culture or the Church really renounces headship.* But you might also be familiar with the term patriarchy, which is commonly railed against by feminism and even by those in the church. Patriarchy, by definition for Christians, is marriages headed by husbands and churches headed by men, both of which are designed by God throughout scripture. When someone blames the patriarchy for the ills of society or the church, they are blaming God's design.

From creation, many textual clues from the account in Genesis and other scriptures make the case for headship and thus patriarchy from the beginning.

1. Eve is created as a helpmeet for Adam. She is created second rather than at the same time. Paul affirms this in 1 Corinthians 11 by discussing creation order (Genesis 2, 1 Corinthians 11).
2. Adam names Eve. Adam also names the animals over which he has dominion. Parents also name their children over who they have authority (Genesis 1, 2).

3. Eve comes from a part of Adam. Man is created in the "image and glory of God," while woman is created in the "glory of man," though both are created in the image of God (Genesis 2, 1 Corinthians 11).
4. God brings Eve and presents her to Adam, foreshadowing a father giving away the bride to the husband. She passes from her father's authority to her husband's authority (Genesis 2, Numbers 30).
5. The comparison of the creation accounts in Genesis 1–3 might show that only Adam received the commands from God in the garden based on how Eve was deceived.

We learn that Eve was deceived, but Adam chose to sin (Genesis 3, 1 Timothy 2), and we can see this in how she was deceived through subtle wording differences: "The Lord God commanded the man, saying, 'From any tree of the garden you may eat freely; but from the tree of the knowledge of good and evil you shall not eat, for in the day that you eat from it you will surely die.'"—"The woman said to the serpent, 'From the fruit of the trees of the garden we may eat; but from the fruit of the tree which is in the middle of the garden, God has said, "You shall not eat from it or touch it, or you will die."

6. Genesis 2 indicates that the man separates from his parents to create the family unit: "For this reason a man shall leave his father and his mother, and be joined to his wife; and they shall become one flesh."

The man breaks off from his parents to establish his own family unit and is joined together with his wife as his helpmeet. The husband is the leader, and the wife is the follower. She takes his name as a sign that she is part of his family. When we decide to follow Christ, we take on His name as we follow Him as Christians.

7. Ephesians 5 demonstrates that marriage reflects Christ and the church. Marriage was present prior to the fall. Therefore, man is created in the image of God and joined in perfect matrimony, which means there must be headship prior to the fall to reflect the eventual marriage of Christ and the church.

8. John 1 indicates that Jesus was present in the beginning. Jesus existed in the beginning and had authority over man, which foreshadows the marriage of Christ and the church (Genesis 1–2, 1 Corinthians 11).
9. When God comes to the garden to talk to Adam and Eve after they sinned, He calls only for Adam (Genesis 3).
10. God told Adam he would surely die if he ate of the fruit. The pattern of the other punishments given to Adam and Eve due to sin is a pattern of increase (Genesis 3).

- The ground was cursed, and Adam needed to work harder as he was already commanded to tend to the garden.
- Eve's pain was greatly multiplied in childbirth. The term greatly multiplied means that it was already present in lesser amounts. Some have an incorrect view that pain is bad, but the ability to feel pain is a protective mechanism of the body against harm, such as avoiding hot stoves, sharp edges, and physical damage to the body. Women's pain in childbirth increased from little to much.
- The second half of Eve's punishment is from the tree of knowledge of good and evil—"Yet your desire will be for your husband, and he will rule over you." This punishment to Eve is an increased temptation to rebel against (or submit) to her husband in the context of her prior relationship (headship-submission). The same Hebrew word for desire (*tĕshuwqah*) used in Genesis 3:16 and Genesis 4:7 (for Cain's desire to tempt him into sin) is used again in Song of Songs 7:10 for sexual desire.[1]

11. Adam is punished for listening to the voice of his wife and for eating the fruit. If Eve were in the same position as Adam, then Adam would have just been punished for eating the fruit and not for both listening to his wife and eating the fruit (Genesis 3).

Aside from these reasons, the concept of headship is the Bible forms quite a few unique relationships.

- Mark 12:10: Have you not even read this Scripture: "The stone which the builders rejected, This became the chief corner (*kephale*) stone."

- 1 Corinthians 11:3: But I want you to understand that Christ is the head (kephale) of every man, and the man is the head (kephale) of a woman, and God is the head (kephale) of Christ.
- Ephesians 5:23: For the husband is the head (kephale) of the wife, as Christ also is the head (kephale) of the church, He Himself being the Savior of the body.

God as the head of Christ is a headship relation between divinity. Christ as the head of man and Christ as the head of the Church (Ephesians 5) is a headship relation between divinity and humans. And man as the head of woman and the husband as the head of the wife (Ephesians 5) is a headship relation between humans. Outside of Genesis, the theological reasons for headship given in scripture in 1 Corinthians 11 rest on the order of creation, the origin of woman (from man), from the fall, and as new creations in Christ.[2]

Overall, scriptural evidence supports the headship-submission model. It is consistently affirmed throughout the course of the scriptures in each of the five distinct phases of biblical history.

1. Creation (Adam and Eve)
2. Post-fall (after Adam and Eve sinned)
3. Pre-Mosaic law patriarchs (Abraham, Isaac, Jacob, and their descendants)
4. Mosaic law (the rest of the Old Testament)
5. Christ and His resurrection (the New Testament analogy of Christ and the church)

Although this might offend the modern sensibilities of equality, this is the structure that God put in place for His followers. The goal of Christians is to be like Christ—to be holy and set apart from the world through sanctification. The Bible tells us that the headship and submission of the husband and wife is like that of Christ and the church. A marriage that follows this model is a direct witness of Christ and the church to the world.

This is not to say that men and women do not have the same value in the eyes of God—they certainly do. But God ordained order and roles in the church and marriage. The husband's position in God's design is the head in the family.

When the Bible and culture are at odds with each other, do you tend to side with culture, or do you side with God? Is salt still salty if it loses its saltiness? How can a light illuminate anything if put under a bushel? (See Matthew 5:13–15.) Who are we to argue with the order He has chosen?

Some common arguments against headship even from those in the church are as follows:

- Some say that there was no headship prior to the fall and that Adam and Eve were equal.
- Some say that headship is a result of sin via God's punishment of Eve in Genesis 3 and therefore less than ideal.
- Others claim that Christ's sacrifice reset the roles of husband and wife, cancelling headship.
- Other arguments focus on the nature of the word submission in Ephesians 5 where Christians are to submit to one another and that we are all one in Christ in Galatians 3.

We already noted that headship existed prior to the fall through the preponderance of textual clues in Genesis 1–3.

Many passages also affirm the headship-submission model all throughout the New Testament: Ephesians 5, Colossians 3, Titus 2, 1 Corinthians 11, 1 Corinthians 14, Titus 2, and 1 Peter 3. Ephesians 5 elaborates that the headship-submission of the husband and wife is supposed to reflect Christ and the church. Another scripture that disproves the theory of a change in marriage order is the prescription for leaders in the church in 1 Timothy 3. The elders and deacons of the church are required to be the husbands of one wife and rule their households well.

As scripture is consistent with itself, both Paul and Peter draw a distinction of the general body of believers from the family's headship-submission model. The argument that the husband and wife are equal falls flat on its face due to the overwhelming evidence against it. For instance, even if Ephesians 5 was conceded, six other scriptures still affirm it with only one that approves mutual submission. Furthermore, these scriptures would contradict each other.

Another strong test of scripture is to look at what those close to Jesus and the early church taught about marriage and the church assembly. The pastoral letters of 1 and 2 Timothy and Titus affirm this structure in marriages as well as the churches.

In conclusion, headship is a part of God's design. How headship is supposed to be used is the next question, which we will address in the next section.

AUTHORITY IS GIVEN TO LOVE

Headship is one of the foundations of marriage, so we need to understand authority to have a better picture of the responsibilities that come with it. In the marriage relationship, the husband was assigned by God with the higher position. With a higher position comes more responsibility. A classic cliché tells us, "With great power comes great responsibility."

Yeah, that's not in the Bible, and the origins possibly date back to France in the eighteenth century.[3] But it's definitely a biblical concept. Luke 12:48b tells us, "From everyone who has been given much, much will be required; and to whom they entrusted much, of him they will ask all the more."

This is taken from the parable of the talents or minas in Matthew 25:14–30 and Luke 19:12–27. Not everyone has been given the same amount of talents or gifts. The talents that we have are important, but what is more important is what we do with those gifts. In the marriage relationship, the husband, who is tasked with being the head, has more responsibilities to handle.

As the leader of your relationship, the buck stops with you. If your marriage has a problem that needs to be addressed, God will come to you for an explanation. Genesis 3:9 tells us, "Then the Lord God called to the man, and said to him, 'Where are you?'"

Authority is composed of two parts: power and responsibility. The concept of why authority exists is simple. God is the Creator of all. He is the ultimate, sovereign authority who made all things and who determines what is right and what is wrong. God is love. His characteristics work in concert with His character. This means the position of authority is given to love those under their authority. For instance, God used His authority to send Jesus to die for our sins so that we can repent and be reconciled to God. Romans 5:8 tells us, "But God demonstrates His own love toward us, in that while we were yet sinners, Christ died for us."

The cultures of the world value the power of authority over the responsibility of authority. "But Jesus called them to Himself and said, 'You know that the rulers of the Gentiles lord it over them, and their great men exercise authority over them. It is not this way among you, but whoever wishes to become great among you shall be your servant, and whoever wishes to be first among you shall be your slave; just as the Son of Man did not come to be served, but to serve, and to give His life a ransom for many'" (Matthew 20:25–28).

Jesus is not denigrating authority or cancelling it. The phrase, "It is not this way among you," indicates that authority is affirmed among Christians. Rather the use of the power of authority must be approached with humility to truly fulfil the responsibility of authority.

Those in authority are tasked to treat those under their authority with love. This is a horizontal relationship where those under authority are treated as if their position were the same as those in authority. For instance,

- Jesus no longer calls us slaves but friends (John 15:12–17).
- The husband is called three times in Ephesians to treat his wife as if he were treating his own body (Ephesians 5:28, 29, 33).
- Governments are responsible for the welfare of their citizens and for punishing evildoers (1 Peter 2:13–17).

On the other hand, those under authority are called to respect, submit, and obey those who are in authority above them.

- Jesus submits his will to the Father (Luke 22:42, Matthew 26:39–46).
- Christians submit to the Father/Jesus (1 Corinthians 11:3).
- Wives submit to husbands (Ephesians 5:22–24, Colossians 3, Titus 2, 1 Peter 3, 1 Corinthians 14).
- Christians submit to the government (Romans 13, 1 Peter 2, Titus 3, 1 Timothy 2, Luke 20).
- Children submit to parents (Ephesians 6).

This is true for all cases where one is under authority except when an authority commands or requests something that overtly goes against God's laws, such as not preaching the gospel or a clear sin, such as stealing, coveting, murder, and so forth.

The images below show how these relationships work.

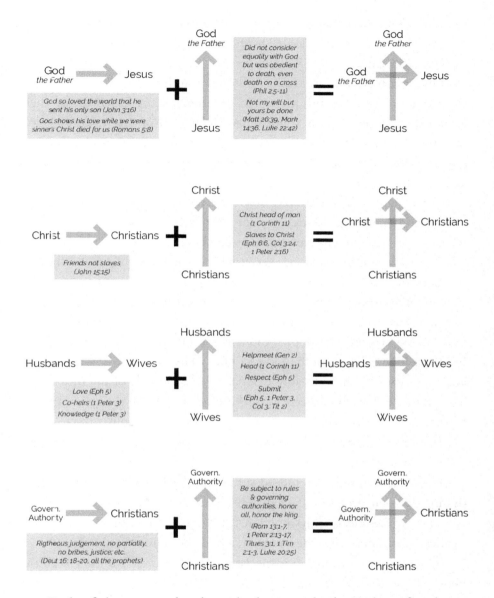

Each of these examples show the horizontal relationship of authority used to love while those under authority are called to respect and submit as a vertical relationship. When Jesus came to earth, He submitted to the Father's will to the point of death on a cross, and the Father demonstrated twice that He loved His Son by sending a voice from heaven in Matthew 3:17, "This is my beloved son, in whom I am well-pleased." Christ used His authority to love the church so much that He sacrificed himself for us so that "we might become children of God" (John 1). The church submits to Christ by obeying His commands.

Similarly husbands are called to use their authority to love their wives sacrificially toward sanctification, and governments are called to use their authority to govern rightly (punishing evildoers—Romans 13). Wives are to submit to their husbands as to the Lord, and as subjects under the government, we are to submit to the government if it doesn't conflict with the commands of God, such as evangelism (Acts 5).

Put together, these examples show the powerful imagery of the cross. The second example is the archetype of marriage: the Christ and the church, which husbands and wives are called to emulate.

Finally, what is the difference between headship, leadership, and authority?

Both positions of headship and leadership have authority to make decisions and the responsibility to love. However, headship and leadership differ in that all heads are leaders, but not all leaders are heads. If it were the case that a leader could become a head, then those with leadership skills could usurp the head's position. This is not found in scripture. The Bible consistently uses the analogy of the head and the body, especially to describe Christ and the church. The church follows the directives of the head, which are the commands of Christ: to evangelize, baptize, and make disciples of all nations.

In biblical marriage, all husbands are heads and thus leaders of their wives. If a husband does not act as the head by taking leadership in the marriage, the marriage can indeed suffer from lack of direction. Yet other dysfunctions can arise too. If a wife rebels and tries to be the head, problems will arise as two heads is dysfunctional. Likewise, if the husband abdicates the head position or the wife usurps it, a body without a head is dead.

The position of headship is special in the scriptures. For the rest of the book, I'll mostly refer to headship as leadership, but keep in mind, they not the same thing. Headship has the innate synergy of working together with the body for a purpose.

CULTURAL BLINDERS ON AUTHORITY

Does the fact that authority figures abuse authority mean that authority is evil? Of course not! God is the one who has created authority. Authority is good. The fact that authority figures abuse authority means they are sinful and fallen. This does not make the position of authority itself evil.

Too often, we as humans conflate our bad experiences with authority into thinking that authority is evil. Unfortunately most authority figures are looked upon with distrust because the abuse of authority for selfish gain in our culture is all too common.

If you suggest that a husband has authority in marriage to anyone in society, they will almost immediately cry abuse. Patriarchy is decried by society as evil. Christians fall prey to the constant barrage of patriarchy is bad. Again, patriarchy simply means husband-led marriages and male-led churches, which are God's design.

The Bible does not given recommendations for the political realm—only marriages and the church—so this can be a point of misunderstanding. Patriarchy in society tends to refer to any man in a position of authority. Today many Christians preach against patriarchy when they do not realize that they are calling part of God's plan for marriage and the church evil. It makes sense that the world wants to call evil that which God has created as very good, but Christians should never do that. Isaiah 5:20–21 tells us, "Woe to those who call evil good, and good evil; Who substitute darkness for light and light for darkness; Who substitute bitter for sweet and sweet for bitter! Woe to those who are wise in their own eyes and clever in their own sight!"

Many Christians can fall prey to several cultural blinders on authority.

- Power, not responsibility, is lauded as the most important part of authority. This goes back to Jesus's statement that the Gentiles lord their authority over them. (See Matthew 20:25.)
- Those with authority or power are seen as better than those without. If you suggest a husband has authority in marriage, Christians who are uncomfortable with authority will always jump to the argument that men and women are equal. A God-given position of authority does not mean that one is better than another—all sin and fall short of the glory of God, and all of us need a Savior.
- They are under the impression that any authority held by men is bad. The patriarchy is reviled. Real and made-up abuses of

authority are commonly used as examples of how the structure itself—not the abuses—is bad.
- Authority and power are fine in the hands of women but not in the hands of men. We can also see this in the justice system when men who commit crimes of abusing authority tend to receive longer and harsher sentences than women who commit the same crimes.
- Responsibility without authority or power is always tasked to the men/husbands. In other words, men usually get most, if not all, the blame when something goes wrong, even if they didn't have any power to get results.

The first two are extremely important because they show that most people still have a Gentile mindset toward power and status as the most important parts of authority. They fail to understand what the Bible says about it. Authority is a position granted by God, and it does not make one better or worse than another. It simply imparts them with additional responsibility and the power to use love to meet those responsibilities.

To put these blinders into perspective, here is what many Christians believe about authority.

- Feminists and liberals accept authority but invert gender roles. The wife is in charge of the marriage.
- Egalitarians (those who believe men and women are equal) reject male authority in word and deed. Consequently, in the vacuum of authority, they accept feminism.
- Complementarians accept authority in word but reject authority in deed. The husband is a neutered figurehead. Note that complementarianism was created in the 1980s by The Council on Biblical Manhood and Womanhood in response to so-called abuses of authority and likely because of the poisoning of the word patriarchy.[4]

The culture and even parts of the church have various interpretations of the nature of authority in the light of cultural blinders that do not agree with scripture.

Here are a couple of helpful ways to view authority.

- Change your perspective from "How does this benefit me?" to "How does this benefit us?" The husband is called three times in Ephesians to treat his wife the same way he treats his own body (Ephesians 5:28, 29, 33).
- If you're in authority, don't tell someone to do anything that you are not willing to do yourself. First be a leader by modeling correct behavior just as Christ did for us. Then delegate as necessary.
- Embrace the difficult nature of the sanctification process. If you sinned or made an error, be humble enough to admit it and repent. If she made an error, be ready to make her aware of it kindly and call her to repent. Ephesians 5:25–27 tells us, "Husbands, love your wives, just as Christ also loved the church and gave Himself up for her, so that He might sanctify her, having cleansed her by the washing of water with the word, that He might present to Himself the church in all her glory, having no spot or wrinkle or any such thing; but that she would be holy and blameless."

Our God is not a God of disorder or confusion but of peace (1 Corinthians 14:33a). Authority is given to bring about order through a final decision maker. The goal of that decision maker is to love those with his decisions and follow God's example of *agape* love. Love is such a loaded word in today's culture that it seems almost better to use two of the other translations from the Hebrew and Greek: loving-kindness and charity. Romans 2:4 states, "Or do you think lightly of the riches of His kindness and tolerance and patience, not knowing that the kindness of God leads you to repentance?" Romans 5:6–8 says, "For while we were still helpless, at the right time Christ died for the ungodly. For one will hardly die for a righteous man; though perhaps for the good man someone would dare even to die. But God demonstrates His own love toward us, in that while we were yet sinners, Christ died for us."

Romans outlines the qualities under which authority is to be wielded. These are kindness, goodness, and patience. It should be given freely, without manipulation, and with kindness in the worst circumstances to give God the opportunity to turn others' hearts toward Himself. This is the powerful calling and responsibility that has been given to the husband in marriage.

Chapter 5
GENDER DIFFERENCES AND MARITAL ROLES AND RESPONSIBILITIES

BIBLICAL MARITAL ROLES AND RESPONSIBILITIES

The scriptures outline numerous prescriptions for marriage, each according to the husband and wife as they differ from each other. A deeper look into biblical roles and responsibilities will prepare both Christian men and women for the marital covenant if they desire to wed.

Let's look at biblical roles and responsibilities to understand how God desires a marriage to function.

Teachings on men/husbands

Ephesians 5:23, 25–33 states, "For the husband is the head of the wife, as Christ also is the head of the church, He Himself being the Savior of the body. . . . Husbands, love your wives, just as Christ loved the church and gave Himself up for her to make her holy, so that He might sanctify her, having cleansed her by the washing of water with the word, that He might present to Himself the church in all her glory, having no spot or wrinkle or any such thing; but that she would be holy and blameless. So husbands ought also to love their own wives as their own bodies. He who loves his own wife loves himself; for no one ever hated his own flesh, but nourishes and cherishes it, just as Christ also does the church, because we are members of His body. For this reason a man shall leave his father and mother and shall be joined to his wife, and the two shall become one flesh. This mystery is great; but I am speaking with reference to Christ and the church. Nevertheless, each individual among you also is to love his own wife even as himself, and the wife must see to it that she respects her husband."

- The husband is the head/leader/authority of the wife.
- A husband is to exhibit sacrificial love to his wife in order to make her more holy, which means guiding her to repentance when she has gone astray.
- This passage states three times that a husband is to love his wife as his own body or as himself.
- A husband is to feed and care for his wife. Other translations use the terms nourish and cherish.

Colossians 3:19 commands, "Husbands, love your wives and do not be embittered against them."

- A husband is not to be bitter or harsh with his wife.

First Peter 3:7 says, "You husbands in the same way, live with your wives in an understanding way, as with someone weaker, since she is a woman; and show her honor as a fellow heir of the grace of life, so that your prayers will not be hindered."

- A husband is to live with the understanding that his wife is weaker.
- A husband is to honor his wife as a co-heir in the grace of life.

First Corinthians 7:3–5 instructs, "The husband must fulfill his duty to his wife, and likewise also the wife to her husband. The wife does not have authority over her own body, but the husband does; and likewise also the husband does not have authority over his own body, but the wife does. Stop depriving one another, except by agreement for a time, so that you may devote yourselves to prayer, and come together again so that Satan will not tempt you because of your lack of self-control."

- A husband is not to withhold sex from his wife.

First Timothy 5:8 says, "But if anyone does not provide for his own, and especially for those of his household, he has denied the faith and is worse than an unbeliever."

- A husband is to provide for his family.

These are the passages in scripture that show the roles and responsibilities of a husband. God has very high standards but knows that not everyone may meet those standards. For those looking for leadership positions in the church, the Bible mandates additional expectations of godliness. All Christian men should strive for these things, in my opinion.

For elders:

> It is a trustworthy statement: if any man aspires to the office of overseer, it is a fine work he desires to do. An overseer, then, must be above reproach, the husband of one wife, temperate, prudent, respectable, hospitable, able to teach, not addicted to wine or pugnacious, but gentle, peaceable, free from the love of money. He must be one who manages his own household well, keeping his children under control with all dignity (but if a man does not know how to manage his own household, how will he take care of the church of God?), and not a new convert, so that he will not become conceited and fall into the condemnation incurred by the devil. And he must have a good reputation with those outside the church, so that he will not fall into reproach and the snare of the devil (1 Timothy 3:1–7).

For deacons:

> Deacons likewise must be men of dignity, not double-tongued, or addicted to much wine or fond of sordid gain, but holding to the mystery of the faith with a clear conscience. These men must also first be tested; then let them serve as deacons if they are beyond reproach. Women must likewise be dignified, not malicious gossips, but temperate, faithful in all things. Deacons must be husbands of only one wife, and good managers of their children and their own households. For those who have served well as deacons obtain for themselves a high standing and great confidence in the faith that is in Christ Jesus (1 Timothy 3:8–13).

Overall, the trend for the elders and deacons is that men aspiring to these offices should strive to be paragons of the faith. This laundry list of qualities shows a man who is fully bearing the fruits of the Spirit. One of the main reasons that I included these passages is because both elders and deacons must rule their own households well: their wives and children. This reinforces the commands to husbands that they must be the leader in their marriage.

Teachings on women/wives

Ephesians 5 indicates one of the responsibilities of the husband as a sacrificial leader is to help to make his wife more holy. This means that a husband must know the roles and responsibilities of the wife so that he can remind her or call her to repentance when she has gone astray.

Thus you must learn and know these roles and responsibilities for a wife so that you know what you are looking for in a single Christian woman if you are a single man. If you are already in a relationship or marriage, you need to know these qualities so that you can fulfill your biblical roles and responsibilities to honor God.

Genesis 2:20 states, "The man gave names to all the cattle, and to the birds of the sky, and to every beast of the field, but for Adam there was not found a helper suitable for him."

- A wife is the helper or helpmeet to her husband.

Ephesians 5:22–24, 33 tells us, "Wives, be subject to your own husbands, as to the Lord. For the husband is the head of the wife, as Christ also is the head of the church, He Himself being the Savior of the body. But as the church is subject to Christ, so also the wives ought to be to their husbands in everything. . . . Nevertheless, each individual among you also is to love his own wife even as himself, and the wife must see to it that she respects her husband."

Colossians 3:18 says, "Wives, be subject to your husbands, as is fitting in the Lord."

- A wife should submit to her husband as to the Lord.
- A wife should submit in everything as to the Lord.
- A wife should respect/reverence her husband.

First Peter 3:1–6 says, "In the same way, you wives, be submissive to your own husbands so that even if any of them are disobedient to the word, they may be won without a word by the behavior of their wives, as they observe your chaste and respectful behavior. Your adornment must not be merely external—braiding the hair, and wearing gold jewelry, or putting on dresses; but let it be the hidden person of the heart, with the imperishable quality of a gentle and quiet spirit, which is precious in the sight of God. For in this way in former times the holy women also, who hoped in God, used to adorn themselves, being submissive to their own husbands; just as Sarah obeyed Abraham, calling him lord, and you have become her children if you do what is right without being frightened by any fear."

- A wife should submit to her husband, even if he is disobedient to the word, so that he may be won without a word by chaste and respectful behavior.
- A wife's adornment should not be merely external but a gentle and quiet spirit should be a priority.
- A wife's example of calling her husband lord and did not walk in fear.

"Older women likewise are to be reverent in their behavior, not malicious gossips nor enslaved to much wine, teaching what is good, so that they may encourage the young women to love their husbands, to love their children, to be sensible, pure, workers at home, kind, being subject to their own husbands, so that the word of God will not be dishonored" (Titus 2:3–5).

- A wife is to love (*philandros*) her husbands and children.
- A wife is to be a sensible, pure, worker at home and kind.
- A wife is to be subject to her own husband.

"The husband must fulfill his duty to his wife, and likewise also the wife to her husband. The wife does not have authority over her own body, but the husband does; and likewise also the husband does not have authority over his own body, but the wife does. Stop depriving one another, except by agreement for a time, so that you may devote yourselves to prayer, and come together again so that Satan will not tempt you because of your lack of self-control" (1 Corinthians 7:3–5).

- A wife is not to withhold sex from her husband.

"It is better to live in a desert land than with a contentious and vexing woman" (Proverbs 21:19).

"A constant dripping on a day of steady rain and a contentious woman are alike; He who would restrain her restrains the wind, and grasps oil with his right hand" (Proverbs 27:15–16).

"It is better to live in a corner of the roof than in a house shared with a contentious woman" (Proverbs 25:24).

"An excellent wife is the crown of her husband, but she who shames him is like rottenness in his bones" (Proverbs 12:4).

"As a ring of gold in a swine's snout so is a beautiful woman who lacks discretion" (Proverbs 11:22).

"The wise woman builds her house, but the foolish tears it down with her own hands" (Proverbs 14:1).

- A wife should not nag.
- A wife should not be contentious or quarrelsome.
- A wife should have strength of character.
- A wife/woman should have discretion.
- A wife should not tear down her own home but rather build it.

"An excellent wife, who can find? For her worth is far above jewels. The heart of her husband trusts in her, and he will have no lack of gain. She does him good and not evil all the days of her life. . . . Charm is deceitful and beauty is vain, But a woman who fears the Lord, she shall be praised. Give her the product of her hands, and let her works praise her in the gates" (Proverbs 31:10–12, 30–31).

Proverbs 31 does not give specific directions to the wife but shows ways a wife *can* operate within the context of her marriage. The qualities espoused are excellence, trustfulness, diligence, a homemaker, charity, running a business (if any) from the home, wisdom, and kindness.

Overall, the main thing that we should gather from biblical marital roles and responsibilities is that they take a lot of work. Men must work hard at being a good leader. Many men find it difficult to understand, feed, and care for a woman. Most women are not naturally submissive or respectful. Most women have a hard time doing what is right if they have a sinful husband.

The great part about the scriptures is that they expose our weaknesses and temptations to help us grow to be more like Christ.

Each of these roles and responsibilities are distinct for the husband and the wife and, most definitely, are not politically correct. But we have a choice about our allegiance. Do we choose the standards of the God who made us, or do we do what society tells us we should do?

GOD'S ROLES AND RESPONSIBILITIES FOR MARRIAGE ARE UNCONDITIONAL

We must notice that God's roles and responsibilities are unconditional. For instance, let's look at the Ephesians 5 passage on marriage.

> Wives, be subject to your own husbands, as to the Lord. For the husband is the head of the wife, as Christ also is the head of the church, He Himself being the Savior of the body. But as the church is subject to Christ, so also the wives ought to be to their husbands in everything (Ephesians 5:22–24).

> For the husband is the head of the wife, as Christ also is the head of the church, He Himself being the Savior of the body. . . . Husbands, love your wives, just as Christ loved the church and gave himself up for her so that He might sanctify her, having cleansed her by the washing of water with the word, that He might present to Himself the church in all her glory, having no spot or wrinkle or any such thing; but that she would be holy and blameless (Ephesians 5:23, 25–27).

There are no "if" statements in this passage. Wives are to unconditionally submit to their husbands as to the Lord. Husbands are to unconditionally and sacrificially love their wives toward sanctification.

This means if a husband is acting in a sinful or evil manner, the wife does not have a card that allows her to get out of respecting or submitting to her husband or to neglect her biblical roles and responsibilities. Similarly if the wife is acting in a sinful or evil manner, the husband does not have a card that lets him get out of loving or honoring her. Sure, if your spouse asks you to participate in sin, then you can refuse, but you should not act in a nasty or angry way toward them either.

The reason for the unconditional commands is simple. If a husband or wife is acting poorly, such as a negative attitude, withholding sex, or behaving sinfully, what type of attitude and actions will influence them to change their poor behavior? What does God recommend elsewhere in the scriptures?

Jesus preaches in Matthew 5 that you should bless your enemies and pray for those that persecute you. Paul supports this in Romans 12. When you treat someone well who is treating you badly, you exert a positive influence on them that the Holy Spirit can use to convict them and change their ways. The same is true of fulfilling your marital roles and responsibilities, even in the face of a bad attitude, anger, contempt, and other negative emotions or actions. This is precisely why 1 Peter 3 commands wives to win their unbelieving husbands through submission; chaste and respectful behavior; and a gentle and quiet spirit.

One of the biggest problems in relationships and marriage is that we allow the other person to influence how we're feeling by their negative emotions and actions instead of stepping back and allowing the Holy Spirit to work through us and exhibit love, joy, peace, patience, kindness, goodness, faithfulness, humility, and self-control when we are offended or abused. If only we would step back, calm down, and ask God to help us to be kinder, humbler, and gentler when those in relationships and marriages are treating us poorly. It would turn our relationships around.

The goal is to honor God first by doing what He commands even when we are being treated unfairly or poorly. Most husbands and wives like to try to do it their own way by playing power games or one upping each other with poor treatment. It never works and almost always makes the situation worse. Sometimes when counseled with scriptural advice, they double down on acting poorly. Why not simply try it God's way instead of trying to do it yourself? You were never meant to do it alone. That's why we have the Holy Spirit as a helper so that we can do it God's way.

Chapter 6
MARRIAGE IS OPTIONAL

MARRIAGE IS OPTIONAL PER THE BIBLE

Now that you better understand marriage within a biblical framework, each Christian man has a choice in life of whether or not to pursue marriage.

Many different opinions exist about marriage in our culture today. Singleness is lauded by some. Since the rise of no-fault divorce in the 1970s, a man or woman can simply opt out of a marriage in the culture. Unfortunately, this seems to have made marriage a bad idea for many because the laws on divorce, custody, and alimony tend to be biased heavily toward women, depending on the judge.

Others, especially in the church, insist marriage is the only way. They believe you are unsuccessful or a failure in life if you are not married. Even some in the church will declare that a man is not a man until he is married. The rise of man boys and men who live in their parents' basement playing video games is synonymous with not becoming a man and stepping up and taking responsibility by having a wife and kids.

Fortunately, the Bible speaks to us as Christians about our choice to be married or not.

> But I say to the unmarried and to widows that it is good for them if they remain even as I. But if they do not have self-control, let them marry; for it is better to marry than to burn with passion. . . . But I want you to be free from concern. One who is unmarried is concerned about the things of the Lord, how he may please the Lord; but one who is married is concerned about the things of the world, how he may please his wife, and his interests are divided.

The woman who is unmarried, and the virgin, is concerned about the things of the Lord, that she may be holy both in body and spirit; but one who is married is concerned about the things of the world, how she may please her husband. This I say for your own benefit; not to put a restraint upon you, but to promote what is appropriate and to secure undistracted devotion to the Lord (1 Corinthians 7:8–9; 32–35).

Those who choose to stay single can wholeheartedly serve God. Those who choose marriage enter a covenant relationship that is reflective of Christ and the church. Paul recommends staying single if possible as it is better, but if you marry, you still do well. Don't allow yourself to be shamed into marrying or not marrying.

Aside from your faith to Christ, deciding whether to find and choose a wife is going to be one the biggest decisions of your life. A wife will literally be one flesh with you and a part of everything that you do. The weight of this decision is heavy, but if you find a potential wife who is virtuous, it can be a time of great joy and delight too.

Every man and woman should read the scripture, pray, and think long and hard about whether to marry.

MARRIAGE IS THE NORM, AND THE ALTERNATIVE IS CELIBACY

One of the biggest points to consider about marriage is sex drive. Most men and women have a sex drive. As Paul indicates to the Corinthians, it is better to marry than to sexually burn.

Several implications of this need to be considered. Male and female sexual desire is not sinful. Man was created for woman and woman for man, according to Genesis and 1 Corinthians 11. The desire to be together in marriage, regularly have sex, and have a family is healthy.

But sexual desire is very easily tempted and exacerbated in today's culture. Almost every form of media—TV, movies, the internet, and books, such as romance novels—along with friends and other sources offer potential temptation. Marriage is the beautiful outlet that God created for the male and female sex drive. Prevalent temptations encourage us to fornicate, commit adultery, and covet that which is not ours.

Marriage is likely the norm for most men and women. Across societies with marriage, over 90 percent of men and women usually end up married. Paul's target audience was a man or woman with a high sex drive who is constantly tempted. If someone has a low sex drive or no sex drive, celibacy might be a likely choice for them. In other words, it is better to marry than to constantly be tempted and sometimes fall into sexual sin.

Marriage is not a solution for a lack of self-control. Someone with a pornography or romance novel addiction—some of the most common addictions for Christian men and women—will still struggle with these addictions after they are in a relationship or married. Although you might have a high sex drive, you must learn to control it and resist temptation when single while preparing for marriage. You do not want to bring any type of addictions to a relationship or marriage as they will cause you endless heartache because they will hurt not only you but also your spouse.

CHASTITY UNTIL MARRIAGE: GOD'S WAY IS THE BEST WAY

Likewise, Christians who choose marriage are to abstain from sexual immorality before marriage and be faithful to their spouse in marriage.

> Do you not know that your bodies are members of Christ? Shall I then take away the members of Christ and make them members of a prostitute? May it never be! Or do you not know that the one who joins himself to a prostitute is one body with her? For He says, "The two shall become one flesh." But the one who joins himself to the Lord is one spirit with Him. Flee immorality. Every other sin that a man commits is outside the body, but the immoral man sins against his own body. Or do you not know that your body is a temple of the Holy Spirit who is in you, whom you have from God, and that you are not your own? For you have been bought with a price: therefore glorify God in your body (1 Corinthians 6:15–20).

> For you know what commandments we gave you by the authority of the Lord Jesus. For this is the will of God, your sanctification; that is, that you abstain from sexual immorality; that each of you know how to possess his own vessel in sanctification and honor, not in lustful passion, like the Gentiles who do not know God. . . . For

God has not called us for the purpose of impurity, but in sanctification. So, he who rejects this is not rejecting man but the God who gives His Holy Spirit to you (1 Thessalonians 4:2–5, 7–8).

Marriage is to be held in honor among all, and the marriage bed is to be undefiled; for fornicators and adulterers God will judge (Hebrews 13:4).

The scriptures are clear on this. God made sex to be enjoyed in the committed and holy union of marriage. Although sex is pleasurable and intimate, it is destructive outside its proper context.

God wants to us to obey His commands first and foremost to demonstrate to us the purity of a relationship with Him. Most of the major and minor prophets speak to us about how Israel and Judah constantly defiled themselves with foreign gods in prostitution and adulterous relationships. God's character and His faithfulness to us in His design shows His glory.

Similarly, any type of compromise that is popular in the world leads to heartbreak and dissatisfaction. Simply look at the state of the culture and the world. Many people, even Christians, might say that you need to supposedly test drive before you buy but look at the state of their lives and souls. People also say that what is in the past should stay in the past, but that is a naive view of the consequences of premarital sex because of the strong correlation between premarital sex and divorce rates, which I will address later.

God has commanded us to flee sexual immorality prior to marriage to protect us from the negative consequences of pre-marital sex. God's way of doing things might seem to limit us from enjoyable experiences now, but if we delay gratification and use self-control, we will experience the fullness of what they should be later.

Remaining chaste prior to marriage is hard. We might be ridiculed by the world for it. But it is never a bad thing to follow God's plan. In fact, science—our human understanding of how things work—often confirms God's plan as the best for marriage.

Studies like the one below track measures of perceived marital stability, sexual quality, communication, and marital satisfaction.[2] Research found that delaying sex, especially sex until marriage, increases the quality of all the factors.

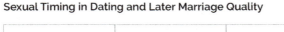

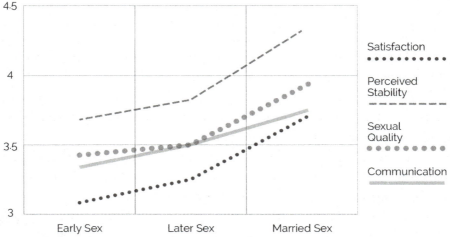

Source: *Journal of Family Psychology*[1]

Some of the potential reasons for this is that the delay in sex eliminates strong emotional entanglements that might interfere with the ability to evaluate and vet a potential spouse. It is easy to overlook learning about the faith, character, values, and commitment of a spouse if one jumps straight into sex. Likewise, waiting until the covenant and commitment of marriage to enjoy the intimacy of sex helps to strongly bind the married couple together as God intended.

We do not need to buy into the world's supposed wisdom by supposedly test driving before you buy to know that God has our best in mind.

AVOIDING THE PITFALLS OF PRE-MARITAL SEXUAL TEMPTATIONS

Although we discussed avoiding pre-marital sex, avoiding other pre-marital sexual temptations is usually difficult for men and women in our highly sexed culture. Christian men and women often become involved in pornography, romance novels, and even unchaste or less-than-modest pictures, videos, and postings on social media.

As we saw in the last section, unchaste behavior dishonors God and can lead to less perceived marital stability, sexual quality, communication, and marital satisfaction. Pornography, romance novels, and similar sexual items will often be disruptive to marital sex and intimacy.

Since Christian men and women struggle in this area, we will mention ways to combat this. The Christian walk is about taking off the old and putting on the new. If you constantly focus on taking off the old, the old basically becomes a temptation to you. All your attention is constantly focused on avoiding pornography, but your mind is so focused on pornography that you're tempting yourself to watch pornography.

> When the unclean spirit goes out of a man, it passes through waterless places seeking rest, and not finding any, it says, "I will return to my house from which I came." And when it comes, it finds it swept and put in order. Then it goes and takes along seven other spirits more evil than itself, and they go in and live there; and the last state of that man becomes worse than the first (Luke 11:24–26).

If you only remove porn, romance novels, or other sexually charged material from your life but don't replace that void with healthy habits, you can fall back into familiar sinful patterns.

The goal is not to simply remove a bad habit but to also instill good habits. Dwelling on "not looking at porn" and even "praying about not looking at porn" means that the subject is on your mind. This focus of attention on the temptation can actually further tempt you to do it again! Paul discusses this very concept in Ephesians 4 about taking off the old and putting on the new. You need to shift your focus away from the old and onto the new.

> But you did not learn Christ in this way, if indeed you have heard Him and have been taught in Him, just as truth is in Jesus, that, in reference to your former manner of life, you lay aside the old self, which is being corrupted in accordance with the lusts of deceit, and that you be renewed in the spirit of your mind, and put on the new self, which in the likeness of God has been created in righteousness and holiness of the truth (Ephesians 4:20–24).

The goal must not simply be taking off the old. You must also put on the new. Remove the sinful habits and create new godly habits. Don't focus on sin but on pleasing God.

What is putting on the new?

- How are you using the gifts of the Spirit that reside within you in the church?

- How are you serving other people and doing good works?
- How are you evangelizing and getting discipled or discipling others?
- What commands of the scriptures are you focusing on so that you can grow more holy?

Since you're thinking about relationships and marriage:

- Have you been studying the scriptures about marriage and what God expects of you?
- Have you been putting those into practice already?
- How can you be more Christlike as a potential husband in marriage?

Meditating on and doing the new takes your mind and focus off the old, which removes the temptations from in front of you. An addict will continue to make poor choices outside of intervention, but those who have accepted Christ have a new master. You might fall into sin here and there, but you can change: you are not under compulsion anymore to be addicted to the desires of the flesh. The Holy Spirit is your helper. This improves as you actively put on the new. You don't have time to worry about temptations when you're doing the things above. It's the process of sanctification.

MALE AND FEMALE SEXUAL DESIRE IS NOT SINFUL

Modern Christians have erred in promoting the concept of purity culture. One of the common verses used to support this is the verse on lust in Matthew 5. This so-called purity falls into the camp of gnostic heresy, which states that desires of the body are sinful and fallen.

> You have heard that it was said, "You shall not commit adultery"; but I say to you that everyone who looks at a woman (*gune*) with lust (*epithumeo*) for her has already committed adultery with her in his heart (Matthew 5:27–28).

> What shall we say then? Is the Law sin? May it never be! On the contrary, I would not have come to know sin except through the Law; for I would not have known about coveting (*epithumia*) if the Law had not said, "You shall not covet (epithumeo)." But sin, taking opportunity through the commandment, produced in me

coveting (*epithumia*) of every kind; for apart from the Law sin is dead (Romans 7:7–8).

Notice the difference in translation of the Koine Greek word epithumeo/epithumia as both lust and coveting even in the same Bible version. This is common throughout most English translations of the Bible. Likewise, in Koine Greek, the word for both "woman" and "wife" is *gune*.[3]

Examining the Koine Greek reveals that Matthew 5 and Romans 7 parallels the Ten Commandments, which is why Jesus said, "You have heard that it was said. . . . " as most of the crowds that He preached to would have heard the Torah at temple readings.

> You shall not commit adultery. . . . You shall not covet your neighbor's house; you shall not covet your neighbor's wife or his male servant or his female servant or his ox or his donkey or anything that belongs to your neighbor. (Exodus 20:14, 17).

Therefore, a more accurate translation of the Matthew 5 passage would be to say that any [man] who covets another man's wife or a husband who covets another woman commits adultery with her in his heart. In other words, if you desire another woman or wife that is not yours, you're committing adultery with her in your heart.

A single man cannot commit adultery with a single woman. The scripture in 1 Corinthians 7 tells us that if a man and a woman burn with passion for each other, they should marry!

This is not to say that if you are a single man that you can't make an idol out of a single woman. But it is far from a condemnation in the way that many in the church say that if you experience sexual attraction to a single woman that you are sinning. Sexual attraction stemming from sexual desire is part of how God created humans. It should be the impetus for you to ask her out on a date if she's a Christian so that you can see if she's a possible candidate for marriage.

DO NOT START A RELATIONSHIP WITH AN UNBELIEVER

This is direct advice from scripture.

> Do not be bound together with unbelievers; for what partnership have righteousness and lawlessness, or what fellowship has light with

darkness? Or what harmony has Christ with Belial, or what has a believer in common with an unbeliever? Or what agreement has the temple of God with idols? For we are the temple of the living God; just as God said, "I will dwell in them and walk among them; And I will be their God, and they shall be My people. Therefore, come out from their midst and be separate," says the Lord. "And do not touch what is unclean; And I will welcome you" (2 Corinthians 6:14–17).

This is a huge problem among Christian men and women today. You find someone you click with who is beautiful or handsome and who wants to be with you. Then you find out they're not a Christian. You reason to yourself that it's okay to be with them or to just hang out as friends. You think that maybe if they come to church, they will convert because you're missionary dating. Then you start spending more and more times with them, and soon you're in a relationship. You tell yourself that it's okay and nothing will happen with them, but then you find yourself in increasingly compromising situations.

Then you have a huge tug-of-war within yourself because you want to stay true to God, but you're already physically, emotionally, and mentally in a relationship with this person. It will hurt so badly to extricate yourself from the person that maybe you should stay together rather than follow God's command to not be with them.

This is not uncommon. First Corinthians 15:33–34 warns us, "Do not be deceived: 'Bad company corrupts good morals.' Become sober-minded as you ought, and stop sinning; for some have no knowledge of God. I speak this to your shame."

Bad company corrupts good morals. Missionary dating doesn't work. Rather than converting them, you will likely be placed in compromised moral situations. Two Christians who like each other will already struggle to avoid pre-marital sex, but what happens when it's only you and the non-believer wants to have sex? You're setting yourself up for failure.

This is not to say that you shouldn't evangelize non-Christian women. Jesus did with the Samaritan woman at the well (John 4). But you should not enter a relationship with any non-Christian woman. If she becomes a Christian and has shown a pattern of sound faith and conscience that is consistent with this, the relationship can possibly work. But I still advise against this because it's easy for immature Christians to fall prey to compromise and ulterior motives.

Those Christians who eventually marry non-believers against the counsel of the scriptures have very difficult lives because their character and values don't match up. They might want to raise your children the way they want rather than with Christian morals and values. They might not treat you or the children well because they don't use the Bible as their standard. You will have many more fights and conflicts because you are not on the same page.

You might have a strong chemistry with many attractive people out there, but don't buy the lie that you should be in relationships with them. Heed the wisdom of the Bible and avoid starting a relationship with an unbeliever. If you're a believer in a relationship with an unbeliever, break up with them now. It will be hard on you because you have created a bond that should not have been started, but it will be better in the long run.

Finally, one of the huge issues with starting a relationship with an unbeliever is that you're taking yourself off the market. If an attractive Christian woman wanted to be with you, you're making yourself unavailable because you're already in a relationship. Who knows how many other potential prospects you might have missed because you were in a dead-end relationship with an unbeliever? Don't make this mistake.

It's better to stay single and prepare for marriage until you find a Christian who wants to be with you.

SECTION THREE
BIBLICAL MASCULINITY

Chapter 7
WHAT DOES IT MEAN TO BE A MAN?

WHAT DOES IT MEAN TO BE A MAN?

What does it mean to be a man?

Men are being thrust in one direction by our culture and are treated disrespectfully and as if they are irrelevant.

The left rails against toxic masculinity, which is interpreted as anything that ranges from the patriarchy to micro-aggressions to privilege and other made-up concepts to make all men feel bad about who they are. The right says you should be chivalrous and respect women. You should man up and marry them and put their own happiness above your own. The church has similar notions to the left or right, depending on where you attend. They expect you to get married, have a family, and sacrifice, sacrifice, sacrifice.

But what does the Bible say about masculinity?

This is what the Lord says to the husbands and fathers of Israel about how to lead their families:

> Now this is the commandment, the statutes and the judgments which the Lord your God has commanded me to teach you, that you might do them in the land where you are going over to possess it, so that you and your son and your grandson might fear the Lord your God, to keep all His statutes and His commandments which I command you, all the days of your life, and that your days may be prolonged. O Israel, you should listen and be careful to do it, that it may be well with you and that you may multiply greatly, just as the Lord, the God of your fathers, has promised you, in a land flowing with milk and honey.

> Hear, O Israel! The Lord is our God, the Lord is one! You shall love the Lord your God with all your heart and with all your soul and with all your might. These words, which I am commanding you today, shall be on your heart. You shall teach them diligently to your sons and shall talk of them when you sit in your house and when you walk by the way and when you lie down and when you rise up. You shall bind them as a sign on your hand and they shall be as frontals on your forehead. You shall write them on the doorposts of your house and on your gates (Deuteronomy 6:1–9).

This is what the Lord told Joshua about how to lead the Israelites into the Promised Land:

> Be strong and courageous, for you shall give this people possession of the land which I swore to their fathers to give them. Only be strong and very courageous; be careful to do according to all the law which Moses My servant commanded you; do not turn from it to the right or to the left, so that you may have success wherever you go. This book of the law shall not depart from your mouth, but you shall meditate on it day and night, so that you may be careful to do according to all that is written in it; for then you will make your way prosperous, and then you will have success. Have I not commanded you? Be strong and courageous! Do not tremble or be dismayed, for the Lord your God is with you wherever you go. (Joshua 1:6–9).

David told Solomon the following:

> As David's time to die drew near, he charged Solomon his son, saying, "I am going the way of all the earth. Be strong, therefore, and show yourself a man. Keep the charge of the Lord your God, to walk in His ways, to keep His statutes, His commandments, His ordinances, and His testimonies, according to what is written in the Law of Moses, that you may succeed in all that you do and wherever you turn, so that the Lord may carry out His promise which He spoke concerning me, saying, 'If your sons are careful of their way, to walk before Me in truth with all their heart and with all their soul, you shall not lack a man on the throne of Israel.'" (1 Kings 2:1–4).

Paul told the Corinthian church in 1 Corinthians 16:13–14, "Be on the alert, stand firm in the faith, act like men, be strong. Let all that you do be done in love."

From the Old Testament to the New Testament, a concept spans the pages of the Bible: a boy who matures into a man should fear the Lord, be taught the commands of the Lord, obey the Lord, be strong and courageous in the commands of the Lord, and be alert and stand firm in the faith. This is what it means to be a man.

Despite what many other people—even Christians—claim to know about what so-called real men should do, the Bible is clear in its definition of who a man should be. A man is not defined by who the world wants him to be or even who those in the church want him to be if that definition conflicts with scripture. He is defined by his unwavering faith in God, whether as a single or in marriage.

Husbands and fathers are the leaders of their wives and children, so they need to be able to stand firm in the faith and teach their family to follow the Lord. This was one of the failures of Adam: he chose to eat the fruit instead of refusing the fruit from Eve.

One of the biggest insults you can give a man is to call him a coward. Even Jesus acknowledges this in Matthew 10:32–33. "Therefore everyone who confesses Me before men, I will also confess him before My Father who is in heaven. But whoever denies Me before men, I will also deny him before My Father who is in heaven."

Those who are afraid (cowards) to acknowledge Jesus before men will not be acknowledged by Him before the Father. Men should be strong and courageous to obey what the Lord has commanded them, and this translates into whether he chooses celibacy for the Lord or to be married and raise a family.

Now that we know what it means to be a man, let's look at our identity and purpose as men.

IDENTITY IN CHRIST

Now that we know about the scriptures and what they say about marriage and attraction and how those concepts work in real life, we need to take a step backward. While we need to know about all these details, we must not forget the two most important things: our identity in Christ and why God has us on earth in the first place.

It would not be an exaggeration to say that a root cause of many problems in society is fatherlessness. The out-of-wedlock birth rates in the United States have risen to 40 percent. First-marriage divorces have climbed to 40 percent, and total marriage divorces are up to 50 percent. We covered some of those statistics in the first couple chapters.

The lack of a father in a child's life gives rise to a whole host of dysfunction—poverty, drug and alcohol abuse, poor emotional and physical health, low educational achievement, crime, early sexual activity, teenage pregnancy, and more. Some fathers are deadbeats and absentees, but other fathers have been ejected from their family because their partner or wives wanted child support, alimony, divorce, or custody of the kids.

On a large scale, all of us are affected by fatherlessness. Our culture and society regularly trash husbands and fathers as deadbeats, make them the butt of jokes, call them clowns and worthless, and disrespect them in general. We seek to drown the needs that we have as children learning about life by filling it up with things of the world.

Jesus primarily talks about God as our Father. If nothing else, so as not to profane the title God ascribes to Himself, this alone stands as an excellent reason not to disrespect the inherited title that God gives to human fathers. He could have referred to God in any other way—love, goodness, righteousness, justice, mercy, grace, humility, joy, peace, patience/endurance, or self-control—but He chose fatherhood. Romans 6, 7, and the culmination in 8 address the Father's adoption of us as Christians through Jesus's blood as children of God.

> So then, brethren, we are under obligation, not to the flesh, to live according to the flesh—for if you are living according to the flesh, you must die; but if by the Spirit you are putting to death the deeds of the body, you will live. For all who are being led by the Spirit of God, these are sons of God. For you have not received a spirit of slavery leading to fear again, but you have received a spirit of adoption as sons by which we cry out, "Abba! Father!" The Spirit Himself testifies with our spirit that we are children of God, and if children, heirs also,

heirs of God and fellow heirs with Christ, if indeed we suffer with Him so that we may also be glorified with Him (Romans 8:12–17).

When we become Christians, we are adopted by God the Father into His family. This gives us a new purpose.

And Jesus came up and spoke to them, saying, "All authority has been given to Me in heaven and on earth. Go therefore and make disciples of all the nations, baptizing them in the name of the Father and the Son and the Holy Spirit, teaching them to observe all that I commanded you; and lo, I am with you always, even to the end of the age" (Matthew 28:18–20).

Our identity is adopted children of the Father, part of the bride of Christ. This identity gives us purpose. Our new mission as Christians is ultimately to evangelize, baptize, and make disciples so that they, too, can become children of God. This is the ministry of reconciliation as it says in 2 Corinthians 5.

For most men, a wife and family are also a part of that mission. This is an additional duty to God that we have as husbands: to adhere to the roles and responsibilities of a husband. All these areas need to come together in one coherent whole to love God with all our heart, soul, mind, and strength. In other words, to paraphrase 1 Corinthians 10:31, "Whether therefore you eat, or drink, or whatever you do, do all to the glory of God."

This is the correct identity we need, and we will see that this mentality helps us develop as Christian men.

JESUS SAYS, "FOLLOW ME"

The relationship between Jesus and the church serves as a guide to male and female relationships and marriage. The analogy of husband (Jesus) and wife (the church) in Ephesians 5 provides a strong background for how we are to walk in male-female relationships that lead to marriage and in marriage. This goes against many things in our popular culture and even in the current church today.

The notion in popular culture is that men romantically pursue women. This thought has also pervaded the Church in the form of the idea that Jesus is my lover or that husbands should romance their wives because Jesus and God continually pursue you. This is false. The Father and Jesus both call us, or rather present us with the opportunity to follow, but it is up to us to acknowledge the call and choose to follow.

> Now as Jesus was walking by the Sea of Galilee, He saw two brothers, Simon who was called Peter, and Andrew his brother, casting a net into the sea; for they were fishermen. And He said to them, "Follow Me, and I will make you fishers of men." Immediately they left their nets and followed Him. Going on from there He saw two other brothers, James the son of Zebedee, and John his brother, in the boat with Zebedee their father, mending their nets; and He called them. Immediately they left the boat and their father, and followed Him (Matthew 4:18–22).

Jesus had just traveled out of the wilderness where He was tempted and had started to preach the gospel in the surrounding areas. In other words, Jesus started His God-given mission. The disciples saw Jesus on His mission; He invited them to come join Him in the journey, and they wanted to follow Him.

In the context of male-female relationships, remember from the beginning that God created woman to be a helpmeet to man. Jesus demonstrates His mission and presents a clear vision of how He was going to task His disciples when they follow Him: to be fishers of men. In the same way, a man who asks a woman out on a date should already be working toward His God-given mission—evangelize, make disciples, use their spiritual gifts to build up the Body of Christ, and lead ministry. He should also have a clear vision of where she fits into his life as his helpmeet as she will help him on his mission. She will also need to fulfill her biblical roles and responsibilities. Jesus does not chase after us nor should men chase after women. This flies in the face of all romance that is popular in the culture and church. Consider the claims of Jesus that He is the bread of life in John 6.

> Therefore many of His disciples, when they heard this said, "This is a difficult statement; who can listen to it?" But Jesus, conscious that His disciples grumbled at this, said to them, "Does this cause

you to stumble? What then if you see the Son of Man ascending to where He was before? It is the Spirit who gives life; the flesh profits nothing; the words that I have spoken to you are spirit and are life. But there are some of you who do not believe." For Jesus knew from the beginning who they were who did not believe, and who it was that would betray Him. And He was saying, "For this reason I have said to you, that no one can come to Me unless it has been granted him from the Father."

As a result of this many of His disciples withdrew and were not walking with Him anymore. So Jesus said to the twelve, "You do not want to go away also, do you?" Simon Peter answered Him, "Lord, to whom shall we go? You have words of eternal life. We have believed and have come to know that You are the Holy One of God" (John 6:60–69).

Jesus challenges all those were following Him about His role and place in the kingdom of God. His invitation is the still same: Follow me and continue to follow me. Yet He let those who were not interested walk away. The same is true of God in Romans 1 where He allows humanity to be given over to their sinful passions and lusts if they don't want to seek Him.

Consider the father's actions in the parable of the prodigal son (Luke 15). The son decides he wants his inheritance to go party. The father allows him to go off on his own. The father does not chase after him to persuade him otherwise. Only when the son makes the choice to come back to the father does the father see him in the distance, come out of his house, and run toward him with arms open wide.

The pervasive romantic attitude that men are supposed to pursue women runs contrary to the Father and Jesus's actions. Both culture and some in the church would have us believe that Jesus continues to chase after us at all costs. This is only true in the example of the parable of the lost sheep where the shepherd goes to apprehend a sheep that wandered away, yet in that case that sheep was already under the shepherd's care (Luke 15). Only after we are committed in marriage are we responsible to seek after that which is lost when it is ours. This mirrors the roles and responsibilities of marriage.

The biblical model for relationships is that men demonstrate and invite, and women choose to respond to that invitation. If a man asks a woman out on a date and she turns him down, should that man continue to try to be romantic and chase after her? Of course not! A man cannot say or do anything to convince a woman to like him more. Even if by some measure, he wears down her resistance, and she capitulates, such a relationship will not work out in the long run because she likely did not have a genuine desire to be in the relationship with him. Whether or not she acts on it, she will want to leave as soon as the next best thing comes along.

No matter how much you as a man might want to be in a relationship with a woman, she also needs to want to be in that relationship with you. She has to want to follow you out of a genuine desire to be with you. We will expand on this in the next section.

- Jesus leads, the church follows. Men lead, women follow.
- Jesus doesn't chase after us. Men should not chase after women.

The goal of a single Christian man should be to wholeheartedly carry out his God-given mission and invite a woman on a date (or to be courted) to see if she wants to follow him.

GOD AND JESUS LEAD PERFECTLY BUT . . .

Dating/courtship and marriage are not as simple as assuming only one person is ever at fault. Each person has different roles and responsibilities, but how a husband and a wife respond needs to be evaluated separately.

Unfortunately, in the church many of the problems that come up in the marriage will be heaped on the husband because he is the head of the marriage and supposedly has responsibility for the whole marriage. This is partly influenced by culture, feminism, and the supposed abuses of men as they are willing to absolve or ignore any culpability that the wife might have in the matter. This is one way that the church can technically cling to the biblical concept of headship while covertly serving and catering to a feminist agenda. In reality:

- In any situation, a husband can choose to act in a godly or ungodly manner.
- In any situation, a wife can choose to act in a godly or ungodly manner.

- Our actions can influence our spouse, but they never *cause* someone else to do something.

For example, consider God leading the Israelites and Jesus leading the church (his disciples and future believers). No Christian would claim that God or Jesus did not lead perfectly. However, the Israelites and the disciples did not always follow perfectly. Quite the opposite, they had hard hearts and messed up constantly.

The Israelites were prone to wander away from the Lord instead of following Him, and God allowed them to suffer the consequences of their actions. When they walked out from under the protection of his authority, the surrounding nations invaded and subjugated them many times throughout Judges and the prophets. Similarly, the disciples often had other ideas of what the Messiah looked like, which is why Jesus rebuked them for their lack of faith or their fear in their circumstances.

Ephesians 5 states that Jesus is the head of the church as husbands are the head of marriage. One of the greatest temptations is that those under authority are prone to rebel when disagree or feel differently according to their understanding. 1 Peter 3 addresses how to treat wrongdoing by an unbelieving husband, which falls in line with the roles and responsibilities of a Christian wife to her Christian husband.

> In the same way, you wives, be submissive to your own husbands so that even if any of them are disobedient to the word, they may be won without a word by the behavior of their wives, as they observe your chaste and respectful behavior. Your adornment must not be merely external—braiding the hair, and wearing gold jewelry, or putting on dresses; but let it be the hidden person of the heart, with the imperishable quality of a gentle and quiet spirit, which is precious in the sight of God. For in this way in former times the holy women also, who hoped in God, used to adorn themselves, being submissive to their own husbands; just as Sarah obeyed Abraham, calling him lord, and you have become her children if you do what is right without being frightened by any fear (1 Peter 3:1–6).

A wife might be unhappy whether or not a husband is leading properly, but according to the scriptures, her response should be the same: to have a gentle and quiet spirit, to have chaste and respectful behavior, and to be submissive and obedient to her husband in order that God might be glorified and that such behavior might potentially win a husband for the Lord.

A husband might be unhappy whether or not his wife is submissive, but according to the scriptures, his response should be the same: love her and live with her in an understanding way as she is weaker and honor her so that his prayers aren't hindered.

The goal, above all, is to continually to put God first in all circumstances and to stay faithful to His Word. After all, this is why Paul recommended that people not marry in the first place, and why he also suggested that those with wives should live as if they had none in that same passage (1 Corinthians 7). Our goal is holiness, not happiness. Staying faithful to God's commands might bring unhappiness in the short-term and potentially even in the long-term. That's why long-suffering/patience is part of the fruit of the Spirit.

Scripture is full of examples of this. Joseph was sold into slavery, falsely accused of rape, and spent years in a dungeon (Genesis). David was chased for years by Saul but chose to righteously spare Saul's life even when he had the opportunity to kill him (1 Samuel). Job lost everything that he had, was afflicted with sores, and his wife and friends told him to curse God and die. The prophets were often on the run from the kings of Israel and Judah who wanted to disobey God (Elijah, Elisha, and Jeremiah). Hosea was told by God to marry an unfaithful prostitute. Jesus Himself was persecuted by the religious leaders, and many disciples left him (John 6). The disciples were persecuted, often to death, for the sake of Jesus.

This is rather self-explanatory but needs repeating: you can't change someone. Only God can do that, and we don't control God although we can certainly pray for His intervention.

In the meantime, we must focus on ourselves. Our goal as Christians is to make godly choices, steward our own lives well, and let God change the hearts and minds of others through our actions. We should keep this in mind in a relationship or marriage.

Chapter 8
CULTIVATING MASCULINE LEADERSHIP

YOUR NEW MISSION FROM GOD

If you have been reading closely, our original mission from God along with His intent for marriage was to take dominion over the earth and be fruitful and multiply. When Jesus came, this mission gained a new dimension.

> And Jesus came up and spoke to them, saying, "All authority has been given to Me in heaven and on earth. Go therefore and make disciples of all the nations, baptizing them in the name of the Father and the Son and the Holy Spirit, teaching them to observe all that I commanded you; and lo, I am with you always, even to the end of the age." (Matthew 28:18–20).

The new dimension has an added spiritual component; our goal is to win nonbelievers to Christ through the Holy Spirit to make disciples. This is the analogy in Ephesians 5 where Christ and the church is compared to the husband and the wife.

When we become distracted from our Christ-given mission, issues tend to creep into our lives. Many Christians are fond of imparting non-Christian values to marriage, such as:

- Communication in marriage is critical to success.
- Marriage is hard work.
- Marriage is about love (feelings).
- To have a successful marriage, you need to do X, Y, and Z.

These are not necessarily true. A husband that is focused on living out God's mission for his life with his wife following and helping will be fruitful irrespective of their communication or their hard work because their communication will automatically improve as they are pursuing Christ's mission. Walking in Christ's mission for us manifests the fruit of the Spirit: love, joy, peace, patience, kindness, goodness, faithfulness, humility, and self-control. (See Galatians 5:22–23.)

We can easily be distracted by all the different cultural and even so-called Christian advice out there about marriage, but do not lose sight of your mission from God. As the head of the marriage, the husband must continually seek God's mission for him and his family. Your wife is to be your helpmeet in this.

What this often looks like for husbands is serving in the church, leading Bible studies, outreach, and even possibly being a deacon, elder, or serving in other leadership position if that is your calling. You should be actively using your spiritual gifts within the Body of Christ. There are many different gifts of the Spirit, so actively explore them in your Bible to find out which ones you have. Volunteer or even take charge or create ministries in the church to use them.

If a potential woman or prospective wife is not on board with your mission from God and is not interested in helping you with it, that tends to be a red flag. This conflict of interest will eventually pit your loyalty to God against your loyalty to your wife. Don't make this mistake.

GOD'S METHOD OF MARRIAGE IS A PROCESS THAT BUILDS ON ITSELF

God did not make a mistake in His design of marriage. One of the reasons why a strong, masculine leader is attractive and helps as a driving force in marriage is because it prepares you for increasing leadership and responsibilities.

- You are under the leadership of your parents and become independent as an adult.
- You are a leader of one (yourself).
- You are a leader of two (a relationship and marriage with a wife).
- You are a leader of a family (wife and children).
- You are a leader of a clan or community (grandchildren and even in the church).

As you can see, this is a gradual process and one that builds upon itself. If you are not independent, you can't be a leader of yourself. If you cannot lead yourself well, how will anyone want to follow you? If you're not an effective leader of yourself and your wife, then your children will likely run roughshod all over you.

This is where your mission for Christ comes into play. He has tasked us with evangelism and making disciples and using our spiritual gifts in the church and community. The more do these things, the more we are effective at stewarding what He has given us. As we do what God has called us to do and step out in faith, we are responsible for everything that has been given to us. We become mature in Christ. As we become mature in Christ, we can start imparting our maturity to others. This is the essence of leadership.

YOU ARE THE LEADER

First, we need to address mindset. Leadership is imparted to a husband by the Creator. As I've observed the feminized Church, I've found that men and husbands are constantly tripped up by several issues regarding the position of headship.

- **Qualifications:** God does not require qualifications. He takes anyone who is willing to serve Him. Moses had a couple of false starts in Exodus. God used the shepherd boy David to rule His kingdom. Jesus chose fishermen and a tax collector as His disciples. You don't need to be qualified, but you must be willing to follow Him.
- **Justification:** What you do does not make you qualified. ~~We have been saved by grace through faith so that no one can boast about works.~~ God has made the husband the head of his wife. You do not need to be accountable or look to anyone other than God because He gave you that role.
- **Worked for:** You have the position already offered to you from God. You do not need to jump through any hoops to be in the position.
- **Permission:** You don't need permission from your wife, yourself, or church leaders to be the leader. If you find yourself constantly asking for permission, you are abdicating your role as the leader and letting everyone else decide what you should be doing.

If you're waiting for something to happen for you to be the leader, you'll be waiting for eternity. If you choose to be married, God says you are the leader. You must be willing to walk in what He called you to do. This is different from leadership positions in the church (1 Timothy 3), which have qualifications and standards for the position. The position of husband does not require any of these, but they are excellent qualifications and standards to strive toward.

Leaders have a mission. What did God do when we were stuck in our sin? He sent His Son Jesus to sacrifice Himself for our sins. Part of that plan was to save us and then to invite us to partner with Him in His mission: spread the gospel and make disciples of all nations.

How do you fit into that plan? What are your gifts of the Spirit? How will you use them in the church?

How are you developing spiritually so that you can be the effective leader that God has called you to be? The spiritual disciplines require time and effort to grow in: understanding the scriptures, prayer, fasting, meditation, and so on.

Leaders are made, not born. Jesus's ministry was short but powerful. We don't know much about His early life until He was about thirty years old, but once He was thirty, He ministered powerfully for three years until His death and resurrection. David's life was the same. He was a shepherd boy for a long while, but God was able to use him mightily later in his life. Joseph was sold into slavery, worked as a household slave, and was thrown into prison before his powerful ministry started. Even if you have been in relative obscurity, God can use you if you are willing.

It takes a lot of work to develop leadership qualities to lead men and women. You need to find and seize the opportunities that come up. Leading Bible studies is one of the easiest ways to do this, but other opportunities in the church, such as organizing and serving in food and clothing drives, volunteering and mentoring those in the youth group, and various other ministries are all great places to serve. Find a mentor, such as an older Christian man who is further along in the journey than you.

Do everything for the glory of God. (See 1 Corinthians 10:31.) It requires strength, fortitude, and courage to take those stands for your faith. It involves putting yourself out there and making mistakes. It means taking risks and being bold.

UNDERSTANDING LEADERSHIP

First, men are tasked to wield authority with love in marriage. How does this play out?

For the most part, leadership is easy. You make decisions after carefully considering the consequences of your actions. You use wisdom, diligence, and prudence to choose the righteous path. The difficult part of leadership is always in the face of conflict. This is where leadership is truly tested and why Moses, Joshua, David, Jesus, and many great men in the Bible consistently lauded strength and courage under pressure to choose to love God and follow His commands. Actions you take should be characterized by love and by the fruit of the Spirit.

> But the fruit of the Spirit is love, joy, peace, patience, kindness, goodness, faithfulness, gentleness, self-control; against such things there is no law. Now those who belong to Christ Jesus have crucified the flesh with its passions and desires (Galatians 5:22–24).

> Love is patient, love is kind and is not jealous; love does not brag and is not arrogant, does not act unbecomingly; it does not seek its own, is not provoked, does not take into account a wrong suffered, does not rejoice in unrighteousness, but rejoices with the truth; bears all things, believes all things, hopes all things, endures all things. Love never fails; but if there are gifts of prophecy, they will be done away; if there are tongues, they will cease; if there is knowledge, it will be done away. (1 Corinthians 13:4–8).

For example, the quintessential display of leadership always comes when emotions and tensions run high, especially during conflict and arguments.

Can you be gentle and peaceful? Can you take a step back from the conflict and calm down so that you are patient? Can you reign in any jealousy? Can you refrain from bragging or arrogant behavior? Can you take into account each viewpoint instead of seeking your own selfishness? Can you stop any provoking behaviors?

One of the best things you can do is seek to fully understand what the other person (or girlfriend or wife) is feeling in that situation and why she has made a particular decision. Anger and other negative emotions do not help you.

Second, examine your leadership style. Even some of the most important Christian leaders of our day seem to have subtly fallen for the feminist mantra.

Wayne Grudem is a professor of theological and religious studies and one of the co-founders of Council on Biblical Manhood and Womanhood, the organization that coined the term complementarianism. He is also one of the general editors for the English Standard Version (ESV) Bible. In his book, *Countering the Claims of Evangelical Feminism: Biblical Responses to the Key Questions*, he attempts to address a biblical response to feminism:

> The biblical ideal is that the husband is to be both loving and humble in his leadership. The wife is to be both joyful and intelligent in her submission. Practically, this means that they will frequently talk about many decisions, both large and small. This also means that both the husband and the wife will listen to the other's unique wisdom and insight related to the decision. Often one will defer to the other in the decision; rarely will they differ greatly in the decision (for the Lord has made them "one flesh").[1]

Ironically, this description aligns more with egalitarianism than with complementarianism. If he were talking about the model used in scripture, he would have stated that the husband makes the decisions as the head, and the wife offers her advice as the helpmeet. Some might think this is nit-picking, but the insidious nature of the wording creeps into marriages in multiple ways.

Intelligent submission was coined to counter the feminist argument that a wife who submits to her husband is a doormat. Regardless of whether a wife's submission is intelligent or not, the feminists will still hate it. There's no use arguing with people who think the Bible is wrong. Unfortunately, the counter of intelligent submission to the idea of the wife as a doormat can damage marriages, which we will see in a bit.

Unlike the Myers-Briggs Type Indicator, which is not scientifically reliable, the Big Five personality test has received more scientific validation. Like most personality tests, it has a limited scope but we can see general trends of human behavior from looking at different traits.[2] One of the traits listed is conscientiousness or efficient and organized versus easy-going and careless. Generally, a man that tends toward stronger conscientiousness will be very structured in his mission for God and his life while a man that leans toward low conscientiousness will be less structured.

In the church, some pastors might criticize the more-structured man who leads by expecting tasks done in a certain way as controlling. They laud the less-structured man with a lax or easy-going leadership style as the "right" type of leadership style. This simply is not true. A man with a very structured leadership style with a wife who fully submits to that leadership is a godly marriage. Under the guise that wives are not doormats to a structured and direct leadership style, those in the church can sow discontent into the marriage by telling the husband and wife that they are wrong and not following biblical principles when, in fact, they are doing it well.

Usually those in a structured marriage won't pay much attention to this talk, which is good. The big problem is when the man likes more structure but the wife likes less structure marriage. The preaching or commentary from the church in this case will sow discontent and motivate the wife to rebel against her husband because he is sinning when he is not. This can destabilize marriages and potentially lead to divorce. The wife should be told to submit to her husband, be respectful, and stop rebelling, and the husband might be counseled to have a less structured style and to be more understanding to his wife.

Single men can save themselves some grief by identified what type of leadership style they have and by making sure they do not marry a woman who conflicts with that leadership style.

A more-structured man usually gets along well with a woman who likes structure while a less-structured man usually connects better with a woman who likes less structure. But issues tend to crop up when a man is more structured and a woman likes less structure. They can also occur when a man is less structured and a woman likes more structure. In the first case, the wife tends to rebel against her husband and the church often supports her. In the second case, the wife tends to start trying to mother her husband for his lack of structure instead of being his wife. This can manifest as nagging, contentiousness, and disappointment when she thinks he should be doing things the same way she does.

These mixed-structure marriages can work effectively, but both the husband and wife need to be aware of and reign in their temptation to sin. The husband as the leader has the obligation to be understanding of his wife's personality in this case, and the wife has the responsibility to resist the temptation to rebel, nag, be contentious, and disappointed.

The wife should understand why she needs to submit to her husband in a scenario, but this might not always be possible. In fact, we as Christians often do not need to be intelligent in our submission. When God tell us to do good works, do we need to question why we need to do good works? Is it because God is good? Is it because we are a shining light for others? Is it because these things are profitable for men (Titus 3)? Is it because God planned them in advance for those who are called in Him (Ephesians 2)? All these things are true and why we do good works, but we don't need to know why we need to do good works in order to do them.

When we see someone suffering or homeless, do we need to be intelligent in our compassion for him? Or do we need only to act on what God has put in our hearts for those less fortunate? In fact, in many cases, if you think about the actions you will take, you can often talk yourself out of being compassionate or doing what is good. "I don't need to do anything because someone else will help them or give them clothing or money."

Furthermore, we need to understand faith. Faith builds trust even when we don't understand. Consider Hebrews 11, which is colloquially called the faith chapter. This chapter lists many instances of faith, but Abraham is one of the biggest inspirations. Abraham did not need to know where he was going when God told him to leave for a foreign land. He walked by faith. And trust through faith is what we ultimately want to inspire in our marriages and relationships with others.

Let's not pretend that we need intelligence to obey God. God uses those who are willing to follow Him. Most of His followers throughout the Bible have been unintelligent people who acquired spiritual wisdom as a result of their pursuit of God They did not possess it beforehand. Proverbs says throughout the book that the fear of the Lord is the beginning of knowledge and wisdom, and the fear of the Lord leads us to obedience first even if we don't understand why. It's nice to know why you are doing something, but this isn't necessary for doing what is righteous or good.

Third, there is no such thing as too much submission.

This is an extension of the response to anti-doormat theology or the idea that wives should not submit too much lest they are doormats. This makes no sense scripturally.

- Could Jesus submit too much to God when He was here on earth? No, He followed the Father's will even to death on a cross. Would you call Jesus God's doormat?
- Can the church submit too much to Christ? No. That would be absurd. Would you call the Church Jesus's doormat?
- Ephesians 5 tells wives to submit to their husbands in *all things* as to the Lord.

Complementarians often like to make a case for too much submission or that wives need to be intelligent in their submission. They use feminist terminology, such as doormat, servile, subservient, and other words with negative connotations to tear down the concept of submission to husbands if it doesn't meet their standards. This is incorrect. They are appealing to emotions—to a person's heart rather than to their mind or spirit.

Submission cannot be taken too far. But there is such a thing as false humility in submission. For instance, a husband might have a certain leadership style for his family, and the wife is doing well in that structure. After she has talked with a mentor, read a book, or read a blog or two on the topic of submission, she now has the impression that she was not submitting properly to her husband before. Instead of working well within her husband's structure for the family, she becomes a self-proclaimed doormat in which she never expresses her opinions and changes how she acts with her husband under the pretense of being more submissive.

What typically ends up happening is that this leaves the wife and the husband feeling poorly about everything and generally unfulfilled in their relationship. Then the husband has an awkward conversation with his wife and tells her he just wants his wife back and that she was acting weird in their relationship. Such examples are often used to show that being a doormat or subservient in a marriage is negative. But this is false.

What happened is that the wife was embroiled in the insidious nature of false humility. The wife unilaterally decided that she knew the right way to be a helpmeet to her husband. Although she had the right intentions of being submissive to her husband, she was rebellious in relating to how her husband wanted the marriage run in the first place. The wife wanted to submit on her terms, not follow his framework for applying submissiveness in the household. Thus conflict came up between them, which needed resolution.

Wives often have the impression that being a doormat or subservient is a negative thing from this experience. But they miss the fact that they were being inadvertently rebellious in this scenario. They were listening to other people, books, or blogs about how to submit to their own husband instead of listening to their own husband about how to submit to him.

When a Christian wife who has gone through this experience sees a marriage with more structure, she often believes that the other wife is in sin because she is being a doormat or subservient. This wrong impression causes wives to attempt to butt into other people's marriages to correct this sin when they might be introducing dysfunction or malcontent into an otherwise godly and healthy relationship.

The church should recognize and affirm the authority of the husband in the marriage relationship lest they create discontent and rebelliousness when there is none. If wives have questions about how their husband is leading their marriage, they should consult their husbands instead of asking everyone else. Husbands should learn this well and impart this knowledge to their wives so that this false teaching does not deceive them.

HEART, SOUL, AND STRENGTH (ALL-IN)

Now that we've covered many of the basics, we will address practical life skills that make you a competent leader. This section is entitled heart, soul, and strength because that's how you are to love God, and by loving God with everything, you also become a strong candidate for marriage yourself. So what does this look like?

> "Teacher, which is the great commandment in the Law?" And He said to him, "'You shall love the Lord your God with all your heart, and with all your soul, and with all your mind.' This is the great and foremost commandment. The second is like it, 'You shall love your neighbor as yourself' (Matthew 22:36–39).

And you shall love the Lord your God with all your heart, and with all your soul, and with all your mind, and with all your strength.' The second is this, 'You shall love your neighbor as yourself.' There is no other commandment greater than these (Mark 12:30–31).

And he answered, "You shall love the Lord your God with all your heart, and with all your soul, and with all your strength, and with all your mind; and your neighbor as yourself" (Luke 10:27).

In all these passages, Jesus is quoting from the Law of Moses in Deuteronomy 6:5.

You can see a slight difference in the wording between Matthew, Mark, and Luke. Matthew was writing from the Jewish perspective while Mark and Luke were writing to Gentile audiences. Hebrew culture only uses the term heart as it was more holistic, but Greek thought embraces the idea of both heart and mind.

We can think about it as loving God with *all* the dimensions of our being. One way to think of this is the various dimensions of our being—physical, mental, spiritual, and emotional. You want to cultivate excellence in all these categories.

- Heart – Mental and emotional to attitudes and actions: Take your thoughts and emotions captive to Christ. Use your free will to do good, and excel in your studies and job. Follow God's statutes and align yourself toward Him as opposed to being friends with the world.
- Soul – Spiritual: The soul and spiritual growth is clear. This refers to the scriptures, prayer, fasting, meditation, using your spiritual gifts in the church, and following God's mission for you.
- Strength – Physical: Cultivating the temple of Christ as healthy and strong. This is doubly important if you plan to marry. You will need to be a protector. You can do this by lifting weights, gaining muscle, learning how to fight, cultivating the protector mentality, disciplining yourself, and keeping your body healthy.

You will need to improve and grow in all these different aspects, and they synergize with being a strong masculine leader, protector, and provider.

Are you all-in for God, especially in cultivating future roles and responsibilities of marriage if that is your desire?

YES AND NO (BE DECISIVE)

The simplest way to understanding how to love God with all your heart, soul, mind, and strength is learning to say how to say "yes" and how to say "no" to the right things. As a Christian, the most common example is how to say no to temptations and yes to the things of God. This is a struggle for many Christians that does become easier as you practice it.

Saying yes is not usually a problem for most people, but you will have a difficult time in life if you have difficulty saying no due to peer pressure. You don't have to conform to everyone else's expectations, but you should keep them in mind if they are in your best interest. Knowing how to use your time wisely and knowing what you like and dislike so that you can say yes or no is important. You can learn a big lesson from the popular book, *How to Say No without Feeling Guilty*.[3]

The hard part about saying yes and no is when your roles or responsibilities start to increase. For instance, if you have a wife or kids and have difficulty saying yes or no in certain situations, they will have a field day and run all over you. Ultimately, this goes back to setting boundaries and standards and being firm about them. You're the leader.

It is best to learn how to say yes and no firmly while you are still single. If you are single and reading this book, you should keep this point in mind when you do things. Although Jesus's statement about yes and no is about vows, the same concept applies in these circumstances as well: "Let your yes be yes and your no be no." (See Matthew 5:37.)

Ultimately, your allegiance is to God for any of your roles and responsibilities. Your goal is holiness. Most temptations tend to focus on the short term. Say no to them and work with God's plan for the long term. The short-term pleasures of this world are nothing compared to eternity. So, too, with most decisions related to the future. We save money because it is useful in the long run for a car, house, or kids rather than spending it on frivolous things. We want to invest in what gives us good returns and not be on the negative side of compounding interest. Many make the decision to go to college because the career prospects tend to be better for someone with a college education than for those without a college education even though you're studying hard for years.

All these things need to be kept in mind when you are making decisions. The reason God gave us free will is so that we can evaluate the consequences of our decisions. We can rise above being ruled by our instincts and emotions. We can make long-term decisions by saying no now so that we can be fruitful later. Learning how to say yes to God, especially in the context of saying no to your wife, kids, family, and friends, is hard but beneficial in the long run. Take up your cross and follow Christ first with your decisions.

How can you learn to grow in godliness and be decisive about the choices you make in your life?

YOU ARE NOT YOUR ACTIONS, BUT YOU ARE YOUR HABITS (BE DISCIPLINED)

It's okay to make mistakes if you repent and learn from them. The following common maxim is present in many different forms and is attributed to many different speakers:

> Watch your thoughts, they become words;
> watch your words, they become actions;
> watch your actions, they become habits;
> watch your habits, they become character;
> watch your character, for it becomes your destiny.

This is obviously based in part on the scriptural concept of sowing and reaping. It's also very similar to the way 2 Peter 1 explains how faith develops into love.

> Now for this very reason also, applying all diligence, in your faith supply moral excellence, and in your moral excellence, knowledge, and in your knowledge, self-control, and in your self-control, perseverance, and in your perseverance, godliness, and in your godliness, brotherly kindness, and in your brotherly kindness, love. For if these qualities are yours and are increasing, they render you neither useless nor unfruitful in the true knowledge of our Lord Jesus Christ (2 Peter 1:5–8).

The point is that even though we are redeemed and saved by Christ as Christians, we still sin. Yet Christ's blood has broken us free from the power of sin over our lives. The process of sanctification is about continually taking off the old and putting on the new.

God still loves you even when you sin. It's okay to sin if you are humble and repent of your sin. We all make mistakes, both intentional and unintentional. The problem is when we continually keep making the same mistakes over and over. This becomes a huge issue. The process is the habit which is repeatedly easily and becomes poor character, which leads to backsliding into immorality.

We can do nothing by ourselves, but through the Spirit all things are possible. The Holy Spirit is our helper so that we can repent of our actions and even of our bad habits. We need to continually focus on taking off the old and putting on the new. The new is not simply just adding good things to your life but walking out God's mission for you.

How can you learn to be more disciplined and self-controlled in your walk with Christ?

Chapter 9
THE ORIENTATION OF A MAN TOWARD A WOMAN

TAKE WOMEN OFF THE PEDESTAL

There is a tendency for men to put women on a pedestal, in both the church and the culture. This can be seen in several ways, which have likely risen from the feminization of Christianity and influence of the culture.

- Women are referred to as angels in popular culture and even the church.

Angels are neither male or female but usually have male names in the scripture (e.g. Michael, Gabriel). Spiritualizing women as angels treats them as morally virtuous when all men and all women have fallen short of the glory of God. If a man enters a relationship with a woman and thinks of her like this, the relationship is almost always doomed from the start because the roles are reversed.

- "Happy wife, happy life."

This idolizes a wife's feelings—instead of what God says—as the barometer of a godly marriage instead of God.

- "Gotta ask the boss."

Even joking, this is outright heresy from men. The husband is the leader in marriage.

- Self-deprecating behavior, especially from the pulpit. Examples include "I couldn't do anything without my wife," and "My wife is my better half," and "I don't know how my wife puts up with me."

It gets a couple chuckles, but you're insulting your wife for choosing you as her husband. What woman wants to be with a man who thinks of himself as incompetent or inferior? Or who puts up with you because it's her duty? Are you a mischievous child or something?

- "I'm lucky to be with her."

Proverbs 18:22 tells us, "He who finds a wife finds a good thing and obtains favor from the Lord." Proverbs 19:14 further adds, "House and wealth are an inheritance from fathers, but a prudent wife is from the Lord." No, you're not lucky. You're blessed by God.

- "Women civilize men."

This is an interesting phrase that conservatives and even Christians tend to quote because they want the boys watching porn and living in their mother's basement to become men. They use this saying to tell men that they should man up and marry and have the responsibilities of a family. But the opposite is true: men civilize women.

As we saw earlier, there is a correlation between ghettos and the fewest husbands and fathers. These are also the populations with the highest crime and violence, worst high school graduation rates, earliest age of loss of virginity, and similar statistics.[1] Men, especially husbands and fathers, have an extremely positive effect on young boys and girls, raising them into responsible adults.

Examine what place women hold in your mind overall compared to what the Words says. In some cases, men, especially young men and beaten-down husbands, hold unhealthy views of women and idolize them. This often plays out negatively for them in relationships because the wrong mindset leads to the wrong actions; instead of acting as the leader, the man or husband abdicates his role, leading to discontent and strife.

ATTITUDES AND ACTIONS

Now that we've covered many of the basics of the faith, let's start to put together some practical knowledge about understanding male and female human nature. Let's start first with understanding how attitude plays a role into actions.

Jesus said, "Are you still lacking in understanding also? Do you not understand that everything that goes into the mouth passes into the stomach, and is eliminated? But the things that proceed out of the mouth come from the heart, and those defile the man. For out of the heart come evil thoughts, murders, adulteries, fornications, thefts, false witness, slanders. These are the things which defile the man; but to eat with unwashed hands does not defile the man" (Matthew 15:16–20).

Jesus tells us that what defiles us proceeds from the heart as they come out and manifest into attitudes and actions.

- Heart → heart postures or attitudes → actions

The heart is what man determines to do based on thoughts and feelings. That influences his attitude toward different things, which typically manifests in actions.

To use another of Jesus's analogies, the heart is like the roots of a tree; the attitudes are like the tree itself, and the actions are the fruit of the tree. Since we cannot see into someone's heart, the attitudes that they have toward themselves and others will be how the tree looks. We can usually tell if a tree does not have healthy roots: its leaves start to die off and the bark starts to rot. This leads to bad fruit, but the cause isn't the tree. The dying leaves, rotting bark, and bad fruit are all affected by the bad roots.

The reason why we need to look at both the attitudes and the actions is simple. We see someone do something sinful or incorrect, but if we know they have the right attitude toward it, they can repent or apologize and improve. An attitude with a lack of humility will be the result of pride; they will not admit any wrongdoing. But a correct attitude toward sinful behavior is based in humility; they are willing to be corrected and can make changes from there.

You can use this tool to examine if someone is a cultural Christian versus a true Christian. For instance, here are two different scenarios when a woman who you want to date or marry might have the same actions but have totally different underlying motivations.

- Heart wants to honor God by being obedient to his Word and loving others.

- Attitudes demonstrate patience, kindness, goodness, humility, and loving.
- Actions manifested in her desire to serve at church and other functions.

On the other hand, you might encounter a cultural Christian who might be involved with church, but she isn't following God.

- Heart is self-absorbed and is looking for a husband for selfish reasons.
- Attitudes might display impatience, lack of kindness, and a lack of humility, especially when she doesn't get her way while dating or in a relationship.
- Actions may still show that she serves at church and other functions, thus giving the appearance that she is a legitimate Christian when she truly is not in her heart.

As you can see, on the surface, the actions might look the same, but the underlying attitudes show the true story. Two of the responsibilities of a wife are similar: respect and submission. Respect is an attitude while submission is an action. A woman who respects her husband will be much more likely to submit to him whereas those who don't might rebel or be contentious when they disagree.

As Christians, our fear, respect, and reverence of God motivates us to follow him. His laws include submission to earthly authorities when it is due as long as they don't command us to disobey the scriptures. The same attitude should be present in those who fear God in any relationship they are in, whether it is Christians to the church, wives to husbands, or us to our workplace and employer or any institution in which we are engaged. When we lose respect, we start down the road to rebellion. After all, if we don't respect those in authority above us, we are more likely to gossip, slander, and fail to submit if circumstances get difficult or if our feelings get hurt.

Don't simply look at a woman's actions but also examine her underling attitudes. What she says and what she does will reveal her heart. Her actions should be congruent with what she believes. But even if she's saying and doing the right things, the situation is a ticking time bomb if her attitude does not align with that. People can only fake for so long before their true nature comes out. First Timothy 1:5 tells us, "But the goal of our instruction is love from a pure heart and a good conscience and a sincere faith."

This verse from Timothy is excellent because it presents the three things that are essential to living in agape love. These are a pure heart cleansed before God, the Spirit working in us as only God is able to make our conscience good, and sincerity or unfeigned faith that eliminates the falseness so that our attitudes align with our words and actions.

If you are a single Christian man searching for a wife, beware of a Christian woman with a poor attitude toward the roles and responsibilities of a wife, such as respect and submission. Likewise, beware of a lack of virtue, a lack of knowledge of the scriptures, and a lack of faithfulness to the spiritual disciplines. These are yellow and red flags.

If you are a Christian single man who is dealing with a girlfriend or if you have married this type of wife or if you came to the Lord after marriage, you will likely walk a hard road indeed. Remember this: it is easier to head off a bad attitude than it is to deal with disrespectful behavior. Proverbs 15:1 tells us, "A gentle answer turns away wrath, but a harsh word stirs up anger." Romans 2:4 states, "Or do you think lightly of the riches of His kindness and tolerance and patience, not knowing that the kindness of God leads you to repentance?"

The ability to diffuse a bad attitude before it escalates into heightened emotions and disrespectful behavior will be your best weapon. Remember to put on the fruit of the Spirit in these circumstances. Be firm as the leader of your marriage in your correction or chastisement but express it kindly and honorably to her.

SUFFERING IS NORMAL

One of the common themes that we see throughout the Old Testament is the promise of God that if Abraham and Israel followed His commandments, they would be blessed and prosperous.

> It shall come about, if you listen obediently to my commandments which I am commanding you today, to love the Lord your God and to serve Him with all your heart and all your soul, that He will give the rain for your land in its season, the early and late rain, that you may gather in your grain and your new wine and your oil. He

will give grass in your fields for your cattle, and you will eat and be satisfied. Beware that your hearts are not deceived, and that you do not turn away and serve other gods and worship them. Or the anger of the Lord will be kindled against you, and He will shut up the heavens so that there will be no rain and the ground will not yield its fruit; and you will perish quickly from the good land which the Lord is giving you (Deuteronomy 11:13–17).

This is where much of the so-called prosperity gospel comes from in first-world Christianity. It is a seductive lie that if you are obedient to God, He will bless you. Some examples of this include:

- If you obey God, you will be happy.
- If you give [money] to God, He will multiply your finances many times over.
- You can name it and claim it or ask God for something, and He will give it to you.

Certainly, these promises were given in the Old Testament, but what about the New Testament? If you obey God, will you be happy?

"These things I have spoken to you, so that in Me you may have peace. In the world you have tribulation, but take courage; I have overcome the world" (John 16:33).

Now you followed my teaching, conduct, purpose, faith, patience, love, perseverance, persecutions, and sufferings, such as happened to me at Antioch, at Iconium and at Lystra; what persecutions I endured, and out of them all the Lord rescued me! Indeed, all who desire to live godly in Christ Jesus will be persecuted. But evil men and impostors will proceed from bad to worse, deceiving and being deceived (2 Timothy 3:10–13).

Everyone who desires to live a godly life in Christ Jesus will be persecuted! God does not promise Christians the fleeting feeling of happiness, which is different from the fruit of the Spirit, peace and joy. Far from it. We should prepare to suffer as Christians for our faith. Even Jesus told us that those who are his disciples will be hated by the world. Yet we are to cling fast to His teachings for salvation. We are to evangelize and make disciples. What do the scriptures say about generosity?

> Now this I say, he who sows sparingly will also reap sparingly, and he who sows bountifully will also reap bountifully. Each one must do just as he has purposed in his heart, not grudgingly or under compulsion, for God loves a cheerful giver. . . . Now He who supplies seed to the sower and bread for food will supply and multiply your seed for sowing and increase the harvest of your righteousness; you will be enriched in everything for all liberality, which through us is producing thanksgiving to God. For the ministry of this service is not only fully supplying the needs of the saints, but is also overflowing through many thanksgivings to God (2 Corinthians 9:6–7, 10–12).

Our generosity multiplies our seed to increase our harvest of righteousness and thanksgiving to God. It does not promise us money or other worldly riches. Rather, we are storing up treasures in heaven.

What do the scriptures say about prosperity?

> Do not worry then, saying, 'What will we eat?' or 'What will we drink?' or 'What will we wear for clothing?' For the Gentiles eagerly seek all these things; for your heavenly Father knows that you need all these things. But seek first His kingdom and His righteousness, and all these things will be added to you. (Matthew 6:31–33).

The context of the above passage is anxiety about basic human needs, such as food, drink, and clothing and not money or worldly riches. Jesus showed a practical application of this in Luke 10 when He sent out the seventy disciples—don't take a money or a bag or sandals but instead eat whatever food and drink is provided to you.

As humans, we have the tendency to think that God hates us or that we did something wrong if we have problems. The scriptures do not promise that if we obey God, we will be happy, rich, or that He will give us *our* desires (though He might). The main thing that we are promised is suffering and persecution for choosing to follow Jesus. It is important to remove the expectation that God will make us happy because this can severely cripple our faith if our life circumstances become hard or extremely difficult.

How many Christians and even non-Christians have turned away from God because they faced difficult circumstances? I'm sure many of us can think of several people who have turned away from God in these situations. But we should instead rejoice and give thanks in our hard circumstances because we can be a witness to those around us in the culture and even the church that we are different. Our joy amidst suffering—even in prison (Acts 16) like Peter, Paul, and the other disciples—shows that God has changed us and delivered us. That's God's *will* for us. 1 Thessalonians 5:16–18 encourages us, "Rejoice always; pray without ceasing; in everything give thanks; for this is God's will for you in Christ Jesus."

All of this is to say that sometimes the battlefield will come to us where we least expect it. Our relationships with our friends, our family, and even in our relationships and marriages can become strained and lead to suffering or even persecution.

This is not a reason to be angry with God, but it is an opportunity for us to witness and show the love of God during the suffering and persecution so that we can win those close to us for Christ. God calls us to do the right thing, and He can win our family, friends, or spouse to Him. But He also doesn't promise us that He will. We need to take it on faith that He will use our righteous actions to continually work in them.

Like Joseph, David, Job, Paul, and the rest of the disciples, we need to keep in mind that our loyalty is to God and His commandments first, no matter how bad our circumstances around us become. These men suffered and were persecuted even for decades on end. But they stayed faithful, and God mightily used them. The Christian life is hard. Embrace it and don't become bitter, impatient, or tired. Continually seek God for His help among the hardships that you encounter and put on His peace and joy.

Finally, if you need to complain, remember that complaining always goes up and not down. David pours out his heart to God in the Psalms, which teach us about the difficult times in his life. Any of his complaints, fears, worries are all going to God. They are not going to his wives, children, advisors, or those around him. David is called a man after God's own heart. Heed his example. Complaining is destructive to those around you. If you must vent or complain, find some trusted Christian brothers who can lend you an ear and give you godly counsel and encouragement.

This is the resilience that we need to develop as Christians that make us even more fervent for the gospel rather than to turn our backs on God. Marital troubles and divorce are certainly some times where the going gets rough, but God desires our obedience even in the midst of suffering.

HONOR AND LOVE INSTEAD OF RESPECT

The concept of respect is thrown around a lot in popular culture. Both non-Christian and Christian women claim that men should respect them, and lots of Christian men claim that men should respect women. But this is not what the Bible says about respect. "Nevertheless, each individual among you also is to love his own wife even as himself, and the wife must see to it that she respects (*phobeō*) her husband" (Ephesians 5:33).

The Greek word used for respect is phobeō. Out of the ninety-three times that phobeō is used in the New Testament, it is only used about reverence or respect a few times. The other references refer to fear of God, fear of the king, or fear of things.

This same Greek word is also used in 1 Peter 3, which talks about how wives are supposed to act even if their husbands are unbelievers:

> "In the same way, you wives, be submissive to your own husbands so that even if any of them are disobedient to the word, they may be won without a word by the behavior of their wives, as they observe your chaste and respectful (phobos) behavior. . . . For in this way in former times the holy women also, who hoped in God, used to adorn themselves, being submissive to their own husbands; just as Sarah obeyed Abraham, calling him lord, and you have become her children if you do what is right (*agathopoieō*) without being frightened (phobeō) by any fear" (1 Peter 3:1–2, 5–6).

Agathos is a fruit of the Spirit (goodness in Galatians 5:22), and *poieō* is a verb that means to make or do. Thus, agathopoieō literally translates to mean one who does what is good. Wives who submit to and respect their husbands do what is good.

Wives who do not respect their husbands do not submit to them. Women who do not submit to their husbands do not fear God or their husbands. They not only disrespect their husbands, but they also disrespect God by not obeying what He has commanded. This is a rational fear from a lack of submission and obedience to the headship and authority structures that God has implemented on the earth.

Husbands are not to respect their wives. They are called to love them and honor them. First Peter 3:7 exhorts husbands, "You husbands in the same way, live with your wives in an understanding way, as with someone weaker, since she is a woman; and show her honor (*timē*) as a fellow heir of the grace of life, so that your prayers will not be hindered."

We are called many times throughout the scripture to honor (*timē*) many different people: Honor our father and mother (listed in the Ten Commandments, Matthew 15, Ephesians 6), honor the Son (John 5), honor all people (1 Peter 2) and honor widows (1 Timothy 5). Honor is the esteem and dignity that is given to every person even to the level that you honor Jesus.

This is the type of attitude that Jesus had about authority: to love and honor rather than to exercise authority to lord it over others.

> But Jesus called them to Himself and said, "You know that the rulers of the Gentiles lord it over them, and their great men exercise authority over them. It is not this way among you, but whoever wishes to become great among you shall be your servant, and whoever wishes to be first among you shall be your slave; just as the Son of Man did not come to be served, but to serve, and to give His life a ransom for many" (Matthew 20:25–28).

The *timē* value of Jesus's life is the way we should honor others as the *timē* that the Pharisees gave Judas to sell out Jesus was the thirty shekels of silver (Matthew 29:6–9).

Respect is an overall attitude toward the one in authority that leads to humble submission. This is the attitude that a woman should have toward her father prior to marriage and the attitude that she should have toward you after marriage. You can screen for this key quality when vetting a wife.

This tends to be a big issue with Christian men with stronger mother figures or absent father figures. They go into a relationship looking for *love* from their wife, and they will *respect* their wife. This creates a dysfunctional relationship pattern with inverted roles in marriage. If you respect your wife, you are inadvertently placing her in authority over you, which means you are making her an idol. Men who claim to respect their wives have relationships where their wife is the implicit boss, and they will often become increasingly unhappy and dissatisfied with the marriage over time. This is an inversion of relationship roles and contrary to scripture. Do not fall prey to this cultural idolatry trap.

GOOD INTENTIONS ARE NOT ENOUGH FOR RELATIONSHIPS

Every man has had a situation where they meant to do something good that turned out badly either in words or actions. This often leads to the other party becoming discontent or angry, which in turn makes you angry because you didn't mean to cause harm or hurt feelings. The cycle continues.

This is one of the big reasons that family, friendships, and even marriages can have division in them for years. Good intentions lead to a poor result, which lead to frustrated emotions, which lead to negative actions from both parties, which lead to huge blow ups. This is a negative behavioral cycle.

One of the hardest things to do is to realize that even though you had good intentions, miscommunication might have caused problems. As humans, we will never ever be perfect at communicating, and this is even truer with the opposite sex. It is easy for misunderstandings to creep in and cause confusion and hurt in relationships.

This is the importance of cultivating the fruit of the Spirit in your life: love, joy peace, patience, kindness, goodness, faithfulness, gentleness/meekness, and self-control. (See Galatians 5:22–23.)

In times of misunderstanding or confusion, the fruit of the Spirit help you take a step back and re-evaluate. You need faithfulness and love to understand that you need the Spirit in these situations. You need self-control and patience to reign in the hurt and anger. You need humility to understand that you might have unintentionally caused hurt yourself even if you don't mean to and that an apology is warranted. And you need kindness and goodness to respond righteously, considering everyone's concerns. Proverbs 15:1 reminds us, "A gentle answer turns away wrath, but a harsh word stirs up anger."

Also, consider Jesus's statement about how to handle judgment.

> Do not judge so that you will not be judged. For in the way you judge, you will be judged; and by your standard of measure, it will

be measured to you. Why do you look at the speck that is in your brother's eye, but do not notice the log that is in your own eye? Or how can you say to your brother, 'Let me take the speck out of your eye,' and behold, the log is in your own eye? You hypocrite, first take the log out of your own eye, and then you will see clearly to take the speck out of your brother's eye. (Matthew 7:1–5).

Jesus is not saying to not judge anyone. Many people in the world distort the verse. He is instructing us to remove all the logs from our eyes before going after any of the specks in the eye of our family, friends, or wife. Otherwise, you look like a hypocrite.

Remember that you can't change people, but you can change how you respond to people. Christianity is about every one of us as Christians taking off the old and putting on the new, which is a witness for Christ.

If things have been a certain way for years on end, then it will take a lot of time to remove those old habits and patterns and put on the new. Don't try to rush the process. Remember that you can't change people, but you can change how you respond to people. You can only do what you can do, which is control your attitudes and actions and let God work on their heart.

Cultivate the fruit of the Spirit in all circumstances, especially when you feel like you are losing control. Spiritual maturity will change how you approach conflict.

Chapter 10
ATTRACTION

THE BIBLE ON ATTRACTION

What does headship and authority have to do with marriage and attraction? That is a great question.

Attraction is one of the most misunderstood concepts for Christians. The position of many pastors on this topic is what they think *should be* attractive as opposed to what *is* attractive. An example of this is the paradigm of godliness is sexy, which will be thoroughly debunked in the next chapter. The importance of attraction is understated by the Christian church, which leads to many poor recommendations to young men and women who want to be married. We will look at what the Bible says both directly and indirectly about attraction, the traits that are attractive, and what this means for the Christian man who desires to be married.

Why does this matter? The simple fact is that everyone—non-Christians and Christians—want to marry (or be with) someone to whom they are attracted. Men generally do not ask out women who they don't find attractive, and women generally don't go on dates with men they don't find attractive. Attraction can be considered an important factor as a force that helps to drive marriage.

What is the Biblical case for this? The following passages in 1 Corinthians give us further insight here.

> Now concerning the things about which you wrote, it is good for a man not to touch a woman. But because of immoralities, each man is to have his own wife, and each woman is to have her own husband. The husband must fulfill his duty to his wife, and likewise

also the wife to her husband. The wife does not have authority over her own body, but the husband does; and likewise also the husband does not have authority over his own body, but the wife does. Stop depriving one another, except by agreement for a time, so that you may devote yourselves to prayer, and come together again so that Satan will not tempt you because of your lack of self-control. But this I say by way of concession, not of command. Yet I wish that all men were even as I myself am. However, each man has his own gift from God, one in this manner, and another in that. But I say to the unmarried and to widows that it is good for them if they remain even as I. But if they do not have self-control, let them marry; for it is better to marry than to burn with passion (1 Corinthians 7:1–9).

Do not be bound together with unbelievers; for what partnership have righteousness and lawlessness, or what fellowship has light with darkness? (2 Corinthians 6:14).

Paul desires that all Christians stay celibate to devote themselves fully to the Lord, but that it not the case for many Christians. To avoid sexual immorality, the scriptures advocate that each man have his own wife and each woman have her own husband. What causes us to long or to burn? The answer is sexual desire, and sexual desire is inflamed by a person of the opposite sex who we think is attractive. This is God's design.

Why would Paul have to urge the Corinthian believers not to be unequally yoked? If it were the case that being a godly Christian equates to being attractive enough to be married, then Christians would only naturally marry other Christians because they would only find other Christians attractive. Paul implies that Christians also find non-Christians attractive and want to marry them, even if they're not believers and against their better judgement. Christian men can find non-Christian women attractive, and Christian women can find many non-Christian men attractive as well. For example, tons of non-Christian celebrities are certainly attractive. Such attractive non-believers are ungodly and should not be considered for marriage. Yet because of so-called love, some Christian men and women disobey God's command not to be unequally yoked.

==Being a Christian and being godly are not attractive in and of themselves.==

Many mainstream churches and pastors preach that being godly and having Christian values is attractive. This is false. If godliness were attractive, both Christians and non-Christians would be falling over themselves to marry the most pious believers, such as nuns and priests. This is not the case. It is important to recognize this deception as it creates negative expectations for those who wish to be married.

Often Christians see our sex-focused culture and downplay the role of sexual attraction in marriage. This is a bad idea. In fact, burning with passion is the only reason given in the New Testament to marry. Marriage is distinctly different from friendships because the husband and wife can have sex and create a family. Sex is an integral part of the marriage to bind it together and increase intimacy. It is a mistake to marry someone that you do not find sexually attractive because they will want to have sex with you. If you find that the person that you are dating is not sexually attractive to you and/or you are not sexually attracted to them, it is a mistake to marry them.

The idea that abstaining from sex or the pleasure of physical intimacy in marriage in Christianity is desirable has its roots in asceticism and Gnosticism. These are heresies that have tried to infect Christianity throughout the millennia. These heresies try to persuade Christians that anything related to the body or pleasure is evil when, in fact, God created man and marriage to be good.

THE CREATION OF MARRIAGE AND ITS RELATION TO ATTRACTION

One of the concepts that has stumped Christians for ages is the role of attraction in marriage. The scriptures tell us that God primarily looks at the heart and that beauty and physical appearance can be vain. Thus many Christians fall into the trap of ignoring attraction when searching for a spouse when attraction is supposed to be synergistic to God's design. Let's walk through this together.

First, we need to understand that marriage is an earthly institution, according to Jesus.

> On that day some Sadducees (who say there is no resurrection) came to Jesus and questioned Him, asking, "Teacher, Moses said, 'If a man dies having no children, his brother as next of kin shall marry his

wife, and raise up children for his brother'". . . . But Jesus answered and said to them, "You are mistaken, not understanding the scriptures nor the power of God. For in the resurrection they neither marry nor are given in marriage, but are like angels in heaven" (Matthew 22:23–24, 29–30).

Jesus lets us know that there is no marriage in heaven. Ephesians 5 describes marriage as created by God to reflect the nature of Christ and the church. Revelation 19 tells us of the wedding of Christ and the church, which is one of the final events before the new heaven and new earth. Marriage is present at Creation and present at the end of the old heaven and old earth, which brings it full circle from Genesis 2 to Revelation 19.

Since marriage is an earthly institution, what is the purpose of that institution? God's commands to man were four-fold in the first Creation account in Genesis 1 and 2:

- **Rule and subdue the earth:** "Then God said, 'Let Us make man in Our image, according to Our likeness; and let them rule over the fish of the sea and over the birds of the sky and over the cattle and over all the earth, and over every creeping thing that creeps on the earth. . . . and subdue it; and rule over the fish of the sea and over the birds of the sky and over every living thing that [am] moves on the earth'" (Genesis 1:26, 28b).
- **Be fruitful and multiply:** "God blessed them; and God said to them, 'Be fruitful and multiply, and fill the earth'" (Genesis 1:28a).
- **Cultivate and keep the garden:** "Then the Lord God took the man and put him into the garden of Eden to cultivate it and keep it" (Genesis 2:15).
- **Obey:** "The Lord God commanded the man, saying, 'From any tree of the garden you may eat freely; but from the tree of the knowledge of good and evil you shall not eat, for in the day that you eat from it you will surely die'" (Genesis 2:16–17).

Genesis 2 gives us more details about the ordering of creation. Man was created first, but there was no helper suitable for him. Hence God created a helper suitable for him. Adam was tasked by God with four different commands.

1. The first command: Adam could fulfill this himself; he took dominion over the beasts as they came to him and gave them names.
2. The second command: Adam could not fulfill this—to be fruitful and multiply—without a helper.
3. The third command: Adam could keep the garden by himself as he did prior to Eve.
4. The fourth command: Adam was tasked with the job of headship when Eve was created.

God created marriage as the vehicle to carry out His commands. Since marriage is an earthly institution, the attraction of each sex in marriage reflects God's creation and commands.

WHAT MEN AND WOMEN FIND ATTRACTIVE

With all of that in mind, what is attractive to both sexes? What are men attracted to?

If you look over the scriptures and reality, it would be accurate to say that men are primarily attracted to physical beauty and femininity. Proverbs often warns men against the seductiveness of attractive, morally deficient women; it condemns their immorality not their beauty.

- Physical beauty includes a woman's face and body, waist-to-hip ratio and curves, symmetry, skin quality, and youth, according to many Old Testament passages.
- Femininity includes feminine demeanor; long(er) hair; feminine clothing, such as dresses and skirts; and so on. Man was made for woman, and woman was made for man (Genesis 2–3, 1 Corinthians 11). Femininity has a very sexual aspect, which is seductiveness, which can be used for good in marriage or evil outside of marriage.

Men are very straightforward to understand. The physical beauty of a woman is very appealing to men, often to the point where they can make poor decisions and sin because they are seduced or enthralled by morally deficient women. These two aspects are sexually attractive to men.

What are women attracted to?

People have tried to categorize attractive traits in quite a few different ways. One is the PSALM/LAMPS mnemonic:

- Power
- Status
- Athleticism
- Looks
- Money[1]

Another model uses four different categories:

- Power and status
- Charisma and confidence
- Appearance (looks, style, etc.)
- Resources (especially money)[2]

Still another lists eight attractive traits:

- Physical presence: appearance and body language
- Personality: humor and ambition
- Social value: leadership and social intelligence
- Sexual potential: desirability and sexual confidence[3]

If you look at the scriptures and reality, it would be accurate to say that women are primarily attracted to multiple different qualities and traits. Based on the descriptions in the Bible, they tend to fall into these categories.

- **Leadership:** God created a man to be the head of the marriage (Genesis 1-3, Ephesians 5, 1 Corinthians 11, Colossians 3, Titus 2, 1 Peter 3) and rule and subdue the earth (Genesis 1 and 2). The main traits that tend to be attractive to women in this category are leadership, power, and the status that comes with it.

Common examples in popular culture that demonstrate these traits are doctors and nurses, bosses and secretaries, teachers and students, and other men in leadership positions, whether these are political, business, or celebrities. Even in the church, women tend to be attracted to the pastor or the worship leader while being less attracted to the janitor, the parking lot attendant, or the church greeter because of leadership, power, and status.

- **Protector:** Men were tasked to protect their families in the scripture, especially in obedience to God's commands, such as Adam in the garden and the warring and fighting done by men in the Old Testament (Genesis 2, Deuteronomy 24). This includes spiritual protection, such as keeping families safe from committing evil (e.g., Adam and Eve, Christ and the church, husbands and wives, parents and children). This might also include traits related to the ability to physically protect and make a woman feel safe when she's with her man such as height, muscle tone, body build, and athletic ability.

It should be no surprise that women tend to gravitate toward men who are excellent at sports, fighters, physically imposing, and who have an attractive beach body. The captain of the sports team and the head cheerleader is certainly a valid cliché.

- **Provider:** Men were tasked by God in the Old and New Testaments to work to provide for their families as Adam was tasked to cultivate and keep the garden even before the fall (Genesis 1-3, the Law, 1 Timothy 5). There is a healthy attraction for a woman who is concerned about the ability of a man to provide for her and the family.

Gold digging is a common example in culture of this concept being taken too far. Family studies also show that if a wife is the primary breadwinner of the family or makes more than the husband, the marriage is much more unstable because the wife is more likely to divorce.

- **Masculinity:** Women tend to be attracted to masculine personalities and traits (Genesis 2-3, 1 Corinthians 11, the patriarchs, David). Man was made for woman, and woman was made for man. This includes traits, such as confidence, boldness, strength, mastery, ambition, risk-taking, independence, humor, excellence, and many others. Masculine personalities are also strongly associated with power and status. This also includes fashion sense and style, which usually signal that a man is well-integrated into society. (Note: Masculine traits are present in all of the above).

We now have an understanding of what is attractive, according to the roles and responsibilities of each gender in marriage. Let's connect the dots.

Men are primarily attracted to physical beauty and femininity. God created woman for man, and one very good aspect of that is to appreciate the beauty of His creation. Man was the last part of God's creation, and we can see the beauty in all His creation: the earth, the sky, nature, and the animals. But perhaps the ultimate beauty He saved for last: woman.

Feminine looks, demeanor, and dress are attractive to most men, especially if paired with seductiveness in a woman. After all, men don't want to marry another man. They want to marry a woman. As an aside, scientific studies have shown that across all cultures, men are primarily attracted to the traditional hourglass waist-to-hip ratio ranging from about .6 to .8.[4] Although our human understanding is unsure of the reason for this, it could potentially signal increased fertility or lack of disease.

The phenomena that explains the way that women evaluate different traits in a man in comparison to other men to determine his attractiveness is called hypergamy. This term was originally used to describe a woman's preferences for marrying up in social castes in India, but recent social sciences use it to indicate a woman's preferences for marrying up in power, status, education, and similar traits.[5] In a study across dozens of countries, Cashdan reviews mating strategies and concludes that they are different between the sexes.[6] Men tend to prefer women who are young and attractive while women tend to prefer men who have it all: wealth, high status, attractiveness, education, and power.

These various traits tend to signal that a man is a great choice for marriage because they follow the commands of God to "rule and subdue the earth" as well as to "protect and provide for a family." For instance, have you ever noticed that women highly prefer a man to be taller than she does? They also prefer that he makes more money than she does and that he is more popular or famous than she is. Has there been a woman who was happy if her man was less educated than she was? When is the last time you saw a woman excited to date down? These types of things rarely happen.

Men and women look for different attractive traits in the opposite sex, and they evaluate those traits differently. To men, beauty has a large component of objective reality. A woman is beautiful even when compared to other beautiful women. There is some subjectiveness in preferences, such as color of the eyes, hair, and body shape. But to women, men are attractive in the sense that they are comparing one man to other men and evaluating him against her own qualities. In some ways, men are competing against each other and against the woman herself before she finds him attractive.

The scriptures give us truth about many different subjects, and it should logically come as no surprise that the Bible accurately depicts what men and woman want in the opposite sex in a mate. After all, God is the one who created man, woman, and marriage.

It is *not* wrong for both men and women to be attracted to physical appearance. Some churches and pastors demonize male and female sexuality and minimize the importance of superficial traits, such as physical appearance. Criticizing men and women for this is effectively criticizing God for how He made us. That's not right.

THE FULL CONTEXT OF ATTRACTION AND MARRIAGE

A Christian might ask, "Why should I do all these things? Doesn't simply pursuing God prepare me for marriage?" Let's take another look at the same scripture passage we looked at earlier.

> But I want you to be free from concern. One who is unmarried is concerned about the things of the Lord, how he may please the Lord; but one who is married is concerned about the things of the world, how he may please his wife, and his interests are divided. The woman who is unmarried, and the virgin, is concerned about the things of the Lord, that she may be holy both in body and spirit; but one who is married is concerned about the things of the world, how she may please her husband. This I say for your own benefit; not to put a restraint upon you, but to promote what is appropriate and to secure undistracted devotion to the Lord (1 Corinthians 7:32–35).

You need to understand that solely focusing on God does not prepare you for marriage. Enhancing our godly attributes increases our ability to work in cohesive unity with our mission from God. Likewise, enhancing our marital attributes increases our ability to work in cohesive unity within marriage. Those attributes are the things described above, which maintains the attraction between a man and a woman. While ungodliness will reduce the marital attributes from carrying their full weight within a Christian marriage, the same can be said of attraction: the lack thereof can often negatively affect our ability to express godliness within a Christian marriage. For instance, if a spouse becomes lazy about maintaining their figure in marriage, this decrease in attraction can lead to a decrease in the frequency of sex.

Part of our obedience to God in the marriage relationship is learning how to emulate Christ and His church. As you obey God by learning and practicing His roles and responsibilities for marriage, you learn how to both obey God and please your spouse. The overarching goal is obedience to God, and a focus on preparing yourself for marriage simultaneously increases godliness and attractiveness at the same time.

What does God desire for a man who wants to be a husband? That he prepares to be a husband who fulfills his roles and responsibilities in marriage. What are the main roles and responsibilities of a husband in marriage? They are leader, protector, and provider, as we have covered.

- How are you becoming a better leader? Are you taking the initiative to lead Bible studies? Are you deepening your knowledge of the scriptures and excelling in the spiritual disciplines? Are you following God's mission for you in the church? Are you using your spiritual gifts? Are you learning how to lead with love?
- How are you becoming a better protector? Are you protecting from evil? Are you helping to sanctify? Are you learning self-defense? Are you learning how to stand up to others so you can verbally protect your wife from any type of harassment she may receive? Are you working out, gaining muscle mass, and becoming more fit so that you can more effectively protect your family from physical altercations? Can you discern when your wife might be spiritually, emotionally, or mentally under attack and help her?
- How are you working to become a better provider? Are you working on your education, or are you making enough to support and care for a family? Are you excellent in everything you do at work to the glory of God? Are you taking opportunities to network and interview to advance your career? Are you generous with the money that God has stewarded to you to help the church and the poor?

Some of these are proactive and some are reactive. You need to be proficient at both. It's one thing to be a reactive leader, protector, and provider by dealing with problems that come your way and solving them. It's a whole other ball game to be the one to initiate improving your ability to do all of these. For instance, not everyone morphs into a great evangelist or mentor when they become a Christian. Most Christians must take a very proactive approach to be effective at God's mission. An evangelist would do well to constantly practice public speaking, give many speeches, eliminate filler phrases and words, focus on clearly and poignantly engaging and presenting points to an audience, and getting feedback from mentors, friends, and family on how they're improving. You need to be actively pursuing excellence in whatever you do as to the Lord.

God's mission for your life can be part of some of these things too. If you have a heart for the poor then instead of simply feeding and clothing them when you see them (reactive), you can run or even start your church's food bank or clothing drive (proactive). If your church doesn't have a men's ministry, you can start one to help disciple and mentor men (proactive).

Invite, mentor, disciple, and put all you have into serving the Lord. There is an epidemic of passivity in men in the church, which is a huge problem. Instead of shaming men to man up as many pastors do, we need to encourage men to explore their gifts of the Spirit and take control of their own lives to steward them well for God.

Aside from not being reactive but mainly proactive, more questions can be asked beyond these. Consider the traits of masculinity and how they interact with being a better leader, protector, and provider. Consider how style fits in with all these roles and responsibilities. Consider how talent and mastery of different subjects can also play a role. This gives you a great idea of where to start, and the framework for that is focusing on what God desires rather than what you desire.

==Interestingly enough, when you start preparing for the roles and responsibilities of marriage to be a better leader, protector, and provider, women tend to become more interested in you because you're more attractive to them.==

ATTRACTION IS A PREREQUISITE FOR ROMANCE

Romance can be useful during dating and marriage. After all, who doesn't like to make their woman or wife feel good? Romance is typically made out to be some mysterious concept when it is simple to understand. Here are some basic keys.

- Attraction
- Personal
- Appropriate

Attraction: Attraction is required for romance. Men and women often get this wrong. If an attractive man offers a woman flowers out of the blue, she will generally be thankful and appreciate them. But if an unattractive man makes the same gesture, she will generally feel uncomfortable, disgusted, or disgruntled. Why?

Look at it from the point of view of a man. If a beautiful, fit woman does something special for you, most men would be thankful and want to get to know her better. If an obese woman does something special for you, most men would think nothing of it or blow her off, especially if you could tell she was interested in you. Some men might even react with disgust.

Generally, both men and women will only think a gesture is romantic if they are attracted to the person. Unwanted romance tends to inspire feelings of discomfort, creepiness, disgust, revulsion, ickiness, anxiety, uneasiness, awkwardness, and more. I'm sure many men have experienced a woman stating that she feels these emotions from men at one point or another. She is saying that she is not attracted to this man who has expressed interest in her or that he is being too forward.

Personal: Being personal includes some consideration of the qualities that are important to both of you. There are lots of different opinions about how this works. For instance, the five love languages—gifts, quality time, words of affirmation, acts of service, and physical touch—are one way of categorizing personal ways to interact in a relationship in a meaningful manner.[7]

Another example of this would be how you celebrate special days, such as Valentine's Day. Why are you required to buy her roses and take her out to eat at a fancy restaurant? Instead you can plan something highly personal to each other that breaks the mold of what you're expected to do. You don't always have to give a gift or the experience of something that she enjoys either. Perhaps try something new that you have never done before. You could also buy her something that reminds her of the relationship or of you. Don't pigeonhole yourself into what the world or the church expects you to do; combine your personality with creativity to make the event personal. You'll both enjoy it a lot more.

Remember that anything you do must come from a heart of desire and not of works or performance. If you're trying to earn romance or affection, it won't work in the long run. If you do it as work rather than "desire," you are setting up the expectation that she will like you instead of viewing what you do as something that she will appreciate. If she does not acknowledge it or is not thankful, then your expectation failed, and you will become hurt and possibly bitter. This is a clear set up for failure because your expectation won't always be fulfilled.

Appropriate: Appropriateness is important. Doing too much out of the ordinary is a recipe for failure.

If you do too much too soon, this is equated with trying too hard, which is a turn off. This is a common sentiment with both men and women. For example, you might write a love note once a week or once a month, but what if you were writing one every day or multiple times a day? If you've only gone on one date with a woman, would you ask her to marry you the next day?

Too much too soon reeks of desperation, but you do not want to be too little too late either. Be wise about anything you do in the relationship and consider the consequences of your actions when it comes to long-term outcomes.

Chapter 11
BARRIERS TO ATTRACTION

THE INFECTION OF ROMANTIC LOVE VIA
THE PARADIGM OF GODLINESS IS SEXY IN THE CHURCH

Chivalry has generally been ascribed to the period of knights and ladies around 1100-1200s, which is also when the legend of King Arthur came into prominence.[1] Varying codes were developed, including warrior ethos, knightly piety, and courtly manners. We are discussing the courtly manners portion, which was generally ascribed to romantic love or a knight trying to win a lady's affections. You can see where this is going as the knight is already putting the lady on a pedestal by chasing after her.

There is nothing particularly wrong with romantic love (or Greek, *eros*); however, in our culture romantic love is often elevated above the commitment of marriage. In other words, romantic love is the justification for sex when instead God created sex for marriage. This is the cultural notion of following your heart and feelings of romantic love to which waxing and waning attraction is a justification for fornication, divorce, and other immorality. This has crept into the church via the paradigm of godliness is sexy, where a husband's sex life is at the mercy of his wife's feelings.

For example, in *Every Man's Marriage*, Fred Stoeker and Stephen Arterburn of New Life Ministries refer to a wife's sexuality as her "soul essence," which the husband must obey.[2]

> What I'm trying to say is that the "master" defines your rights (and remember again that though we refer to your wife as your "master," it's our shorthand for the fact that becoming one with her essence is actually your God-given master). Why? Because you're called to oneness and her essence sets the terms.[3]

Doug Wilson, in his book *Reforming Marriage*, makes a similar argument that the emotional state of wives is God's way of telling us if a man is virtuous or not:

> In other words, keeping God's law with a whole heart (which is really what love is) is not only seen in overt acts of obedience. The collateral effect of obedience is the aroma of love. This aroma is out of reach for those who have a hypocritical desire to be known by others as a keeper of God's law. Many can fake an attempt at keeping God's standards in some external way. What we cannot fake is the resulting, distinctive aroma of pleasure to God.[4]

President of the Southern Baptist Theological Seminary and board member of Focus on the Family, Dr. R. Albert Mohler Jr. is much bolder about his unbiblical views:

> Put most bluntly, I believe that God means for a man to be civilized, directed, and stimulated toward marital faithfulness by the fact that his wife will freely give herself to him sexually only when he presents himself as worthy of her attention and desire.[5]

In a similar vein, Tim and Kathy Keller, in their book *The Meaning of Marriage*, talk about a supposedly godly temper tantrum:

> Kathy talks of what she calls the "godly tantrum." By this she means not an emotional loss of temper but an unrelenting insistence on being heard. . . .
>
> One day I came home from work. It was a nice day outside and I noticed that the door to our apartment's balcony was open. Just as I was taking off my jacket I heard a smashing noise coming from the balcony. In another couple of seconds I heard another one. I walked out on to the balcony and to my surprise saw Kathy sitting on the floor. She had a hammer, and next to her was a stack of our wedding china. On the ground were the shards of two smashed saucers.
>
> "What are you doing?" I asked.
>
> She looked up and said, "You aren't listening to me. You don't realize that if you keep working these hours you are going to destroy this family. I don't know how to get through to you. You aren't seeing

how serious this is. This is what you are doing." And she brought the hammer down on the third saucer. It splintered into pieces.[6]

Joel and Kathy Davisson talk about lowering the boom in one of their blog posts about "Your Wife Had an Affair, It's Your Fault":

> One of these requirements is that she speak up to her husband, very clearly, and COMMUNICATE to him exactly what he is doing or not doing that is straining the relationship. Has she learned to speak up and REQUIRE that he be a man of God in his marriage by being the husband that he promised to be when he convinced her to marry him?... If a wife has NOT been plain spoken, if a wife has NOT called upon her church leadership to speak to her husband and call him to accountability, if she has NOT asked him to read books or go to counseling, then she has to do this first. First things first. . . .
>
> If she has done all of this, and he is still a manipulative, controlling, and abusive husband. Or if he is simply a retreating, non-responsive husband to her needs who continually ignores her pleas, informing her that she is losing her sanity, then she must act before she becomes embittered.
>
> She must act before she indeed does lose her mind. She must decisively give him what he wants: out of the marriage. What does he want? He wants OUT! In this case, it is time for him to get exactly what he wants, and that is to be put out of the home.
>
> She must engage the law to the fullest extent to extract child support and alimony. If her state can extract this from him with a separation, then separation is the way to go. If her state cannot extract this in a separation only, then she must file a divorce to put his back to the wall.[7]

Your spider senses should be tingling. Are only husbands supposed to be obeying the Bible and not wives? Where is the fruit of the Spirit that these Christian leaders are supposed to be counseling for the wives? Don't the scriptures in 1 Peter 3 counsel the wives of unbelievers to win their husband through pure and respectful behavior, a gentle and quiet spirit, and submission? Why are these Christian leaders so blatantly ignoring the scriptures? The rot inside Christianity runs deep.

Almost every Christian organization seems to buy into the paradigm that "godliness is sexy." Family Life Today, a subsidiary ministry of Cru, has a series by Dave and Ann Wilson called "The Mystery of Intimacy in Marriage" that similarly says, "[A] man's relationship with God is key to unlocking the mystery of marital intimacy."[8]

Christian films are not immune to the lie that godliness is sexy, either. The Christian, marriage-themed film *Fireproof* by the Kendrick Brothers of Sherwood Baptist Church expounds the same model in fictional form as you can read in the following paraphrased summary.

> Fireproof tells the story of a fireman named Caleb (played by Kirk Cameron) whose wife Catherine is going to divorce him to take up with a doctor because he has an internet porn habit and would rather spend their savings on a boat for himself instead of medical equipment for her mother. The husband cleans up his act, kicks his porn habit, starts treating his wife better, and even secretly pays for her mother's medical equipment. When Catherine discovers that it was Caleb instead of her doctor lover who paid for the medical equipment, she decides to recommit to her marriage. In other words, once Caleb became the man God wanted him to be, Catherine's attraction to him was reignited.[9]

Matt Chandler, writing at John Piper's Desiring God website, makes this point explicitly:

> I keep saying it: Godliness is sexy to godly people. The culture tells us physical/sexual attraction is first, then character, godliness, and compatibility follow. I think we get it backwards. I think once character, compatibility, and godliness are there, those fuel attraction in the way that pleases God, and is much safer for our souls.[10]

Dennis Rainey, CEO of Family Life Today, gave an extended treatment of this paradigm on the website *Stepping Up: A Call to Courageous Manhood*. (He has also written a book by the same name.)

> What does all this have to do with romance? Plenty. The success McDonald's has experienced as the world leader of fast-food franchises came about because the company became a careful student

of the customer. In the same way, one key to thriving in your relationship is to understand your wife. This is not to suggest that you should try to manipulate her. Rather, as you invest time and effort to understand your wife, you'll discover how to define romance using your wife's dictionary. I have to admit that I defined romance for years using my distinctly male dictionary. We men spell romance: S-E-X. However, I've learned when I want to communicate romance with Barbara, I'd better understand how she defines the word! As a husband does this, he understands the three nonnegotiables for a romantically satisfying relationship: security, acceptance, and an emotional connection.[11]

Chivalry as a form of romantic love, as virtuous as it might seem to some, can get to the point where it idolizes women and/or your wife. Paul speaks to the fact that husbands have divided concerns about the Lord and their wives, which can tempt them to place their wife above God.

> But I want you to be free from concern. One who is unmarried is concerned about the things of the Lord, how he may please the Lord; but one who is married is concerned about the things of the world, how he may please his wife, and his interests are divided. The woman who is unmarried, and the virgin, is concerned about the things of the Lord, that she may be holy both in body and spirit; but one who is married is concerned about the things of the world, how she may please her husband. This I say for your own benefit; not to put a restraint upon you, but to promote what is appropriate and to secure undistracted devotion to the Lord. (1 Corinthians 7:32–35).

This is the battle of every husband: the concerns of God versus the concerns of his wife. This can manifest in quite a few forms of idolatry:

- Elevating a woman's feelings and emotions above God's commands (i.e., A wife's sex drive is the measure of the godliness of a husband.)
- Working to try to please your wife over God's commands (i.e., giving into a wife's complaints about chores, trying to fix her emotions)

- Putting her expectations over God's commands (i.e., abdicating your role as leader)

The moment that pleasing a woman or your wife is elevated above any of God's commands is the point at which idolatry of the woman or wife has started. This is also the point at which a husband makes himself a slave to his wife: by her emotions, by works, or by her expectations. Unfortunately this also ties in strongly with the belief that godliness is sexy that many Christian pastors and authors seem to have.

C.S. Lewis makes this clear in *The Allegory of Love*:

> The love which is to be the source of all that is beautiful in life and manners must be the reward freely given by the lady, and only our superiors can reward. But a wife is not a superior. As the wife of another, above all as the wife of a great lord, she may be queen of beauty and of love, the distributor of favours, the inspiration of all knightly virtues, and the bridle of 'villany'; but as your own wife, for whom you have bargained with her father, she sinks at once from lady into mere woman. How can a woman, whose duty is to obey you, be the midons whose grace is the goal of all striving and whose displeasure is the restraining influence upon all uncourtly vices? You may love her in a sense; but that is not love, says Andreas, any more than the love of father and son is amicitia. We must not suppose that the rules of love are most frivolous when they are most opposed to marriage. The more serious they are, the more they are opposed. As I have said before, where marriage does not depend upon the free will of the married, any theory which takes love for a noble form of experience must be a theory of adultery.[12]

The elevation of the feelings of romantic love above the moral commands of God, such as the covenant of marriage, leads to thinking that might eventually end in actual adultery. It places romantic love above the covenant of marriage. When that happens, following your heart to divorce or adultery becomes the truth rather than the faithfulness and fidelity of marriage.

Unfortunately, much of the modern church believes women are attracted to godly men of high character who will affirm, serve, emotionally support, listen to, and validate the high worth of their women. Perhaps this is because they believe this is the way it *should be* rather than being faithful to the scriptures and reality.

- The elevation of feelings of romantic love above the scriptures leads to idolatry of a woman or wife's feelings, expectations, or a focus on pleasing her.
- The paradigm of godliness is sexy confuses Christian men and women in marriage, which leads the men to further idolize of the wife.
- Since both aspects are similar to how the world and culture operate, this contributes to the normalization of sin, such as divorce and single motherhood.

The church, pastors, and other Christians tend to peddle false and conflicting information about what is sexually attractive in marriage. This is detrimental to both Christian men and women because it creates a sense of false expectations in the path toward marriage. Christian men are told that they should try to be a nice young man or strive for godliness because that is what attracts a woman and that he will win her in the end. Likewise, Christian women are often told that inner beauty makes a woman beautiful and that the right young man will come around and love her for who she is. Sometimes this advice works out though not usually because of the advice. The general trend by the church to encourage embracing these points, which are outright lies or half-truths, do not help Christian men and women get married.

Sometimes you have to say the truth. Women will attract more interest from men when they are younger, feminine, and maintain an attractive figure and appearance. Men will attract more interest from women if they are a strong, confident leader who is rich and handsome. Men will attract more attention from women if they are tall, muscular, and have a powerful build and know how to fight. Women prefer the pastor, the youth-group leader, and the worship-team members over the janitor, the door greeter, and parking lot coordinator. We do young single men and women a disservice when we lie to them. Instead, emphasize the areas that are under your control—most of them—and not the areas you can't control like facial structure or height.

WORKS AND DESIRE

We can better understand where romantic love goes awry by contrasting the mindset of works against desire. One of the fundamental basics of the Christian faith is that we cannot *do* anything to be saved. We've been saved through grace, not of our own works.

> For by grace you have been saved through faith; and that not of yourselves, it is the gift of God; not as a result of works, so that no one may boast. For we are His workmanship, created in Christ Jesus for good works, which God prepared beforehand so that we would walk in them (Ephesians 2:8–10).

> For we also once were foolish ourselves, disobedient, deceived, enslaved to various lusts and pleasures, spending our life in malice and envy, hateful, hating one another. But when the kindness of God our Savior and His love for mankind appeared, He saved us, not on the basis of deeds which we have done in righteousness, but according to His mercy, by the washing of regeneration and renewing by the Holy Spirit, whom He poured out upon us richly through Jesus Christ our Savior, so that being justified by His grace we would be made heirs according to the hope of eternal life. This is a trustworthy statement; and concerning these things I want you to speak confidently, so that those who have believed God will be careful to engage in good deeds. These things are good and profitable for men (Titus 3:3–8).

In the Old Testament, God instituted the law of Moses so that Israel could seek after God with their whole hearts. However, the law was incomplete. The Israelites could work and sacrifice animals for their sins to obtain mercy and wash away their sins. They could not follow the whole law so that they would never sin. Mercy only dealt with sins; mercy did not *change* the person. Jesus died as a sacrifice on the cross so that we would obtain both mercy *and* grace—unmerited favor from God for salvation from our sins. This is different from the world where you must work, work, and work to earn mercy, favor, and respect.

The works mentality is a pitfall that both immature and mature Christians can fall prey to even after we are saved. For example, the immature

Christian continues to cling to our past perception of ourselves when he or she sins. We allow these thoughts to continue to shackle our soul and our mind. As serious Christians, we are often our own worst critics. If you sin, you know that you have the grace of God. But you sometimes catch yourself internally beating yourself up because of that sin. You think, *I should've known better*, or *I should have been able to overcome this temptation*. Some of us even go to the extent of making promises or pledges to do things for God to help us not sin again.

This is a works mentality. Beating yourself up or making promises to God means that you think you can do something to please God on your own. It's far simpler to accept the grace and mercy of God for your sin, drop the guilt, and walk away from the sin. Constantly beating yourself up is often a cyclical and self-defeating behavior cycle; you keep thinking about how not to sin or the promise you made, which keeps your mind on the sin, which tempts you to sin again. If we only accepted the mercy and grace of God and forgot about the sin, we wouldn't have tempted ourselves to sin again and been able to walk free. A genuine desire to please God will manifest in righteousness and good works instead of dwelling on sin and temptation. This is the freedom of Christ.

A similar dynamic is true in the beginning of relationships. Almost all men have tried or done things to make a woman like them more. Examples include pick-up lines, giving gifts, compliments, spending money on food or trips, and more. When you think about it logically, you can't buy affection or attraction. Nor would you want to.

If you expect a girl to like you for what you do for her, you are treating her like a prostitute. You're spending your time and your money in exchange for her affection or attraction. As harsh as that is to say, relationships and marriage must be founded on desire to function correctly. If you fall into a pattern of exchanging or expecting time or money or sex and affection for something equivalent, then you are either prostituting yourself or her.

It's extremely easy to fall into a works mentality with our family, friends, and our spouse. Any relationship built on works is almost inevitably doomed to fail. This commodification of love usually works for a short time until one person or the other doesn't like the arrangement anymore and then they bow out. In early relationships, a woman might enjoy the time, energy, and money invested in her, but she will eventually just move on once she finds someone she actually likes. You were in the friend zone the whole time because you were never attractive to her; you were just buying her affection for a time.

The dichotomy of works and desire is also an important concept for husbands to understand in their marriages. Working does not work. Biblical marriage is an image of Christ and the church. These same standards apply to the husband and the wife—one of desire and not work.

- You cannot work hard enough to placate your wife's emotions (i.e., make her feel more attracted to you).
- You cannot work hard enough to please your wife (i.e., do enough chores).
- You cannot work hard enough to ever meet her expectations.

Falling into a pattern of works is falling into the temptation of sin. Your works will never be enough. Part of the reason why works fail is fear. If you are working, there is a chance that you will fail. If there is a chance that you will fail, you will fear. If you fear your wife, you are not leading or loving according to the scriptures (1 John 4). You set yourself up to fail.

Does this mean that you shouldn't try to please your wife? Certainly not. But it must come from desire and not working to try to please. We will talk about this more in further chapters.

SOULMATES AND INFATUATION

One of the prevalent concepts in our society is the idea of soulmates. Jesus mentioned to the Sadducees that there was no marriage in heaven. This eliminates the idea of soulmates. Disney movies with Prince Charming are not the Bible. They often espouse concepts that are contrary to the Bible, especially when it comes to romantic love; diluting gender-specific roles and responsibilities; and denigrating men, husbands, and fathers.

Likewise, Christians have also made up their own version of soulmates called "soul ties," which is used to dissuade people from having sex with each other based on an odd interpretation of one flesh. As Paul notes to the believers in 2 Corinthians, we should not be joined in fornication with unbelievers or temple prostitutes.

Sex prior to marriage is extremely intimate and can heighten emotions to a point where you no longer make good choices. This is sometimes colloquially called one-itis or putting a woman on a pedestal as was discussed earlier. This heightened bonding can make it feel as if you're on cloud nine, but it is almost inevitably destructive because you cannot make proper decisions about leading effectively or about the relationship. When you are infatuated with a woman, you might do things that you otherwise would not do to win or persuade her to like you or to want to be with you. As we have seen before, this is detrimental.

If you can recognize that you are infatuated or obsessed with a woman, then that is a sign that you need to back away from the relationship rather than trying to win her or become more involved. It's too easy to fall into situation where the roles are reversed roles and she is the leader and you are the follower. This almost never ends well, especially after the infatuation wears off, and you see her faults and flaws. Allow yourself time and space to come back down to earth before you decide whether or not such a relationship is wise.

THE RISE OF OBESITY

Some very startling facts in the United States regarding obesity follow.[13] This data is somewhat less prevalent in similar first-world countries.

- Percent of adults aged twenty and over with obesity: 37.9%
- Percent of adults aged twenty and over who are overweight, including obesity: 70.7%

As we know, men are primarily attracted to physical appearance in terms of beauty, symmetry, clear skin, and an hourglass figure. Women also desire a component of physical attractiveness in the form of tall(er), muscular, athletic men.

A physically fit body earns us the respect of outsiders, increases our influence in God's kingdom, and ensures that there are no physical psychological barriers that enhance the number of people that we can evangelize or disciple. Like it or not, being overweight or obese does give other people negative impressions, which can sabotage your ministry. Not only that, those who are overweight or obese are much more likely to have health problems down the road that can cut short ministry.

A physically fit body does not make you godlier, but it does make you more effective. Man does look at the outward appearance (while the Lord looks at the heart), which influences his thoughts, feeling, and actions toward that person. (See 1 Samuel 16:7.) No one is perfect even though we strive to be. But that doesn't mean appearance shouldn't play a role in our decision making. If you showed up to a job interview in ratty gym clothes instead of a suit, you probably (deservedly) wouldn't get the job. A crude way of thinking about dating is that it's a form of marketing yourself to the opposite sex as you are interviewing for the position of husband or wife. Excellence with the temple of the Holy Spirit is healthy for both prospective husbands and wives.

From the start, I want to disregard notions about the various causes of obesity, such as laziness, gluttony, lack of self-control, or other factors. Even so, the fact is that those who are overweight and obese are generally less attractive to those of the opposite sex. Obese men and women who have lost lots of weight can tell you the reality of the difference the lost weight made for them. Men are rejected less when asking women out on dates, and women are asked out more because they are now seen as more attractive.

Several studies and books have estimated that compared with normal weight, there is a decreased likelihood of getting married of about 10 to 30 percent for an underweight or overweight person and 30 to 50 percent for an obese person.[14] For every ten extra pounds of weight above normal, there is an increased chance of 10 percent that the person has never dated.

This is one of the big elephants in the room that tends to be discredited when giving advice to singles who want to be married because it is politically incorrect to mention, or it will hurt the feelings of those who are overweight or obese. The reality is that weight is a significant factor in making a good impression so that someone will go out on a date or enter a relationship.

ATTRACTIVE JERKS VERSUS UNATTRACTIVE NICE GUYS

Why does it seem that women tend to flock to jerks? How do they exhibit any desirable traits, such as leadership, protection, provision, or masculinity? Many of us certainly know some jerks who are successful with women who exhibit few, if any, of those traits. In fact, we probably saw a bunch of these guys growing up when we had a crush on a girl in high school, but she liked the popular athlete. She complained that he was a jerk, but she still dated him and not you. These are questions that often come up when women are attracted to non-Christian jerks while they friend zone Christian nice guys.

Very few men and women have all attractive traits of men or women at the highest levels. For example, very few men meet the criteria of being a pastor or worship leader who is also six feet tall or taller, two hundred pounds of solid muscle, a former pro athlete with a high salary, who confidently lead his congregation with high moral standards. Even in the secular world, only a few male celebrities are handsome, well-built, super rich, masculine, and leaders. The majority of men tend to be lower or average in most categories while being above average in just one or two.

So why are jerks more attractive, even to Christian women? These jerks might have some of the physical traits of attractiveness, such as height, muscles, or athletic ability. Some might have impeccable fashion sense. Still others have money to throw around. Usually jerks will have some combination of qualities of leadership, protector, and provision. But what almost all attractive jerks have is a high degree of confidence when interacting with women.

To understand this, we need a basic knowledge of social interactions between the sexes. Flirting is a playful or amusing way to show that you are interested in a member of the opposite sex. One of the main ways to do this is teasing. Teasing that is more playful or lighthearted in nature with the opposite sex tends to signal that a man is romantically interested in a woman. In the Bible and in most cultures, overt sexual advances are highly frowned upon, so flirting is one of the ways to show subtle romantic interest.

Now that we know that, consider the observation of how the sexes tend to interact with their same-sex associates:

- The tendency of women's socialization is to be supportive, agree with each other, and validate each other's experiences and feelings.
- The tendency of men's socialization is to be critical, challenging, ribbing, teasing, and mock insulting of each other.

Jerks tend to act in a masculine manner with women while nice guys tend to act in a feminine manner with women. These jerks will often have confidence in spades and are very charismatic with women. Jerks are attractive to women because they lead the conversation well and tease with confidence. In other words, they have learned social mastery. Women might think that this is mean or wonder what they just heard, but body language betrays interest. The woman is smiling, laughing, touching her hair, and otherwise enjoying herself. She'll likely dish out some teasing back to the man, and if he is all hurt over it, then she loses interest too.

Men, especially Christian men, rarely interact with women by leading a conversation and confidently teasing. Some Christian men who see a Christian woman they like will spend a week or even months or years to try to build up the courage to talk to her, let alone ask her out. This shyness or conversational awkwardness is precisely what gets a man friend-zoned. It's simply unattractive to women. She will also lose interest when you are hurt by her teasing. This is because you are not exhibiting leadership and/or a masculine personality that can take on all challenges.

Nice guys tend to cater to a woman and put her on a pedestal. They will readily agree with what a woman is saying or defer to her opinion. If asked his opinion by a woman, a nice guy will answer in a wishy-washy way instead of with confidence. The pedestal is the exact opposite of what a man should be doing. A man who puts a woman on a pedestal is hoisting her up as the leader in the interaction or idolizing her. He tries to defer to her opinions to garner her favor, which results in the exact opposite effect that he wants. He wants to be her boyfriend, but he is just her friend because he is acting as a friend, like any of her girlfriends. If a woman wants affirmation or confirmation, she will go to her girlfriends for it. A nice guy is just the male version of a woman's girlfriends.

In short, the rise of the LGBT movement notwithstanding, God designed women to be attracted to men, not other women. This holds particularly true within the church. When a man acts in a feminine manner toward a woman, she will not be attracted to him. But if he begins to act toward her as a man, attraction can begin to grow.

The logical conclusion to this is startling to one who has been indoctrinated by the feminine culture we live in but is a common fact of life for one who has a biblically grounded view of how God designed men and women. If you can't lead a conversation with a woman and confidently interact with her in a romantic atmosphere, then why would she agree to be your wife? God has tasked you as the man to be the leader in the marriage and to be fruitful and multiply. If you're too shy or afraid to express your opinions to a woman, then how will you lead her in marriage? If you can't express your romantic interest, how will you be fruitful and multiply in marriage? If her words hurt you, how can she expect you to protect her from true danger?

In a sense, flirting is showing a woman your masculine backbone and ability to lead her. Are your opinions made of nice-guy fluffy gelatin that shapes to whatever mold it fills? Or can you confidently hold a conversation with her, tease her, make her laugh, and *lead* her the way you would lead in marriage so that you can create a family?

The reason why most people think that jerks are attractive to women is because not many Christian men are attractive. The reason this has occurred in the current culture is quite clear. These bad boys tend to retain their masculinity because they don't give a crap about what society says about supposedly toxic masculinity while Christian guys become feminized because they buy into cultural standards of masculinity.

Who will a woman choose—the masculine man or the feminized man? As previously stated, a feminized man is basically just like one of her girlfriends—a person who she can pour out her emotions and feelings to but with whom she has zero attraction and romantic interest.

In reality, the solid men who are masculine leaders, protectors, and providers are almost always snatched up in marriage early, leaving the impression that only jerks are left. The nice guys aren't even considered by women for a date or relationship. It is quite frustrating as a single Christian man to hear other single Christian women complaining about where all the good men are when you're standing right there in ear shot with other single Christian men. That means they consider all of you nice guys within their social circle friends and not potential suitors. As such, you're just a guy to them, not a *man*.

THE INTEGRATION OF YOUR MISSION FOR GOD AND ATTRACTION

One of the most difficult things for many Christian men to do is to properly integrate the information in these pasts few chapters on God's mission for us, how attraction works, and various things that are barriers to attraction. Although we discussed this previously, I believe a recap of this topic is a good idea.

First, I think it is best to deal with some misconceptions about the Scriptures and attraction. An example of this is the argument that working out to build a muscular physique is not in the Bible and there is no command to work on sexual attractiveness. Therefore, as a Christian, why should I do either? It is easy to fall into the trap of absolutes, and this is one of them.

There's much wisdom and discernment in understanding the nature of how God designed things. Sexual attractiveness tends to fall within this realm. While there is no "biblical" command to improve your own sexual attractiveness, there is wisdom and discernment for certain situations.

If I'm a fat, lazy husband who is not striving to be an active participant in God's mission, it doesn't take a genius to see that I am potentially increasing the temptation for my wife to be unhappy and, possibly, divorce me. No, she should not divorce me because she is a Christian, but I'm not doing her any favors. 1 Corinthians 7 says that spouses should not deny one another sex, as it can tempt the other spouse toward sin. While this is not quite the same thing, we should avoid putting stumbling blocks in front of our spouse.

If I, like most men, am not called to celibacy, it would be wise of me to increase the odds that I might attract a mate by dressing nicely, being well groomed, working out, losing fat, gaining muscle, and so forth. It is not a sin to not do any of these things, nor does the Bible tell me to do them. However, viewed through the lens of wisdom, we will realize that women tend to find certain things attractive. Therefore, if one wants to be married, it might be a good idea to do these things. Being too scrawny, or being obese and poorly dressed with bad hygiene makes you less likely to attract a woman than if you take care of yourself, and one could argue that a lack of self-control in this area may be sinful.

Some parts of attractiveness like physical appearance can be thought of in terms of wisdom and discernment, but others are simply beneficial side effects of what you get by giving your all to God.

Let's first examine how actively being on your mission for God results in beneficial side effects like increased masculine leadership and attraction. These are things you *need* to be doing as a Christian:

Evangelism: What better way to become bolder and more confident in your faith *and* get over a timid personality than sharing your faith? This will also help you learn to initiate and engage in conversation, which is helpful for dating. If someone does not respond to the Gospel, it's like receiving a rejection from asking a woman out, except they are rejecting God, not you. This will help give you the mindset that it's not a big deal in the grand scheme of things.

Exercise your spiritual gifts: Go after your mission for God. This will help you learn how take initiative and be more assertive at the same time. If you have a heart for the homeless, help the homeless. If you are musically gifted, serve on your church worship team. If you have administrative gifts, you may be able to help in the office. Learn to be comfortable taking initiative and being assertive to get things done, rather than passively waiting for things to happen.

Discipleship/mentorship: Both giving and receiving. What better way to grow in the faith than having a more mature Christian help you move toward obedience to Christ? While you are being mentored by someone further along in the journey than you, it is likely that there will be people around you who aren't as far along who you can mentor. This is a good way to learn to teach and influence others, which you will do with a girlfriend/wife anyway.

Read and meditate on the biblical marital roles and responsibilities of marriage: What better way to prepare for relationships and marriage than to study the end goal and emulate what God desires? This goes hand-in-hand with discipleship and mentorship. One facet of leading a relationship is spiritual leadership, which often requires teaching and discussions about the Scriptures and the Christian walk.

Don't be afraid to admit when you're wrong and call out (usually privately) Christians when they're wrong: Not only is this part of the sanctification process (see Matthew 18, 1 Corinthians 5, and 1 Thessalonians 5), but it is part of marriage as well. It also cultivates an attitude to honor God first and stand up and be bold when necessary.

Lead and serve in the church: Get out of your comfort zone. Lead a Bible study, serve in the homeless ministry, volunteer with the youth group, whatever utilizes your gifts to put your faith into action. Leading in various capacities teaches you many things you will use in a relationship and marriage. Serving will give you the right attitude to lead by example.

Be excellent in all you do for God's glory: This carries over to your job, where working hard will likely get you promoted. But even if it doesn't, we are called to do our work for God's glory. Excellence is a quality that carries over into numerous facets of life and will help you to lead by example.

Provide and protect: Learn to be able to provide for yourself and, eventually, a family. This includes monetary needs, but encompasses many other things as well. Even if you are single, you can learn to be a protector by standing up for yourself, your beliefs, and your mission for God. Learning to be responsible with money now will prepare you for your future as well.

Many of these things fall into the archetype of the husband God designed for marriage: strong, masculine leaders, providers, and protectors. You're practicing many of the habits and traits that will help you be successful with God's mission and with women.

Timothy, the eventual leader of the Church of Ephesus, had some of these problems in his youth and had to be mentored by Paul toward boldness in the faith.

> For this reason I remind you to kindle afresh the gift of God which is in you through the laying on of my hands. For God has not given us a spirit of timidity, but of power and love and discipline. Therefore do not be ashamed of the testimony of our Lord or of me His prisoner, but join with me in suffering for the gospel according to the power of God (2 Timothy 1:6-8).

Many Christians who attend church regularly are just hearers of the Word and not "do-ers" (James 1:22). When you become a do-er, you start to cultivate many of the qualities that are necessary for God's mission and masculine leadership in relationships.

On the other hand, here are a few suggestions for increasing attractiveness or removing some of the barriers to attraction. These are not necessarily "biblical commands" but they are wise things to do.

Improving physical appearance: Losing weight if overweight or obese, gaining muscle mass through strength and hypertrophy-focused workouts, proper grooming and hygiene, finding a style of clothing that works well for your body, and things of the like.

Improving physical presence: Playing a sport, learning a marital art for the purpose of self-defense, learning how to make solid eye contact, eliminating fidgeting, learning how to speak and enunciate clearly, public speaking, etc.

Improving emotional presence: This can include learning how to not take yourself so seriously while interacting with women, learning how to take jokes and make jokes, learning how to playfully tease women, and learning how to build connection through conversation. You probably already know how to do many of these things with your male friends, but you may not be as skilled in relating to women in these ways. It will likely seem more natural for those who have grown up with female siblings, especially younger sisters.

Cultivating talents and hobbies: Playing music is an obvious one that tends to be attractive to women. Being excellent in your hobbies also overlaps with some of the previous examples.

Many of the masculine traits: Confidence, boldness, strength, mastery, ambition, risk-taking, independence, humor, excellence, and many others, some of which fall under other areas above. Perhaps your boldness and confidence can help a woman to step out of her comfort zone in an activity like skydiving.

Some of the things mentioned above (like gaining muscle or learning martial arts) fall under the category of "protector" for the archetype of strong, masculine leader, protector, and provider. One could argue that these are things a man should be doing if he is serious about having a family. To be fair, I am only going to classify them as "the wise thing to do" rather than saying they are things you *must* do. After all, there are many men who don't workout or know martial arts but are godly husbands who their wives find attractive.

For most Christian men, the primary ones I strongly recommend have to do with physical appearance and presence. These are also good ones to start with, and the ones I believe are most neglected by the Church. They also make the most impact, as physical appearance and presence are big first impressions for either sex. A stylish, strong, muscular, Christian man is going to leave a very good impression as opposed to an obese man who wears baggy clothes and doesn't bother to style his hair or shave.

You can also break these down into various stages in order to give you a better idea of what your issue(s) may be:

- If you're having trouble getting dates, you may need to focus on your physical attractiveness and emotional presence.
- If you're having trouble conversing with dates or maintaining relationships, you may need to focus on your leadership and communication.
- If you've changed significantly in the course of a relationship in a negative manner—extra weight gain, exposure of character flaws, or even if life hasn't gone your way and you reacted poorly—these are things you will need to address to keep a relationship from heading south.
- If you're having trouble finding women to date, you may need to put yourself in places where you will find single, Christian women who are committed to growing in their faith and becoming spiritually mature.

Even if things are going well, why would you not want to do these things? Wouldn't you appreciate your future wife working toward maintaining these things the best she could while being focused on growing in her faith? You bet you would. So why wouldn't you do the same for her?

Having a good physical appearance is not mutually exclusive from being a godly man. However, it is often the case that spiritual discipline and physical discipline synergize with each other. A healthy, strong body is more resistant to physical illness. It will also typically give you a sharper, clearer mind for the things of God. On the other hand, be sure not to turn your physical appearance into an idol like the world does.

At the end of the day, your mission for God should be your primary focus. If you do this, you will begin to develop many of the character traits and qualities you need to grow spiritually, lead a marriage, and even be attractive to your future wife.

SECTION FOUR

THE CULTIVATION PROCESS FROM SINGLENESS TO RELATIONSHIPS TO MARRIAGE

Chapter 12

A FIVE-STEP PROCESS FOR GROWING IN RELATIONSHIP AND SPIRITUAL AND PRACTICAL MATURITY

There are many ways to become spiritually mature. Most of these involve discipleship and the spiritual disciplines, such as reading the scriptures, prayer, meditation, and fasting. Let's examine these actions and habits more in-depth in the scriptures as this provides a solid guideline for the whole process of the Christian walk.

> Now for this very reason also, applying all diligence, in your faith supply moral excellence, and in your moral excellence, knowledge, and in your knowledge, self-control, and in your self-control, perseverance, and in your perseverance, godliness, and in your godliness, brotherly kindness, and in your brotherly kindness, love. For if these qualities are yours and are increasing, they render you neither useless nor unfruitful in the true knowledge of our Lord Jesus Christ. For he who lacks these qualities is blind or short-sighted, having forgotten his purification from his former sins. Therefore, brethren, be all the more diligent to make certain about His calling and choosing you; for as long as you practice these things, you will never stumble; for in this way the entrance into the eternal kingdom of our Lord and Savior Jesus Christ will be abundantly supplied to you (2 Peter 1:5–11).

Aside from the general Christian walk, one of the ways you can apply this to your Christian walk is in the context of relationships.

1. Know what God says about relationships: Faith to moral excellence and knowledge.

2. Know your mission, your dreams, and goals: Knowledge to self-control, perseverance, and godliness in your life.
3. Know your standards for women: Determine the self-control, perseverance, and godliness of the woman you want to marry.
4. Know your standards/boundaries in a relationship: Transform your godliness into brotherly kindness and love.
5. Know how to assertively communicate: Show you can love effectively.

Knowing what God says about relationships is akin to developing your faith to moral excellence and knowledge. Once we follow Christ, we want to know and do what is right. Carrying out our mission for Jesus is about taking the knowledge that we have gained and doing it: using self-control, perseverance, and discipline and ultimately showing godliness in your life. Likewise, knowing your standards for a potential wife is critical to bringing a woman on board who has the same mission as you. Standards and boundaries in a relationship are a way to effectively show love without enabling, and they help you hold each other accountable to the standard of Christ. Finally, use your communication skills to love effectively.

These five steps are how I approach this issue from the perspective of a Christian man who has discerned that marriage is in your future as opposed to celibacy. If you are undecided, be chaste, pray, meditate, and read the scriptures about singleness and marriage in 1 Corinthians 7 for several months. Talk to some godly mentors. Don't make the decision lightly.

KNOW WHAT GOD SAYS ABOUT RELATIONSHIPS: FAITH TO MORAL EXCELLENCE AND KNOWLEDGE

This is the most obvious point but also one of the most neglected. When I talk to and mentor younger Christian men about what they're doing to prepare for relationships, I almost inevitably hear something about school, a job, or money. That's not enough. I've seen enough married couples to know that they did little to nothing to explore what the scriptures say about relationships before marrying. This is to their own detriment.

To get started, spend some extended time studying the follow passages in depth: Genesis 1-3, 1 Corinthians 7, Ephesians 5, Colossians 3, Titus 2,

1 Peter 3, and Proverbs 31. Other passages on marriage, husbands and wives, or male-female relationships include Hebrews 13, 1 Timothy 3, Proverbs 18, Ecclesiastes 4, and some general commands in 1 Corinthians 11-14 and 1 Timothy 2 on church affairs.

You not only need to know these standards, but you need to be these standards. Remember some of the roles back in the chapter on attraction? You want to be a strong masculine leader, protector, and provider. These are the passages that help prepare you for the roles and responsibilities of being married.

The sad state of affairs is that Christians want to be married but don't know God's standards for relationships. They are entering marriage at their own risk. Do not let worldly measures of success cloud your vision of what a godly relationship should be. God created everything, and His Word gives us His truths that bring us joy and peace. He understands us at a fundamental level as we are His creation. But even when we think such truths are uncomfortable, we will understand them as we submit to them and live them out.

No one would suggest that you apply for a credit card before you read the fine print. Nor would anyone suggest you buy a car or a house before you read the terms and conditions on the loan or mortgage. As the leader of your potential marriage, failure to read the fine print of the scriptures means you are also culpable for part of the failure, even if the person you decided to marry is not who you expected.

The scary thought is that if you failed to point out truth about sin as a husband or wife, then you are also culpable for letting that sin slide (Matthew 18, 1 Corinthians 5). This is a hard word for most Christians in relationships because it means that you are responsible for calling out your spouse or significant other if they get off track. Similarly, you are responsible for humbling yourself in the sight of God so that you can come back on track if you sin. Both Christian men and women have a very difficult time doing this, which shows in the sad state of affairs in so-called Christian relationships and the divorce statistics. Not hurting someone's feelings becomes the priority over what the scriptures say.

One of the best ways to implement this section effectively through discipleship is to find a male mentor who is further along than you in the journey. It can be a pastor, elder, deacon, or even a mature married husband and father who lives according to biblical principles and the roles and responsibilities of marriage. They can help guide you along the way.

KNOW YOUR MISSION AND GOALS: KNOWLEDGE TO SELF-CONTROL, PERSEVERANCE, AND GODLINESS IN YOUR LIFE

Your mission is God's mission. That mission is the great commission: to spread the gospel and make disciples. How do you fit into the Body of Christ? The spiritual gifts are found in Romans 12:6–8; 1 Corinthians 12:8–10 and verse 28; Ephesians 4:11; and 1 Peter 4:11. Generally, God will use your natural strengths for His kingdom so look there first. But He will also use you where you least expect it, so be open to His call if He wants you to serve in a certain area.

There's no such thing as being off mission. Men compartmentalize well, so this can be a big issue. One common example is the Sunday-only Christians who go to church, confess their sins, and live the way they want the rest of the week. In other words, we need to be living as if everything we do is for the glory of God, whether it is our job, school, friends, or family. The church is not a building. We take the church wherever we go as we are part of it and represent Christ.

My mission involves making money to financially support ministries, mentoring young men in the church, and evangelizing when I have the opportunity to do so. You might fill other roles, depending on the gifts that God gives to you, but these are the ones that God impressed upon me. When I was single:

- My relationship with God is my top priority: seeking Him in scripture, prayer, and the like. By extension, I help build up the Body of Christ locally at church.
- Build my relationship with my family.
- Search for a wife and explore potential relationships.
- Be excellent at work every day.
- Mentor and interact with young men every day when possible.
- Stay fit and build muscle with exercise and nutrition.

Everything falls under the broad umbrella of serving God although these are some of the different facets of it. These goals could be improved by using the SMART criteria—specific, measurable, achievable, relevant, and time-bound.

Sometimes you need to prioritize certain goals, but that doesn't mean you're removing yourself from God's mission. If you find a girl with the potential for a relationship, I recommend that you set aside time to get to know her. Prioritizing time to be with her will increase as you get to know her. I would not jump up and prioritize for a girl I just met. As the relationship progresses to engagement and marriage, she will be a bigger priority. Know how to prioritize where a spouse fits in your life. This is developing the perspective: a potential wife will be basically family and next after my priority of my relationship with God and His mission for me.

At a younger age, you should recognize that if a family is important in your life, you need to prioritize it early and not let precious chances slip away. If it's a priority, you will be *proactive* in taking action. Most things in life do not simply come to you. You must go out and do them, like your mission for God.

You will always find time for what is important to you. I've known men who have had a family, worked a full-time job, and gone to school—all at the same time. If this sounds impossible to you, it's a sign that you need to work on your self-discipline.

KNOW YOUR STANDARDS FOR WOMEN: DETERMINE THE SELF-CONTROL, PERSEVERANCE, AND GODLINESS OF THE WOMAN YOU WANT TO MARRY

You need to know what God says about who you should choose and how your wife fits into your God-given mission as a helpmeet. Here are some of the scriptural points that I looked for in a wife.

1. **Evidence of a relationship with God:** Carrying out their mission for God. Daily scripture reading, prayer, meditation, and service in the church and community. This is a heart that is seeking after God and is fruitful with good works and the fruit of the Spirit (Galatians 5). Also do not be yoked with unbelievers (2 Corinthians 6).
2. **Evidence of godly earthly relationships in relation to God:** A potential prospect as a wife must understand how God views

earthly relationships and act accordingly. A woman should respect and submit to Jesus (John 14:15), the church (1 Peter 5:5), earthly authorities (Romans 13, Hebrews 13, 1 Peter 2, Titus 3), and parental/fatherly authority (Exodus 20:12, Ephesians 6:1). When a woman understands godly earthly relationships, she also understands the three main roles and responsibilities of biblical marriage: a helpmeet (Genesis 2:18), submission (Ephesians 5, Colossians 3, Titus 2, 1 Peter 3), and respect (Ephesians 5, 1 Peter 3). She should show evidence of the fruit of the Spirit—joy and peace—in these actions.

3. **Evidence of cultivated godly femininity:** She has long hair, veiled when necessary (1 Corinthians 11), purity and reverence in conduct (1 Peter 3:2), inner beauty through a gentle and quiet spirit (1 Peter 3:4), not a slanderer or slave to drink and teaches what is good (Titus 2:3), self-controlled, chaste, good managers of the household, kind, and submissive (Titus 2:4). She is trustworthy (Proverbs 31:11), does him good and not harm all the days of her life (Proverbs 31:12), works with her hands at various tasks (Proverbs 31:13,16–19), brings and provides food and delegates tasks to servants and children (Proverbs 31:14–15), provides for the poor (Proverbs 31:20), wisdom and kindness comes from her tongue (Proverbs 31:26), and is not idle in her household (Proverbs 31:27).

4. **Evidence of chastity in attitude and action:** Preferably a chaste virgin (Deuteronomy 22, 1 Corinthians 6 and 7). I do not think it is worthwhile to have to deal with the drama that surrounds a woman who has previously been intimate with other men. Yet, I would say it is better to marry a Christian woman who has shown she has repented through years of being a Christian than a virgin Christian woman who has done everything but have sex with many men and doesn't think it's a problem. Chastity not only includes virginity but modesty. She avoids fishing for attention from others and similar traits. She keeps herself unstained from the world. (See James 1.)

5. **Evidence of attraction/chemistry**: A woman who strives to be attractive even though it takes work will be a better ambassador

for Christ than one who is given over to sloth and gluttony. This goes both ways, as your potential wife should be attracted to you also. Inward beauty and outward beauty are not mutually exclusive; you want both.

6. **Evidence of a willingness to prioritize the family:** She wants many children: "Be fruitful and multiply and fill the earth and subdue it" (Genesis 1:28b). I don't care if my wife has a career, but she should be willing to lay it aside for her family as necessary (Titus 2:3–5). Age was not a primary consideration for me, but since I wanted to have many children, I knew that a younger woman was better.

Those are the scriptural standards. You can also have other standards as they pertain to your mission. For example, one of my standards is that my wife enjoys working out and healthy nutrition because some aspects of my job are related to fitness. She should also reflect who I am and a helpmeet who is slovenly or obese reflects negatively on my witness. Plus, I'm more attracted to women who are fit.

Compromise on non-negotiables and/or red flags is a recipe for failure.

I tried to compromise a bit with the passion for nutrition and fitness with some women, and it was a failure. It was like the church of Laodicea in Revelation 3 when God tells them that because they are neither hot nor cold but lukewarm, He will spit them out of His mouth. Some women will try to please you, just as men will also try to please women. This is based in works rather than desire. It's not attractive, and who's to say that they won't become complacent stop these actions altogether once you get married? You can't know for sure if they have really changed or if they are just doing it to please you. But it's another story if they started enjoying fitness and healthy nutrition for themselves.

All the other aspects are somewhat negotiable. I want a large family with at least five children, but I might be willing to compromise with three or four children. But I won't settle for a small family. There is some wiggle room with other qualities. Even in these, there needs to be a consideration for godly values. A woman that desires a large family is more likely to be unselfish: she cares about family and is willing to sacrifice time and energy to make that happen.

One of the major red flags for pseudo-Christians is that they are miserly with love. Their attitude toward serving and helping others (including you) is lacking. For instance, they might only want one or two children because they view children as a hassle if they even have children at all. Her attitude and reasoning toward children matter. Does she only want three children because she wants to spend more time on herself and her career? Or does she want three children because she wants to adopt? You need to explore the attitudes behind her decisions to understand her values and character.

KNOW YOUR BOUNDARIES IN A RELATIONSHIP: TRANSFORM YOUR GODLINESS INTO BROTHERLY KINDNESS AND LOVE

Jesus asserts a very firm boundary in John 13 and John 15 at the Last Supper.

> A new commandment I give to you, that you love one another, even as I have loved you, that you also love one another. By this all men will know that you are My disciples, if you have love for one another (John 13:34–35).

> This is My commandment, that you love one another, just as I have loved you. Greater love has no one than this, that one lay down his life for his friends. You are My friends if you do what I command you. No longer do I call you slaves, for the slave does not know what his master is doing; but I have called you friends, for all things that I have heard from My Father I have made known to you. You did not choose Me but I chose you, and appointed you that you would go and bear fruit, and that your fruit would remain, so that whatever you ask of the Father in My name He may give to you. This I command you, that you love one another (John 15:12–17).

Christ tells His church that if they love Him, they should obey His commandments. Ephesians 5 likens Christ to the church as the husband to the wife and tells the wife to obey her husband in all things as to the Lord. *Yet what Christian husband today would tell his wife that if she loves him she would obey him?* Think about that for a moment: could you imagine tell this to your wife or significant other?

We need to reach this point as Christian husbands. When we follow scriptural commands the rest of culture—and maybe even those in the church—will hate us. Can you stand firm on the scriptures even if everyone around you—Christian and non-Christian alike—hates you?

Here are some examples of standards and boundaries that I address early in my relationships with women. I discuss these after a few dates or right after establishing an exclusive dating relationship. These almost always go over well because I am telling a Christian woman how the relationship will progress. But almost inevitably, when I say I have some rules or standards for a relationship, the Christian woman will become tentative and fearful because she thinks I am trying to control them. Once I actually discuss these, however, it builds further attraction and intimacy.

My three main boundaries are:

1. God's Way Trumps All
2. Honesty
3. Embracing the Uncomfortable

Let's look at each one in detail.

- My first boundary is that God comes first in everything and that His scriptures are our guideline.

We agree that God's marital roles and responsibilities are the foundation of our relationship and marriage. Any disagreements are always resolved with God's standards first (the scripture). Then they will default to my authority as the head.

My first boundary with God signals to her that the goal is to please God rather than myself or her. I won't put her on a pedestal and idolize her, and she shouldn't put me on a pedestal and idolize me. This is important because it sets the tone of the relationship. More than half (53 percent) of Christian women now rate their family as a top priority. Only 16 percent of women had faith as their top priority, 9 percent listed health, 5 percent gave career performance, and 5 percent said a comfortable lifestyle.[1] In the same survey, a "women's sense of identity very closely follows their priorities, with 62 percent of women saying their most important role in life is as a mother or parent. Jesus came next: 13 percent of Christian women believe their most important role in life is as a follower of Christ. In third place at 11 perecent is their role as wife." Imagine that: 13 percent of so-called Christian women believe that Jesus is their top priority. How scary is that? Talk about fishing from a small pool. Obviously, this is a sad indication of the priorities of women, and I want to properly establish a relationship from the get go.

- My second boundary is to never lie. Relationships are built on trust. The trust in a relationship is built on truth in interactions with each other.

If I ever find out that one of the building blocks of the relationship was a lie, then it's possible that every other interaction I've had with this person is a lie. You don't really know, and I wouldn't be able to trust the woman. Thus I tell her that if I ever find out that she has lied to me, that will be the end of the relationship. I won't lie to her, and she won't lie to me.

My second boundary is based around the fact that lying is one of the sins that is straight from Satan himself (John 8). For the most part, we are carried away by our own lusts in our human nature. However, lying and deception is a sin that is rooted primarily in Satan, and it is specifically designed to undermine relationships. Deception was the reason that Satan could tempt Eve to eat the fruit. Deception undermined the relationship of Adam and Eve with God and the relationship between Adam and Eve. I do not tolerate lying and deception in my relationships.

> Jesus said to them, "If God were your Father, you would love Me, for I proceeded forth and have come from God, for I have not even come on My own initiative, but He sent Me. Why do you not understand what I am saying? It is because you cannot hear My word. You are of your father the devil, and you want to do the desires of your father. He was a murderer from the beginning, and does not stand in the truth because there is no truth in him. Whenever he speaks a lie, he speaks from his own nature, for he is a liar and the father of lies. But because I speak the truth, you do not believe Me'" (John 8:42–45).

We know the primary identity of God is the Father and His primary attribute is love, but we often don't think about the primary identity and attribute of Satan. His primary identity is a murderer, and one of his chief traits is lying and deception. (See Genesis 3.) Let that sink in for a moment. Obviously, we hold murder up as one of the most serious sins, but lying is not a big deal to some Christians. They believe that it's a piddly matter that you can just ask forgiveness for, and everything will be fine. Our attitude toward lying must be change from nonchalant to hardline if we value relationships.

Note: This is for early relationships and prior to marriage. As a Christian, there is no justifiable reason to divorce a spouse for lying. But holding to this standard will weed out liars.

- My third boundary is to be comfortable with being uncomfortable. I view this as a three-pronged approach: I should be growing in my relationship with God; she should be growing in her relationship with God, and we should be growing in relationship with each other. Growth requires change, which is often uncomfortable, especially in the context of taking off the old man and putting on the new man (Ephesians 4).

My last boundary focuses on relationship growth. This is important because when talking about sensitive topics, the tendency is to want to fudge the truth a bit and start with so-called harmless white lies. But evil can then creep into a relationship. Likewise, admonishment and rebuke will occur within a relationship; humans are not perfect, so we need to deal with the uncomfortable aspect of our feelings when addressing the truth. This sets down the standard that being uncomfortable is positive and complements the second boundary that walking in the truth is the right thing to do even when uncomfortable. Feelings are not the truth of the relationship.

I'm not saying you must adopt these same boundaries, but these were important to me. Strong boundaries facilitate trust within a relationship. You will take the reins of leadership in the relationship when you introduce them.

When I've used these in my relationship, it led to a deeper level of truth and intimacy that was not there before. Obviously this only works with Christians who want to walk in the truth, so each person must decide whether or not they want to follow this standard. It probably won't work well with those who are lukewarm. But you're trying to filter out those women (or men) anyway.

As much as women hem and haw about boundaries and how they hate them, they really do like them. Masculine men are overt in their intentions;

women know their values and where they stand with them. The couple does not play a guessing game, which provides a certain security in knowing truly who a man is. This type of outline of a relationship will foster growth as a leader and attraction as a byproduct. A man who knows what he wants in a relationship and knows the steps to building it is far away ahead of his peers.

In this case, maturity is the ability to lead and build the relationship from the ground up in a godly manner.

KNOW HOW TO ASSERTIVELY COMMUNICATE: SHOW YOU CAN LOVE EFFECTIVELY

I think this is the broadest and most confusing point for most Christian men. It might be helpful to remember the differences in how men and women communicate. Women tend to affirm each other while men tend to be more critical of each other. A scripture verse addresses man-to-man communication. Proverbs 27:17 states, "Iron sharpens iron, so one man sharpens another."

The criticism, the challenging, the ribbing, the teasing, and mock insulting in male camaraderie is to encourage other men to gain strength and courage when they face tough situations. Men are telling each other in so many words: just do it; don't be a scaredy-cat; go all out; we'll think less of you if you don't try, and similar phrases.

Recall what we discussed in the attraction chapter about nice guys versus jerks.

- What do the nice guys do? They're always very complimenting and affirming of women, thinking that is what women want to hear and that it will help strengthen the relationship. They think they need to be her friend and that a woman will recognize how nice he is and accept him.
- What do the jerks do? They criticize women, challenge them, tease them, and mock insult them at times. Women call them jerks because they can seem mean at times, but they secretly like them and their behavior. Why?

Nice guys tend to communicate with women in a very feminine manner like a girlfriend. If you treat her like a girlfriend, then it's no secret that she'll treat you like a platonic girlfriend—not a romantic girlfriend. Jerks tend to communicate with women in a very masculine manner, like a leader. A leader is not afraid to have an opinion and call out anyone who is wrong or needs correction.

This is not a hard-and-fast rule by any means, but what I've found works well is interacting with women—Christian or not—with a 50/50 split of serious communication and masculine banter. Indeed, other percentages can work too. Some married friends prefer a lot more banter, as much as 80 percent, with 20 percent in-depth conversation. Find a division that works for you.

Serious communication recognizes that the relationship always needs to be growing in some form. I might ask and discuss various topics about faith, life, dreams, goals, and specific situations. This is where relevant questions come in, such as finding out the intensity of her faith and if she is a virtuous woman. The masculine banter shows her that she's around a man who can be a leader who she can respect, which is usually quite fun for both of you. Don't take yourself too seriously when you tease her.

Assertive communication focuses on the ability to share your faith as well as your opinions on likes and dislikes. Obviously, there is straight truth from the Bible, and we know that we as Christians should adhere to that. But you can have differences of opinion and still honor each other within a relationship. Thus, part of relationships is sharing your likes and dislikes with the other person. Scripturally this is important to understand. As a Christian man, you will be teaching Christian women that you don't desire love but respect in the relationship.

Women might say, "I love you" to men to communicate their feelings or desire for reciprocal words. The former is good, but the latter is bad. A man should value the statement, "I love you" from the perspective of Titus 2 as affectionate love (Greek, *philandros*) for their husbands which communicates these feelings of love. But in terms of the relationship, respect and submission are paramount for it to function correctly.

Many Christian women assume that men want love because they want to be loved, and most Christian men are unaware that they should not strive for love in marriage, according to scripture. This is because love is held as the standard for worldly relationships, and Christians confuse this feelings-based love (eros) with actions-based love (agape). Mixing the worldly standards with attempted biblical standards is a recipe for failure. This is important for mentoring young Christian men and women. Respect correctly frames authority and thus headship.

If you ever reach the point where you are not encouraging assertive discussion in a relationship, then it's going downhill. The trust in a relationship is being eroded.

Another part of assertive communication is the ability to create a safe space. This is nothing like the safe space of feminists, which means don't hurt my feelings. A real safe space means that if something has gone wrong, then your woman or wife can talk to you about it without a second thought. For instance, if a woman brings up her hurt feelings or opinions with me, I always thank her for doing so, letting her know that I value her communication. This tells her that I am kind and care about what she has to say before we even engage in discussion about the issue, no matter the outcome. This builds trust and does not allow wrongs to fester under the surface until someone blows up.

FIVE STEPS: A SUMMARY

To summarize, we've explored how to effectively apply some of the principles of God's Word to male-female relationships.

1. Know what God says about relationships.
2. Know your mission, your dreams, and goals.
3. Know your standards for women.
4. Know your standards/boundaries in a relationship.
5. Know how to assertively communicate.

All this structured planning is important for men. It helps them determine God's truth, His mission for them in their life and relationships, possible approaches to problems, and gives them overall confidence in being decisive about the path they should take in life.

Compromising standards because of women is generally a very bad idea. I was talking with some men recently about compromising standards and ultimatums and how they are lose-lose situations. For instance, if a woman ever wants you to choose between mission and her, then answering either way is a loss. If you select her, then you compromise your mission and life, and you will no longer be the man that she was attracted to in the first place. If you select your mission, then she'll be angry. She might still be attracted to you, but you can't trust her that well anymore. Repairing that trust is difficult. In general, it's not the answer that matters but addressing the underlying attitude: a woman in a relationship with you or your helpmeet won't even consider making you choose in the first place.

Healthy relationships thrive on boundaries as they create trust. Putting God first, lying as a deal breaker, and an expectation of growth will help weed out poor candidates in the long run. It's assumed I will tell the truth—however blunt—but that I will be as kind as possible. Boundaries must be both proactive and reactive. The proactive approach from a scriptural perspective properly frames a relationship. The reactive approach is part of the sanctification process; if there is sin or offenses, they need to be addressed. For example, if your woman makes an inappropriate comment in public, you need to pull her aside and let her know that her comment was disrespectful.

Assertive communication ties everything together. You can know what the Bible says about relationships. You can know God's mission for you. You can have healthy standards and boundaries in relationships. But if you can't communicate well regarding these and other key subjects, you will not be successful in any relationship. We know that charisma and public speaking are learned abilities, so you need to know how to communicate effectively in conjunction with the fruit of the Spirit, especially in difficult situations.

Once you realize this, you can obviously see that time doesn't do anything to mature a person or to ready him or her for a relationship. As the common maxim goes, women aren't looking for men with potential. They're looking for a man who's already a winner. This will put you on the track to figure out what you are doing, to be confident about what you're looking for, and to pull the trigger when the time comes.

You will be a man who knows what he wants and is not afraid to go after it.

Chapter 13
EXPECTATION PITFALLS TO RELATIONSHIPS

THE CHURCH, MARRIAGE, AND SOCIAL SCRIPTS

By and large, the church as a whole has compromised with the world regarding social scripts, which are cultural influences and social norms that influence the directive and expectations of people within a given society.

For example, a typical economic social script, which influences the timeline of marriage, looks like this:

High school → College → Stable job → Car + House → Family

This social script ranges from fourteen to twenty-five or thirty years for age for a young man or a young woman. This social script tells most young men and women that they shouldn't start a family until they have all their ducks in a row—an education, a stable job, a car, and a house. Then, and only then, should they start a family.

There is no written law or rule that tells everyone they must follow this path, but because of cultural influences and social norms, the vast majority of people in first-world countries go through these steps anyway. That is the power of social scripting—most people want to fit in with the norm, so people will avoid being outliers. They will jump on the bandwagon with everyone else rather than discerning for themselves what is wise for their own life.

Scripture presents the above script as extremely problematic. 1 Corinthians 7 states that Christians should marry if they burn to avoid sexual temptation. Young men and young women start to feel their sex drive and thus passion during puberty at around thirteen years of age. Yet we expect our young Christian men and women to wait to marry until they have all their ducks in a row between the ages of twenty-five to thirty. This is a gap of twelve to seventeen years when Christian men and women have a very strong sex drive. The average age of marriage as of 2015, according to the U.S. Census Bureau, is twenty-nine for men and twenty-seven for women.[1] In some European countries, this average is as high as thirty to thirty-five for both men and women.[2] In most industrialized countries, it will only increase.

Is it any wonder why young Christian men and women are falling into sexual sin—whether pornography, sex out of wedlock, or other sinful behaviors—at very high rates? The church and families pushing these types of scripts have put heavy shackles of expectation on their children to resist sexual temptations for more than a decade while they attempt to put their lives in order before they marry. This is an unrealistic view to push on Christian young men and women who desire to honor God.

Similarly, what is to say that they can even find someone to marry once they hit twenty-five to thirty years of age? Anyone reading this book knows the difficulty of dating and relationships in the digital age. Most young Christian men and women are around their peers and can meet someone with a similar faith at high school and college groups. Once you leave college, a lot of your friendships with other believers tend to fall by the wayside, and work becomes a priority. It's hard to meet other single Christians when life priorities block your way.

This is not to say that we should encourage teen marriages. In some parts of the United States, the pendulum has swung the other way altogether in Christian communities with the promotion of very young marriages. Even shotgun marriages fail at exceedingly high rates because the couple is forced together and left to fend for themselves. The mentality is, "It's their problem as they got pregnant. They can deal with it." This is problematic due to the nature of how we now raise children. In most countries, the age of adulthood is eighteen. Many cultures in the past had coming-of-age ceremonies at the age of puberty or around about thirteen years old, including Jewish bar mitzvahs.

We need to thoroughly teach our children about God, maturity, and marriage before they get married. How many young men and young women can say they were mentored and taught by their parents or the church about relationships, sexuality, and marriage? Very few, I would guess. These can be uncomfortable topics, which parents and the church tend to ignore.

We cannot shelter our children from the hardships of life. We do them a disservice if we expect them to adhere to social scripts or if we push them into marriage too early. Many sinful pitfalls along the way are brushed by the wayside. In the end, it's not about taking an easier road but about preparing them for godliness despite the difficulty of the road. Young burgeoning relationships and newly married couples need family, church, and community support, especially in hard times.

Many other different types of social scripts in our culture normalize behavior that is contrary to the Bible. Some of these are:

- Men pursuing women
- Romantic love as the most important thing in marriage
- Pornography as a healthy activity
- Gay marriage
- Transgenderism
- Sex before marriage
- Cohabitation
- Any divorce
- Disrespect toward men, husbands, and fathers
- Fathers threatening potential sons-in-law over their daughter

Many of these Christians know that these are against what God says in the Bible, but some of these issues can still trip up immature Christians. Even the church has had its fair share of social scripting issues with the influence of books, such as *I Kissed Dating Goodbye*, and ineffective organizations that encourage men to man up, such as Promise Keepers. The "man up" social scripts don't work.

IT JUST HAPPENS VS. COLLEGE ANALOGY

Many Christians and those in the world believe that finding a spouse just happens. A lot of pseudo-wisdom out there states, "if you stop looking for love, it will find you" and similar statements. Some people continually parrot these statements because they sometimes work, but they clearly don't work for everyone.

An analogy that fits well here is the process of college. You extensively prepare yourself to be the best possible candidate not only to get into college but to be successful in college. Students who want to go to college do the following:

- Study to get good grades in high school
- Study for the SATs or ACTs
- Prepare your essays and have others proofread them
- Prepare for interviews and practice interviewing skills
- All this diligence and discipline sets you up for success in your college classes

The same thing is true of Christian marriage.

- Extensively study the scriptures on marriage, roles, and responsibilities
- The test of your faith is figuring out and contributing to God's mission through the church
- Find married mentors who can help you with marriage readiness
- Practice assertive communication and leadership skills to prepare for dates
- All this diligence and discipline sets you up for success in a Christian marriage

This is not to say we should necessarily be actively pursuing marriage, though you can do so if that desire is on your heart. It is more important to focus on God's mission for your life and then see which women might potentially come alongside you in the journey. This ensures that you're not actively chasing or pursuing women, which is not the right mentality for relationships and marriage. A man might do well to marry, but he does better if he serves the Lord without marrying (1 Corinthians 7). If a woman wants to follow you and comes alongside of you in the journey, and you burn with passion for each other, by all means, marry.

Sadly the divorce rates in the church are very close to society's divorce rates. This means that what the church has been doing is too much like what the culture does. The church is not separate from the culture. Most churches recommend some form of marital counseling prior to marriage, but it is not enough. Both the husband and the wife ought to be discipled in their faith, and they should be proactive about understanding and applying the Bible's roles and the responsibilities of marriage.

MANAGING EXPECTATIONS

As the leader in marriage, you need to understand expectations and manage them correctly. This not only goes for your expectations but also for those of your future wife. Remember, Jesus states twice in John 13 and 15, "If you love Me, obey my commandments." This is prior to the church's engagement with Christ and prior to the marriage of the church to Christ.

Christ's sacrifice on the cross when he shed his blood for the remission of sins is the marriage proposal. Our acceptance and repentance from our sins and the indwelling of the Holy Spirit is our seal of engagement, much like an engagement ring in our culture is the promise to be married.

> Also we have obtained an inheritance, having been predestined according to His purpose who works all things after the counsel of His will, to the end that we who were the first to hope in Christ would be to the praise of His glory. In Him, you also, after listening to the message of truth, the gospel of your salvation—having also believed, you were sealed in Him with the Holy Spirit of promise, who is given as a pledge of our inheritance, with a view to the redemption of God's own possession, to the praise of His glory (Ephesians 1:11–14).

When the marriage of Christ and the church finally happens in Revelation 19, the wheat and chaff will be separated as will the sheep and the goats and other analogies Jesus uses in the gospels. Those fake Christians who were unfaithful or who were simply acting like Christians during the engagement period will be cast away, and those who were faithful Christians will become the Bride of Christ (Matthew 17:21–23).

It might be helpful to understand that the Jewish engagement during Jesus's time was different than our engagement today, which is very flippant. You generally needed a certificate of divorce to break engagements at that time because they were as binding as marriage was. Being betrothed was considered to be very serious.

A Christian marriage of a husband and wife is a foreshadowing of Christ and His bride, while Christ's example simultaneously guides us on how to act in a Christian marriage. Ephesians 5 calls this a great mystery. A Christian marriage with the husband and wife in headship/submission and love/respect is very beautiful to the world and a great witness. It's no wonder why the enemy wants to tear it down.

We need to understand that Jesus places expectations on the church and on Christians that make up the church. What commands has he asked us to obey? Go and make disciples of all nations—not simply just evangelize but disciple: mentor and be mentored. Love one another as I have loved you. He also has spoken through His disciples, through the scriptures, and given us roles and responsibilities in the marriage covenant.

This is where the rubber meets the road. As Christians, whether single or married, we need to be able to speak the truth regarding the scriptures into our relationships. This is part of the sanctification process. Some pastors tell Christian husbands that respect and submission are the wife's duty and that husbands shouldn't comment on them. This is false. The husband's duty of sacrificial love is for the sanctification of his wife. He must be committed to holding her to the expectations of God in the scriptures to wash her from the influence of the world and the tendency to rebel, disrespect, nag, and be contentious.

If a man cannot speak to his girlfriend or a husband to his wife about the expectations in the scriptures, this is the same sin Adam committed in the garden. We don't know whether Adam was there when Eve was being tempted. But we do know that when Eve ate the fruit and gave some to him, he chose to be complicit in the sin and eat the fruit instead of rebuking his wife.

Naturally, confronting the wife over sinful behavior means running toward conflict and not away from it. This is difficult, but you must be strong and courageous against sinful behavior. The fruit of the Spirit is necessary in these situations as you walk in kindness and patience to help guide your wife in the process of repentance. Humility and repentance are also necessary if you also chose to be complicit in the sin before or even now.

The scriptures on roles and responsibilities are but the *minimum* expectations for the marriage. Remember that God has given you a mission and gifts of the Spirit. Since your wife is your helpmeet, you must also have expectations of her that you introduce prior to marriage to see if she is the right fit for you. If she's going to become your helpmeet, she needs to hear and agree with these, otherwise it would be a bad idea to marry her. ==You should not marry a woman that doesn't follow well, doesn't submit, actively disrespects her husband, isn't affectionate, or is frigid.== If a man chooses to marry a woman like this, then those consequences are on his head

It is much more difficult for a husband who is married to communicate expectations if he has not done it before. This will be discussed more in depth in the marriage section of the book. The road is long here.

Likewise, wives have expectations of their husbands. Many of these are often according to the scriptures, such as the provider, protector, and masculine leader. You need to figure out if her expectations in these matters agree with your role and responsibility. Unmet expectations, especially when not verbalized, tend to build up bitterness and unhappiness. This is where assertive communication is very useful.

For instance, some women are looking for an excessive provider that some men cannot give. Perhaps that is a polite way of saying that they are gold digging. It would be unwise for a man to marry a woman who has these types of expectations, especially if he does not have a career track that can meet those expectations. Let's also be real. A high-maintenance woman is neither good or bad; some men like high-maintenance women and can have a godly marriage with one. But a man who prefers low-maintenance women should not marry a high-maintenance woman with all the related expectations. This is a recipe for disaster.

Thus, a man should know his own expectations and communicate them, and he should seek out a woman's expectations to see if he can meet them. This will help to screen out poor matches. After the expectations are known, a man must be able to hold both himself and her accountable to them prior to marriage. Indeed, nothing changes once you are married; you both should work to fulfill them to the best of your ability before and after marriage.

MASCULINE IMMATURITY IS PLACING RESPONSIBILITIES BEFORE ROLES

How does one place a responsibility before their role?

We looked at the example in a previous chapter of why women tend to go for jerks over nice guys. This is because jerks tend to have masculine traits, such as boldness and confidence, in spades, as opposed to nice guys who act shyly or cowardly around women. Also, these jerks tend to act masculine around women whereas nice guys tend to act feminine.

One of the typical things that shy men do is to become a woman's friend first and then try to become her boyfriend. This type of man hangs around or tries to befriend a woman while trying to win her favor by:

- Taking her out to places.
- Paying for her meals, clothes, and other items.
- Being emotionally available to her if she is having issues, ironically, often when she has issues with her boyfriend, friends, or family.
- Inviting her to events with him that seem like dates but that are not really dates. She would deny they are dates if asked.

This strategy is not successful. It's a classic case of putting responsibilities ahead of the actual role. A man who acts like this is playing the role of a boyfriend without actually being a boyfriend. Very few women will turn down free food, free things, attention, and support. Yet they do not want to go out with this man when everything is said and done.

If a man was taught the role—or at least emphasized the role—of leadership along with responsibilities, he would know that it is unwise to pursue a woman who doesn't like him back. A leader will not try to push his way into a relationship by trying to get a girl to like him because of what he does. Instead he will take charge. What you have in this case is:

- The man is fulfilling the responsibilities in a relationship.
- The man is not fulfilling his role in a relationship.
- The woman is not fulfilling her responsibilities in a relationship.
- The woman is not fulfilling her role in a relationship.

Of course, since there is literally no relationship, the only one who is actually wrong is the man who is fulfilling the responsibilities of the relationship when there is none to begin with.

Trying to fulfill responsibilities without establishing the roles is falling into a works-based mindset. You're trying to win her over by what you do. If you fall into this pattern, it's very difficult to get out of, but it will never work. You can never do enough to satisfy or make someone happy. It's her responsibility to be in control of those things. In fact, you might be tempting her to sin by doing this as you're setting yourself up for internal conflict between you, her, and any possible future relationship (because she's obviously not interested in you).

When you teach men to act as the leader or head of a relationship, then a man becomes more attractive by being confident and doing the correct things from the outset. He is not trying to back a woman into a relationship. Rather he is focused on finding a woman with whom he wants to fulfill his roles and responsibilities. He is also looking for a woman who is willing to fulfill her roles and responsibilities to him.

CHRISTIAN VALUES AND SELECTIVENESS

When using specific criteria for vetting, one of the big questions that comes up among Christians is the concept of forgiveness.

Let's use the example of a woman's or a man's sexual past. God certainly forgives Christians who repent of their sins and casts them as far as the east is from the west, to paraphrase Psalm 103. Therefore, why shouldn't a man forgive a woman of her sexual past as God does and marry her?

In fact, forgiveness of her sexual past is already a no-win trap, much like the Pharisees who constantly tried to trick Jesus. It makes the man defensive and attempts to shame him about something that someone else did. This is another blame game in the church, where men consistently draw the short end of the stick. Aside from this trap, it is important to understand that there are various reasons why the question is wrong anyway.

While God does forgive our sins and does not impute them against us spiritually, He also might not remove the physical, emotional, or mental consequences of our sins from our lives. We might deal with physical issues from previous sexual encounters, such as STDs or infertility. We will almost always carry emotional or mental baggage from previous sexual relationships. This is not to say that virgins might not have hang ups either. In some cases, some virgins have made an idol out of their virginity or have a mindset that sex is dirty from growing up in church. These issues can also cause problems in the marital bed.

Just because someone is a Christian and forgiven does not make them a suitable or wise candidate for marriage. Ultimately, a man should be looking for a wife that will be his helpmeet. Many women might not be compatible based on their personalities, spiritual gifts, and mission from God. The same is true with her past history.

On the other hand, we are all sinners, and all of us have things in our past that will make us less suitable candidates for some people than others. If you feel comfortable marrying someone with a sexual past and believe that they are truly changed in Christ, then marry them. If you are uncomfortable with someone's sexual past, then don't marry them. The same is true of other issues as well: pornography addiction, cohabitation, alcoholism, drugs, or whatever the case might be. Being selective is not sinful but rather wisely considering your own situation. It would be unwise to try to guilt-trip yourself into marrying someone or even have another Christian try to guilt-trip you, especially if you are uncomfortable or concerned about their past.

The criteria to become a Christian are different than they are to become the wife of a husband and the husband of a wife. You should be selective about who you marry because you will be married to that person for life and tied together in your mission for God. God does not tell you to marry a person with a sexual past, a history of alcoholism, or even a murderer just for the sake of forgiveness. God gives us freedom to choose.

Be wise about your future marriage given your own standards, and even if he or she meets your criteria, take a hard look at their character and godliness.

Chapter 14
MANAGING A HEALTHY RELATIONSHIP

MONEYBALL FOR MARRIAGE:
STATISTICS FOR VETTING TO AVOID DIVORCE

One of the common parroted statistics in popular culture today is that there a 50/50 chance that you will divorce if you are married. This argument is true overall for all marriages but is about 42-45 percent for first marriages. It is used to dissuade people from marrying. Even so, statistics can be misleading.[1]

Unfortunately the church rarely approaches faith from a statistical point of view. This is disheartening to us because statistics almost always support the validity of character and behavior that God teaches us in the scriptures. Let's look at some of the scriptures' instruction and how statistics support them. For instance, these are some guidelines that the Bible gives about who you should marry, including these traits:

- A Christian (2 Corinthians 6)
- Someone with solid character (Proverbs 31)
- Those who are obedient to the Word (Ephesians 5, Colossian 3, Titus 2, 1 Peter 3)
- No sex/chastity before marriage (1 Corinthians 7)

Statistics show general trends in the population at large. Statistics can serve as strong predictors about populations to which they apply, but a statistic does not necessarily apply to any individual person, especially if they do not meet the criteria.

If 50 percent of all marriages end in divorce, your marriage does not necessarily have a 50/50 chance of divorce. Research from The Heritage

Foundation has yielded interesting results regarding the number of pre-marital sexual partners that women have had and how this number correlates to their rate of divorce.

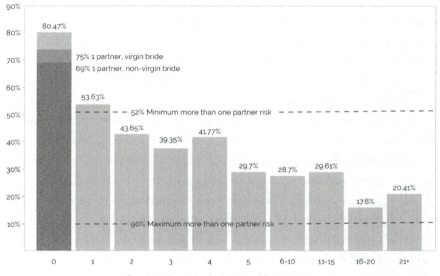

Source: *heritage.org*[2] and *The Social Pathologist*[3]

According to this study, even just *one* sexual partner prior to marriage dropped a woman's chances of a stable marriage from close to 80 percent down to only 53 percent. That's a much bigger difference than the drop between two partners and fifteen partners. This study has been corroborated by other research as well, and the trend is consistent. As one article cited:

> According to new research by the National Marriage Project, more than half of married women who had only ever slept with their future husband felt highly satisfied in their marriage.
>
> But that percentage dropped to 42 percent once the woman had had pre-marital sex with at least two partners. It dropped to 22 percent for those with ten or more partners. . . . It concluded: 'Remember that what you do before you say 'I do' seems to have a notable impact on your marital future. So decide wisely.'[4]

Before we go further, we should discuss what these statistics do and do not mean.

Correlation is not causation: We cannot say that virginity has a causative effect on divorce rates. We do not know that if you control for other variables, such as sexual education, religious affiliation, other behaviors, and similar factors, that you would still see a similar strong effect. But it's clear that sexual choices have some effect on divorce. An 80 percent drop down to 50 percent and then into the 20 percent range is a strong correlative effect. It's likely that all the variables combined that would lead a woman to retain her virginity until marriage play a strong role in avoiding divorce. Men would do well to consider the risk factors themselves and decide whether mitigating circumstances, such as spirituality, evidence of repentance, and godly character, are sufficient reasons enough to make her a low risk of divorce.

Variables affect each other: An example of the interplay of these factors is risk-taking behavior. Those who engage in these behaviors, such as binge drinking, are more likely to try other risky behaviors, such as illicit drugs use and sexual promiscuity. As inhibitions are lowered, people act crazier.

For a potential wife, a woman who is genuine Christian is more statistically likely to be a virgin, chaste, and with the desire to be a wife and mother. This will mean that you will likely find many chaste, virtuous women in a strong community of genuine Christians. Like begets like.

Statistics are not destiny, but they do predict relative risk: Any single person could be an exception to the rule, but everyone who has engaged in a behavior shows patterns.

School and job interviews discuss your past schooling and employment because these are likely predictors of future ability to do well in more advanced schooling or success in your job. Likewise, I'm sure many of us have heard of a story where their grandparents or a friend's grandparents chain-smoked ten packs of cigarettes a day for sixty years and still lived to the ripe old age of 110. On the other hand, many people have had relatives or friend's relatives who died of lung cancer in their forties and fifties. Smoking is a high-risk activity that is known to cause cancer in a large portion of the population. Marrying a non-virgin woman carries a higher risk as well.

A man can make the choice that he won't marry a smoker because she is more likely to die earlier, spend money frivolously on cigarettes, and have more health issues. He might not want to expose his children or himself to second-hand smoke either. The same is true of marrying someone who has been sexually promiscuous. Sure, she could be an exception, and you could have a godly marriage with her if she has repented of her sins and follows Jesus. But you are still taking a risk by marrying someone with a promiscuous past that you wouldn't have if you had married a virgin. If they have not made the choice to continually submit to God, they can easily fall back into old habits, which can include divorce or being sexually promiscuous again.

Common maxims, such as "Once a cheater, always a cheater," emphasize these statistical tendencies. Overall, the past is a consistently reliable predictor of the future.

You can think of such relative risk ratios as yellow or "red flags, depending on your preferences. One yellow flag is questionable. Two might cause raised eyebrows. Three is concerning. Four or more and sirens should be going off in your head. As the saying goes, "If it's not 'hell yeah!' it's a 'hell no!'"

The whole package and relative risk: It is important to assess the background of a woman in a count-the-cost manner if you are considering her as a potential wife. I've mentioned before that a one-and-done mistake made by a repentant person is likely more trustworthy than a virgin woman who has done everything but have sex with her many boyfriends. This is the importance of quality of behavior over the quantity of behavior. People like to get hung up on the quantity of behavior over quality when quality is just as important.

Quality of behavior is also assessed when it comes to past history and tendencies of an individual. Someone who was ignorant of the gospel and had sex but has a testimony where she turned around and now has a history of chastity and good works will be a better selection for marriage than someone who was a so-called Christian the whole time they were continually engaged in sinful behavior.

To further correlate these points, the CDC in their National Center of Health Statistics showed a few general trends that back up the importance of virginity in women. Women with more non-marital sexual partners are:

- More likely to have an STD
- Less likely to have a stable marriage

- Less likely to be happy
- More likely to be depressed

Women Who Have More Non-Marital Sexual Partners Are More Likely to Be Infected with Sexually Transmitted Diseases

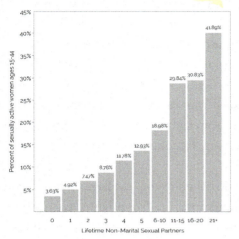

This chart shows the impact or increases in the number of lifetime sexual partners on the chances of being infected by a sexually transmitted disease (STD). The chart covers all sexually active women, some of whom have had sex only with men whom they married. Some 3.6 percent of sexually active women who have had zero non-marital sex partners have contracted syphilis, gonorrhea, chlamydia, genital warts, or genital herpes, or have a self-reported high risk of HIV. By contrast, the STD infection rate of women with 11 to 15 non-marital sexual partners is nearly ten times higher. Some 30 percent of these women have been infected.

Women Who Have More Non-Marital Sexual Partners Are Less Likely to Have Stable Marriages

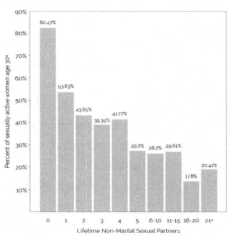

This chart covers sexually active women over the age of 30. Women were defined as having a stable marriage if they were currently married and had been in that same marriage for at least five years. Women who had more non-marital sex partners were less likely to have stable marriage. Over 80 percent of the women who had never had a non-marital partner were in stable marriages. By contrast, only 30 percent of the women with five non-marital sex partners were in stable marriages.

Women Who Have More Non-Marital Sexual Partners Are Less Likely to Be Happy

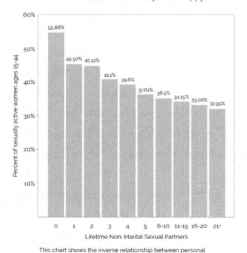

This chart shows the inverse relationship between personal happiness and the number of lifetime non-marital sexual partners. The greater the number the non-marital sex partners, the lower the probability of personal happiness. The chart covers all sexually active women. Some 56 percent of women who have had sex only with men they married report they are currently "very happy." As the number of non-marital sex partners increases, the probability that a woman will report she feels "very happy" shrinks. Only 37 percent of women with five non-marital sex partners report they are very happy.

Women Who Have More Non-Marital Sexual Partners Are More Likely to Be Depressed

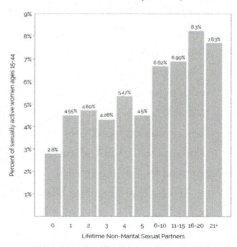

This chart shows the relationship between the number of lifetime non-marital sexual partners and depression. The greater the number of non-marital sex partners, the higher the probability of depression. Only 2.8 percent of women, who have had sex only with men they married report they currently feel "not very happy" or "very unhappy." By contrast, 8.3 percent of women with 16 to 20 non-marital sex partners report they currently feel "not very happy" or "very unhappy."

Source: CDC, National Center of Health Statistics, National Survey of Family Growth 1995[5]

You can see how these all feed into each other. A woman who has been with another man or with many men, aside from her husband, is more likely to be exposed to STDs. She's more likely to compare her husband to other lovers, which can lead to dissatisfaction. She's less likely to bond strongly to her current partner. God knew what He was talking about when He required that women be virgins at marriage in Deuteronomy 22.

Aside from virginity, statistics provide other indicators of stable marriages as follows: [6]

- **Age:** Lowest risk between 25 and 30 years old. Higher outside these ages.
- **Religion:** Catholics > Active Protestants > Non-practicing > Non-practicing Protestants > Other
- **Importance of religion:** Active > Non-practicing

Those committed to their faith or with no faith have stronger marriages than those who are lukewarm.

- **College education:** Graduate > College-educated > Some college > HS diploma > Some high school

Education is a predictor of stable marriages, potentially due to the ability to plan long-term and develop discipline and self-control and see goals to completion.

- **Family background:** Two parents > One parent > No parents

A person with a family background of a father and a mother provides the most stable marriage, which is also a predictor of divorce. Single parents and no parents have children with less stable marriages. Divorced or out-of-wedlock single mothers are *much riskier* than widows or widowers because they have already made poor choices.

- **Children and wedlock:** Children in wedlock > Children within first nine months of marriage > Children out of wedlock

Shotgun marriages are worse than children within marriages but better than having children out of wedlock then not getting married.

- **Age of first sexual experience:** 18+ > 17-18 > 15-16 > 13-14 > 12
- **Cohabitation:** No cohabitation > Cohabitation

- **Income:** Husband earns more > Equal income > Wife earns more
- **Income total:** Middle > Higher > Lowest (Speculation: more cash and prizes for divorcing the highest income earners)
- **Ethnicity:** Asian > Hispanic > Caucasian > Black

Delaying sexual experience obviously improves the chances of a stable marriage. Ethnicity is a hot topic. This does not mean marrying an Asian is better than marrying a Caucasian or a black, especially if you are of a different race. As we'll see in a bit, interracial marriages can do worse or better than normal, depending on the race of the individuals in the marriage.

Some factors include:[7,8]

- **Prior marriage:** No prior marriage is better than a prior marriage.
- **Employment status:** Employed > Part-time > Unemployed
- **Interracial marriages:** Some have a higher likelihood of staying together (e.g., Caucasian man, Black woman) and some have a lower likelihood (e.g., Black man, Caucasian woman; Asian man, Caucasian woman, and others).
- **Country:** The United States is divorce happy compared with many other countries. For example, 50 percent of all Catholic annulments worldwide are in the United States while only about 5 percent of the Catholic population lives in this nation.
- **Ability to resolve conflict:** Never argue > Rarely argue > Regularly argue > Heated arguments
- **Alcohol use:** None > Some > Frequent
- **Drug use:** None > Some > Frequent
- **Mental illness:** None > Having one (depression, schizophrenia, BPD, etc.)
- **Age difference:** Reverse bell curve with the least risk when a man is zero to two years older.
- **Forced premarital sex:** None > Forced sex or rape
- **Length of marriage:** The longer your marriage lasts, the less risk of divorce.

Social attitudes also play a role.

- **False** – Divorce is usually the best solution when a couple can't seem to work out their marriage problems.

- **True** – A young couple should not live together unless they are married.
- **False** – It is okay for an unmarried female to have a child.
- **True** – It is more important for a man to spend a lot of time with his family than to be successful at his career.

Other factors might include:[9]

- **Blue states > Red states:** An increase of more than 27 percent – Red states traditionally have younger marriages, often without solid counseling and discipleship. This does not mean Democrats are better than Republicans, or Republicans are better than Democrats.
- **Arguing about finances once a week:** An increase of more than 30 percent – money issues correlate with increased divorce.
- **If one is a smoker:** You are 75 to 91 percent more likely to divorce than if both were non-smokers or smokers respectively.
- **You and spouse had previous marriages:** You are 90 percent more likely to divorce than if this is a first marriage for both of you. If you both failed at marriage before, you likely chose poorly and/or you have issues with leading another.
- **Wife is 2+ years older – 53 percent more likely to divorce than if husband is one to three years older:** While age does not signify maturity or leadership, often if the husband is older, the wife likely has a higher propensity to follow.
- **No cancer > cancer:** Some abandon their spouse if they have cervical (+40 percent) or testicular (+20 percent) cancer. So much for in sickness and in health.
- **Twins or triplets:** An increase of a +17 percent risk, likely due to increased stress or finances
- **Female serial cohabiters:** More than 40 percent increased risk of divorce if a woman has previously lived with other men. This relates to the other cohabitation risk mentioned earlier.
- **Same-sex marriages:** More than 50 percent and more than 16 percent for male and female same-sex marriages. (Not that any Christians reading this book planned to marry a person of the same sex.)

All of these are different indicators of an increased probability for separation or divorce, and these are all various criteria to look at when evaluating a potential wife. Some are more important than others as you can see by the different percentages.

One important thing to note about these risk factors is that almost all, if not all, actually fit God's standards for marriage. Virginity, having a father and mother, religion, employment status, the ability to resolve conflict, the lack of alcohol and drug abuse, no children outside marriage, the lack of remarriage, and related factors all decrease the risk of divorce. God's standards for marriage are truly meant to bind us together for life and decrease our risk of divorce.

Using a combination of statistics, you can calculate the divorce risk over periods of time. For example, using these criteria, the relative risk of separation at ten years is 2 percent.

- Older than twenty-five
- Has a four-year degree
- Catholic
- With an intact two-parent family
- Lost her virginity to you in marriage
- Was not a single mother
- Does not believe divorce is an option
- Does not believe in cohabitation
- Does not believe that an unmarried woman should have a child out of wedlock
- Believes family time is more important than career advancement

This is not even considering the myriad of other risk factors, including ethnicity, income, income total, employment status, interracial marriages, country, conflict resolution, alcohol use, drug use, mental illness, age difference, and forced premarital sex.

Lots of these are yellow or red flags to keep in mind. No woman is likely to meet all of these criteria, but they are worth investigating as you listen to her words and observe her attitudes and actions and what she brings to a relationship toward marriage.

Can these factors reduce your risk to 0 percent? Not at all. There's always a chance that a person will change. But paying attention to these can likely reduce your odds to more reasonable numbers. Maybe a man wouldn't take a 50/50 shot at marriage, but he would take a 95 to 98 percent (or higher) probability of a stable marriage without the risk of divorce.

Every man knows it: divorce can seriously ruin lives. Therefore, you should understand both how scripture and wisdom come together to make smart decisions when choosing whom to marry.

QUESTIONS TO ASK A PROSPECTIVE WIFE

These questions are to give you an idea of what you need to think about when dating or courting. You don't need to turn into an interviewer, but these can be great topics of discussion to get to know a woman better.

The best way to generally include these into a conversation is to ask a question about the future when you're talking about the past or present. For instance, if you're talking about your families and how your parents raised you and how you behave now, you can ask her what she would teach her future kids about that topic. Current events are a practical way to bring up topics, too, especially related to popular culture, such as how everyone can marry, regardless of their gender. Bring the Bible into the discussion as well.

You are mainly looking for her attitudes and actions when it comes to following your lead, showing respect, how teachable she is, and her compliance to the Bible over culture. Always trust actions over words. Men and women might tell you what you want to hear, but their actions always show their true thoughts. This will point out various yellow or red flags that you need to consider.

Obviously, be prepared to answer these yourself. Some of them have no right or wrong answer, but they are volatile questions. It would be wise to discuss more superficial topics earlier in the relationship and deeper topics as the relationship progresses. If you don't know what the scriptures say about a topic, you need to do your spiritual research first!

STANDARD CHRISTIAN QUESTIONS

- What is your testimony?
- How have you seen God work in your life recently?
- Do you fast?

- What is the value of prayer?
- How have your prayers been answered?
- What have you been learning from your scripture reading recently?
- Are you currently chaste and do you have a past sexual history?
- What are your spiritual gifts?
- How are you using your spiritual gifts?
- What do you think of equality between the sexes?
- Tell me about your past relationships
- What's your favorite hymn and favorite Bible verse and why?
- What story about Jesus when you first read it blew your mind so that you knew this was no ordinary man but the Son of God?
- What are your thoughts about missions? Are you called to missions?
- Do you believe in speaking in tongues, prophecy, miracles, and the gifts of the Spirit?
- Does God speak to you? If so, what has He told you?
- Should women be pastors?
- Should women teach in church?

STANDARD MARRIAGE QUESTIONS

- Will she take your last name?
- After you have children, what are your priorities (order them from highest to lowest): Children, husband, herself, her work/career, her hobbies, God, other family relatives, friends, church obligations. Justify your answer.
- What happens if we have mismatched libidos?
- What are your expectations as to the frequency of sex in marriage?
- What does submission mean to you?
- What are your expectations of the husband in spiritual leadership?
- What are your expectations of the husband in household leadership?
- What are your expectations of teaching children spiritually and mentally?
- How do you plan to teach the children?
- How do you feel about adoption?

- What would you do if you disagreed with a decision I made, and I made that decision anyway?
- What would you do if I made a decision, and you disagreed, and it turned out that I was wrong?
- What are acceptable reasons for divorce?
- Do you believe in soulmates?
- How do you feel about feminism?
- What do you think about the sexual double standard where men are studs and women are sluts?
- What do you think about a marriage in the church with witnesses and a signed covenant, but not a marriage license from the state?
- If your female child wanted to get married at twenty years old, would you encourage her to do so?
- What are your thoughts on egalitarian marriages?
- Who manages the money? Should women have access to the family's money?
- What do you think about polygamy?
- What are your thoughts on the distribution of labor in the household, such as cooking, cleaning, laundry, trash, yard work, and other chores?
- If we get into an argument, how should we resolve it?
- Do you avoid conflict?
- How should a husband handle his wife when she is feeling emotional?
- What do you think the age of responsibility is for children?
- What is a helpmeet?
- Should you ever be alone with a man who is not your husband after getting married?
- What does happiness mean in a marriage? Should marriages seek happiness?
- Are there any topics that are off limits in marriage?
- Should there be full disclosure about your sexual past in marriage?
- Should you share your passwords to your email, Facebook, and other social media when you're married?
- Do you think a husband should check up on his wife if she is out with friends or away from home?

- What should a wife do if her husband has a pornography addiction?
- What should a husband do if his wife has an emotional affair with another man?
- What would you do if your husband asked you to use birth control?
- What would you do if your husband asked you to have an abortion?
- What should a wife do if she has more expertise in an area, but her husband refuses to listen to her advice?
- How should a husband handle it when another man hits on his wife? What if they are mutually flirting?
- What do you think makes women feel loved in marriage? What would make you feel loved?
- What do you think makes men feel loved in marriage? What do you think makes me feel loved?
- What are you attracted to in a man?
- What are men attracted to in a woman?
- Should men/women date more than one person at the same time?
- What would you tell women who want to have it all?
- What would you say to women who are having trouble attracting interest from men?
- What would you say to women who can attract interest from men but can't sustain any relationships?
- What would you say to men who cannot get any dates at all?
- What would you say to men who can get dates but cannot sustain relationships?
- Why do you think men prefer virgin women?
- Why is lying about sexual history such a big deal to men?

QUESTIONS THAT REQUIRE DEEP THOUGHT

- How do you explain submission to a Christian wife if she is in rebellion or to a Christian single that believes in egalitarian marriage or to a non-Christian wife or single?

- How do you explain self-esteem to your kids?
- How do you explain divorce to your kids?
- How do you explain gay marriage to your kids?
- How do you explain abortion to your children?
- How would you explain feminism to your children?
- How would you explain why feminism is bad to Christian wives or non-Christian wives?
- What does Peter mean when he talks about women as a weaker vessel?
- What does it mean in Timothy when it says women are saved by childbearing?
- What would you tell your female children if they wanted to have a career and travel before getting married?
- Is sex in marriage different from sex outside of marriage as in the same act, just a different context? Why?
- How would you explain why God allows suffering in the world to your children? Or to Christians? Or to non-Christians?
- What are your thoughts on free will and/or predestination?
- Can you explain the relationship between faith and good works?
- What would you do if you were married and found out you couldn't have kids? What would you do if you found out your husband was sterile?
- Should a husband or wife have close friends who are divorced? (Statistics show that if you are friends with someone who is divorced, it increases your chances of getting a divorce.[10])
- What should be a husband's response be to his wife if she lies to him, and he finds out about it and confronts her?
- What should a husband do if his wife denies him sex? What should a wife do if her husband denies her sex?
- What should a husband/wife do if the wife/husband is unhappy in marriage?
- What should a husband/wife do if the wife/husband is not attracted to him/her anymore?
- What should a husband/wife do if their spouse wants a divorce?
- What should a husband do if his wife goes behind his back to do something he told her not to?

- What should a husband do if his wife lies about her sexual past before marriage?
- In what type of circumstances should a husband apologize to the wife? A wife to the husband?

OTHER PERSONALITY QUESTIONS AND YOUR PREFERENCES

- What do your closest friends say about you?
- What quirks do you have?
- What are your life passions?
- What are your pet peeves?
- What piece of playground equipment did you play on the most?
- Favorite childhood memory?
- Earliest childhood memory?
- Nutrition
- Fitness
- Other habits
- Homeschooling versus private school versus public school
- Cooking
- Chores at home

Some of these topics might be more suitable for engagement or marriage counseling, or a third party or mentors could bring them up.

TEACHABLE

One of my friends likes to use the FAT acronym for women: *faithful, available, and teachable.* Faithful and available are obvious, but teachable is not often discussed. These are some of the most important traits that you should look for in a potential spouse.

What does *teachable* mean?

One of the primary goals of Jesus's ministry here on the earth was to teach his disciples about the kingdom of God. If you recall many of the stories throughout the gospels, Jesus often chastised his disciples for their lack of faith, such as when they didn't believe His prophecies, corrected them when they were off the mark, such as when they rebuked the little children who came to Him, instructed them, such as when He washed Peter's feet, and otherwise firmly handled their desire to be the greatest disciple.

In other words, a prospective wife must be open to learning and understanding how to be her husband's helpmeet. In other words, in our culture, one of the only words more uncomfortable than submission is the action of submission: obedience. As Christians, we are obedient to Christ's commands.

Older women likewise are to be reverent in their behavior, not malicious gossips nor enslaved to much wine, teaching what is good, so that they may encourage the young women to love their husbands, to love their children, to be sensible, pure, workers at home, kind, being subject to their own husbands, so that the word of God will not be dishonored (Titus 2:3–5).

It is not simply husbands who can teach their wives to be obedient. The older Christian women are supposed to help with that, too. That can be hard to find among Christians in our culturally infested churches.

This is one of the most difficult aspects of headship: learning how to effectively teach a wife and help her be submissive and obedient. This can be done several ways:

- If a woman or wife makes a mistake, kindly point it out and suggest an alternative way that it could have been done.
- If you want something done a certain way, thank her for the effort and kindly point out how you like things done for future reference.
- If certain decisions come up, go through your decision-making process and thoughts with her to teach her how you like things done.
- Encourage her to ask for your input on your preferences, such as how she dresses, and regularly ask for her input as well.

Any prospective woman that you are considering as your wife should be teachable. Making mistakes is okay if we learn and grow from them. Usually the most difficult areas of teachability will include pride, sin, emotional attachment, or disagreement. Be kind and sensitive when approaching her. However, if your woman or wife is not teachable, that is a huge issue. Not only is she not submissive and not obedient, but this tends to lead to other contentious behavior, nagging, and rebellious attitudes and actions. As the Proverbs say, it's better to live on the corner of a roof or in the desert than with such a woman. (See Proverbs 21:9, 19.)

GAMES DON'T MATTER WHEN YOU HAVE THE RIGHT FRAME

People make up a lot of dating rules. They can be useful as heuristics, but they ultimately don't matter. For instances, some of the common games that people play are using pick-up lines, waiting a certain amount of time before responding to a text, ghosting someone, doing certain things to get people to like you more or to make a certain impression, and similar games. These are a façade and masquerade when people are dating or in a relationship that is different from their normal personality and character.

For example, if an unattractive man acts romantically to a single woman, she will often think it's creepy or weird, but if an attractive man acts romantically to a single woman, she will think it's romantic and sweet and likely respond to the overtures so that they can go on a date. This is an important dichotomy to understand; men who act in the exact same way can get different results. This is what is confusing about dating at times.

Usually the so-called rules about what to do or what not to do were made for a specific population: men who are not attractive. One common trope is not to discuss your emotions with women.

Men who are not attractive tend act in a feminine manner with women: they seek to be affirmed and validated by women rather than acting in a masculine manner with them. For these men, discussing their emotions with women comes from a place of just speaking without thinking and expecting her to help clean up the mess as she would with one her girlfriends. This is unattractive.

Perhaps a better thought process would be to only discuss your emotions with women when you're not needy or negative. This is more in line with the internal state of a man rather than trying to manipulate women through outward behaviors. But even this is not a winning strategy because you're trying to work to find what is successful when, in the long run, working does not work. Remember the works and desire mindset that we previously discussed.

Overall, the most important contextual concept to remember is that it doesn't matter much what you say but how you say it and who you are when saying it. If you're in a relationship or marriage and tend to act in a way that is contrary to biblical marital roles and responsibilities, then don't be emotionally transparent with your wife as it will probably come off poorly. No one likes a whiner or complainer, much less your girlfriend or wife. She doesn't need a husband who acts like a girlfriend to dump his emotions on her for affirmation or validation.

It's not wrong to share concerns and emotions with your wife. This is actually beneficial when performed in the proper context. Do it from the perspective and actions of a leader. I personally discuss whatever I want with her because I've ingrained this subconscious habit into myself as a leader. You will almost always have positive results when you do this. From a biblical perspective, this is the difference between knowing you are the leader to actually being the leader.

Your maturity as a masculine leader means that you understand that there's probably nothing you can say that will shake your wife's opinion of you because you have consistently proven yourself as a strong leader, but it takes a wealth of knowledge and experience to arrive at that place.

COUNT THE COST AND DO NOT FEAR

As the final chapter in this section, you need to count the cost, according to Jesus.

> "For which one of you, when he wants to build a tower, does not first sit down and calculate the cost to see if he has enough to complete it? Otherwise, when he has laid a foundation and is not able to finish, all who observe it begin to ridicule him, saying, 'This man began to build and was not able to finish.' Or what king, when he sets out to meet another king in battle, will not first sit down and consider whether he is strong enough with ten thousand men to encounter the one coming against him with twenty thousand? Or else, while the other is still far away, he sends [a]a delegation and asks for terms of peace. So then, none of you can be My disciple who does not give up all his own possessions" (Luke 14:28–33).

Let's be real. In today's world, any wife can call the cops and claim domestic violence so that the husband is arrested due to the Duluth model. Due to no-fault divorce laws, any wife can just up and leave any time and likely take the kids and half of everything. Any man who wants to get married should be concerned about these things.

But it is also true that a husband who is afraid that he might have everything taken away from him will not act rationally in the best interests of the marriage and cannot fully fulfill his biblical roles and responsibilities. If a husband fears that his wife will divorce him, he will not be able to love her to sanctification. He will waver when she sins, and he won't be able to effectively and kindly call her to repentance for fear of what will happen to him if she turns on him. He'll have difficulty pushing back against a culture that suggests, "happy wife, happy life."

Rosenfeld's analysis relies on data from the 2009-2015 waves of the nationally representative How Couples Meet and Stay Together survey. He considers 2,262 adults, ages 19 to 94, who had opposite sex partners in 2009. By 2015, 371 of these people had broken up or gotten divorced.

As part of his analysis, Rosenfeld found that women initiated 69 percent of all divorces, compared to 31 percent for men. In contrast, there was not a statistically significant difference between the percentage of breakups initiated by unmarried women and men, regardless of whether they had been cohabitating with their partners.[11]

Wives initiate most divorces, and several studies have confirmed the above rate of approximately 70 percent.[12] Perhaps one of the reasons for this is the dominant narrative that men are to chase and pursue women, which influences women to marry someone that they might not necessarily like all that much. Perhaps this is because marriage is still attractive as a status and for financial benefit. Whatever the case, it is very different when a woman wants to follow you versus if you must convince her to do so.

This is not to say that those going into a marriage with a positive attitude and without fear will have godly and successful marriages. Everyone has free will, and even many who were disciples of Jesus rejected him when the going got rough (John 6). But a bad attitude and fear will likely lead to eventual marital ruin. In this context, we can say that a husband who does not fear his wife but only fears God stands a much better chance at having not only a godly marriage but having a successful marriage as well. After all, if Jesus is our model, how does he interact with His bride? Does He fear the church or revere His Father?

Each man must count his own cost in terms of marriage as we count the cost in terms of following Jesus. He must evaluate whether he has the capacity to stand strong on the biblical roles and responsibilities of marriage. He must also evaluate whether the woman he has chosen has the qualities and attributes necessary to honor God and her vows over her own feelings and selfishness. He should read the scripture about the nature of women, pray, fast, and consult wise counsel.

Wives today can do the same thing that Jesus's wavering disciples did to Him and even worse: simply up and leave through no-fault divorce while taking half the assets and the children. If a man has any reservations or wavering convictions, it would be unwise to marry. Do not let anyone or anything pressure you to marry if you don't want to. Marriage is one of the biggest life decisions that you can make. You want to be absolutely sure that you are making the best choice for your own good and for the good of the one you choose to marry in the context of your God-given mission.

Chapter 15

FINDING AND CHOOSING A WIFE: A PROSPECTIVE TIMELINE

The wording introduced in this section is not biblical except engagement and marriage. However, it's useful to understand the process of developing a relationship in this messed-up modern culture of Christian dating or courtship. To define the terms that are used in this section, dating is getting to know someone, and a relationship is boyfriend and girlfriend or going steady. Courtship is a blend of these together. It's up to the individual the way they want to approach things. Arranged marriages are also valid and tend to work well.

1. Pre-introductory Phase
2. Introductory Phase (Asking Out)
3. Transitional Phase (Dating)
4. Intentional Relationship Phase (Courtship)
5. Engagement
6. Marriage

The phases are structured a certain way because they focus on facilitating relationship growth while learning about the other person's expectations and guarding your own heart against hurt.

1. Pre-introductory Phase

First, it is important to understand your core identity as a Christian. Much of this has been addressed in the previous chapter on the scriptures, mentality and practical life skills for men. The goal is love God with all your heart, soul, and strength. If you're reading this, I assume the goal is to find a virtuous Christian wife. That also means that one of your missions is to cultivate yourself as a provider, protector, and strong masculine leader.

Let's review the five-step process to maturity here:

- Know what God says about relationships
- Know your mission and goals
- Know your standards for women
- Know your boundaries in a relationship
- Know how to assertively communicate

Aside from the heart (thoughts, emotions, and actions) and soul (spiritual development, gifts of the Spirit), you also need to cultivate physical excellence to be a protector and leader. This includes the body and appearance. This can include:

- Sleep well to be at the top of your physical mental game
- Train hard—lift heavy weights
- Eat healthy food for proper nutrition
- Groom yourself well and find a style of clothes that work for you
- Find hobbies that you enjoy, such as sports or music
- Take up a martial art or self-defense course to learn how to protect yourself and family
- Taking a firearms course may be useful

A Christian might ask himself why he should incorporate these things into his life. Most of these help build discipline and toughness as a leader and protector.

In general, you can think of these as increasing your odds. Let's say you were attractive to 5 percent of Christian women your age. If you gain ten to fifteen pounds of muscle, you might now become attractive to an additional 5 to 10 percent of women your age. By developing proper grooming skills and wearing clothes that fit you well, you might become attractive to another 5 percent of women your age. Perhaps you become the leader of a Bible study, which helps improve your leadership skills, how you carry yourself, and social skills which might add 5 to 10 percent to your attractiveness.

All these things will improve your attractiveness to Christian women. Thus, when you ask them out on a date, they will accept instead of rejecting you. Instead of being attractive to 5 percent (one in twenty), you might now be attractive to 20 to 30 percent (one in five to three in ten). No man is attractive to all women due to personal preferences, but upping your attractiveness increases your overall prospects to get your foot in the door for dating.

The difficulty for most men is the inertia associated with this phase. Many Christian men have been wallowing in mediocrity for five to ten years or more, depending on their age, because they have had no direction in life other than generally serving in the church without any specific focus. It's very hard to break out of such a lifestyle, and it takes a long time.

If you start from a disadvantage, such as being extremely overweight or extremely skinny, if you don't know God's Word, if you don't prioritize prayer, and if you don't know your mission from God, then it might take time to understand and start to grow. This does not prevent you from talking to women, but they might not be attracted to you at first. You should talk to women during these times to improve your interaction with them and to develop your social skills.

Places to look for single Christian women: In my experience, some of these places will yield the best results:

- Young adult ministries at many different churches.
- Inter-denominational events.
- Volunteering at homeless/soup kitchens and at other church outreach activities.
- Attending a college/campus ministry, such as Cru, Navigators, or any other Christian groups on campus.
- Friends and family and others in your network. When the topic of relationships comes up, and ask them if they know anyone who meets your criteria. You can help them out if you know anyone who meets their criteria. If you are friends with any married men, they are usually willing to help out as well.

Other places that can work but that don't work as well include:

- Online dating usually does not work unless you are very physically attractive and are tall. You can try it to see how it works, though, as it has worked for some.

- Hobbies, such as sports, can work, but you might not be able to find devout Christian women in these areas.
- Dancing, such as salsa, swing, or ball room, can be another way to meet women as a much higher percentage of women than men participate in dancing. Even so, your chances of meeting devout Christian women are lower.

A useful model for this stage is the two-thirds rule. In other words, spend no more than about one-third of the time on a plan. Spend two-thirds or more of the time on doing your God-given mission, including focusing on improving your heart, soul, and strength.

The reality is that if you wait until you are perfect to date or to look for the perfect spouse, then you will never get married. The Father works through our imperfections, so it is important to realize that you are looking for someone to grow with rather than a finished product. This is why you need to find someone teachable. If you're reading this, you're teachable because you want to be fruitful at your God-given mission and in your potential search for a spouse. The same is true of women—if you can find one who is willing and enthusiastic in learning, she has significant potential.

2. *Introductory Phase (Asking Out)*

The key in this section to remember is to *engage and invite*. Jesus started His ministry in the surrounding areas, met His disciples, and invited them to "Come, follow me. I will make you fishers of men." (See Matthew 4:19.) That's the model of Christ and the church and husbands and wives. Invite her along on your mission.

This is more of a get-to-know-you phase. If you have just gotten to know a woman and you're not a traditionally attractive man, then you will have your work cut out for you. This is where all your preparation on becoming a strong, masculine leader, provider, and protector will come into play. Here is a list of masculine traits to keep in mind: hard-working, confident, strong, direct, leader, bold, honest, dominant, assertive, unwavering, backbone, courageous, and calm under pressure.

These traits cannot be exemplified on the outside only. You have to internalize them, thereby making them a part of who you are as a man.

One-upping another man does not earn you brownie points from a woman. Trying to impress her doesn't work. When someone tries too hard, it's goofy and awkward. The same is true of a man trying to get a woman to like him. It doesn't work that way.

How you go about your life will attract her to you. For instance, grandstanding about your skills or talents will seem arrogant, which is a turn off. If the subject comes up in a conversation, then it will be natural. Women understand the basics: you're the man, but you don't need to prove your worth or show off your talent.

First contact: There's no such thing as a special line that will win her. What matters most is confidence and effective body language if you're are talking in person. If you are chatting via electronic communication, the main thing is to act like a man instead of a woman. It's better to tease and rib her then it is to agree with her and validate everything she says.

Here are some tips on in-person presentation:

- Keep your body language relaxed. Don't fidget or move around. Pull your hands out of pockets and leave them hanging by your side.
- Stand up straight.
- Make direct eye contact but don't stare. Look away when she looks away.
- Smile genuinely and be easygoing.
- Breathe slowly through your nose into your stomach to stay calm.

If you look good, you feel good, and you're confident. Whatever you say should be fine. If it isn't, then just acknowledge it. "Well, that was awkward." If you don't make a big deal out of it, then she won't either. This takes practice, though. This has more to do with your confidence level then what you actually do or say.

It's helpful to understand that a rejection is simply not a big deal. Ultimately, you want to be with someone who also wants to be with you. Jesus calls for many to follow Him but only some answered that call. If they say they don't want to be with you for whatever reason, that's fine. That's just one person who isn't a good fit for you. You don't need to worry about it.

Compliments: When meeting someone new, don't pay her a generic compliment, such as, "You are beautiful." Many women hear compliments like this all the time. In fact, you shouldn't even talk about their looks at all.

If you decide to pay her a compliment, don't focus on something that she can't change about herself. For instance, instead of complimenting her on her beauty, instead compliment her on her dress selection and how the style or color flatters her. Or if she cooked a great meal, then compliment her on her skill and how it must've taken a long time to develop. A poor compliment focuses on generic beauty because most people are born with certain looks, and most women have heard this type of common compliment before.

Personally, I don't pay a woman compliments in the beginning of the relationship. It's not worth it most of the time because you don't know her well enough. The compliment isn't truly genuine, and she might hear them all the time. It doesn't make you stand out, and if you don't stand out to her, she will group you in with all of those other guys, which will kill your chances. In general, a woman appreciates compliments after she already likes you.

Asking her out on a date: Generally, relationships that start out as friends first don't work out well. They tend to work only if she was attracted to you from the outset. They are also built on dishonesty as you have a secret agenda for the long-term development of the relationship that you haven't told her about. Keep it straight forward and simple.

- First, say her name to make it personal. Some people don't do this, so you connect with her personally from the start.
- Second, briefly describe what intrigued you about her or what you enjoyed (not her beauty). This emphasizes the connection between the two of you.
- Third, express your interest using an I statement. This shows that you are bold and direct about your intentions.
- Finally, make a statement about where you want the relationship to go. I am opposed to asking it as a question, such as "Will you go out on a date?" because this creates pressure by emphasizing her. Instead, word it as a statement and an invitation, which is less pressure on her.

For example, instead of asking, "Would you like to go out to dinner with me?" say, "We should get dinner together." This is like Jesus inviting His disciples. He didn't say, "Come, follow Me?" He told them, "Come, follow Me." A statement rather than a question shows initiative, leadership, and confidence, whereas the question doesn't reveal anything about you to her and instead places her in the lead—she gets to be the one to decide if the relationship progresses. If you don't want to go to dinner, you can just as easily suggest another activity of your choice.

You might be terribly nervous about the inevitable rejections you will face. If she declines your statement, you can always say, "Hey, that wasn't actually an invitation," leaving room for a confident recovery and indicating that she should be the one who wants to invite you rather than you inviting her.

If you have your own way of doing this, then go with that, but this is just a simple way to do it to reduce the pressure of the situation.

If a woman doesn't accept your invitation, then that's okay. It's better to find out now that she's not interested than to find out later. You don't want to be on the road to marriage with someone who is only half-heartedly invested in your relationship.

3. *Transitional Phase (Dating)*

The transitional phase generally encompasses a few dates where you get to know each other better to see if you want to pursue a relationship with this woman and if she wants to be in a relationship with you. Back in the day, they used to call this dating and then going steady once you decided you wanted to be in a relationship. It doesn't really matter what you call it if you understand that getting to know a person does not mean you will marry her.

Christians have a tendency to assume that people should only go on dates if they already have plan that the relationship is headed toward marriage. The reality is that you don't know whether or not you want the relationship to go in that direction until you actually get to know the other person first. Contrary to popular belief, going on a date is not synonymous to a serious relationship or to marriage. Over-exaggerating the importance of dates can negatively affect Christian singles.

Dates: Regarding dates, you should do what you want and not cater to her wishes. Catering to what you think she wants to do sets a bad precedent for the relationship as to who is running the relationship, undermining your role as the leader as nothing more than a figurehead for her wants and desires. Jesus did not ask His disciples what they wanted to do during His ministry; He had plans for His ministry, and His disciples followed Him.

You should avoid typical events, such as going to the movies and going to dinner. This is because these are typical activities and are not very helpful for you to find out more about each other. You should avoid going to a movie as you can't talk during the whole movie so you can't get to know each other. I don't like going out for food and drinks either because you are sitting down. While there's nothing wrong with sit-down places, they tend to favor men who are extremely adept at the art of conversation. Many men who are just getting started with dating struggle with conversation. If you have trouble quickly thinking of topics and easily stumble over your words or become flustered when conversing with someone you are interested in for more than thirty minutes, then you should not place yourself in a situation that demands substantial conversation time.

Activities are useful. You can lead and/or teach the activity if you have some expertise, showing your leadership skills. Selecting activities also allows you to move around from place to place and talk about different subjects while getting to know each other, which is less pressure than a sit-down date. Here are some ideas:

- A Bible study (You're a Christian and will be the head of your household in marriage.)
- Dancing (If you can dance and lead it this is a must.)
- Bowling
- Mini golf or Frisbee golf
- Rock climbing (usually indoors)
- Your sport or hobby of choice
- Board game night (This works well with double dates or groups.)
- The zoo or aquarium if available (more city-based)
- Fruit picking or other outdoor activities (more country-based)
- A walk in the park or at a nature center (Nature is awesome to discuss.)

- Hiking (Generally, a woman won't go alone on a hike with a man she doesn't know, so this might be better for later after you know each other.)
- A night in, which might include the woman cooking dinner (Again, women won't usually do this on a first date, but you can do this on later dates. This also gives you the advantage of experiencing her cooking to see if you like it or not. If you can or want to cook, you can impress her instead.)

You ~~can~~ [must] plan out all the logistics of the date, including time, place, what you want her to wear, and related matters. Women like to be taken care of and don't want the pressure of decisions on dates. You might not like the work involved with this, but if you plan to marry a woman, you'll have to be organized in marriage anyway. You'd better get used to it now—if you can't, then you haven't sufficiently mastered yourself as an effective leader who is ready to date.

Topics of discussion: You can discuss various topics through both electronic communication and in person on dates. If you choose an activity for your date, you will have an immediate subject for conversation: talk about what you did together. Otherwise, I like discussing theology and our life experiences for the first few weeks to months. This allows you to evaluate if you are a biblical match and if she is willing to follow your lead. Do not be afraid to teach her or explain things if you have a different perspective than she does. In fact, this is often positive as it shows you have a backbone and that you're not just going to lie down and agree with everything she says.

If she does not share the same beliefs as you do on critical theological issues, such as headship-submission, or if she is too entrenched in the world and culture and doesn't take being a Christian seriously, then it might be necessary to be up front with her that you can't continue a relationship with her. This is where the list of questions mentioned in the prior section is useful. Questions about theological issues and your personal life can be tough if you're a private person, so be ready to expound on these subjects. If a woman is interested in you, she generally should be more than willing to discuss these topics with you because she wants to know more about you.

Vision and vetting: This is also the time to discuss your vision for your life and your family in terms of God and utilizing your gifts of the Spirit in the church. You also want to find out about her passions and goals and see if she is the right fit for you and your mission.

Discussion on sex: Around the fourteen to twenty-one day mark, I bring up the discussion on libido to open up the topic of marriage, sex, children, and desire with her. While this subject is typically uncomfortable for most men, but it is important. If you have different views on sex and having children, then you might not be the right fit for each other. The husband and wife have a marital debt to each other, according to 1 Corinthians 7. You can delay this discussion until the relationship starts, but you should probably not get into a relationship and then start the discussion with her six months later. If you find out that you are on opposite sides of the spectrum on some of these issues, you have wasted a lot of time

One way to go about this if you are super uncomfortable about this subject is to talk about what your parents taught you regarding marriage, sex, and relationships. You can start here and then go more into depth as needed. In some cases, if you both have strong mentors, they can help lead a discussion on the matter.

Overall, during these next few weeks, you should decide if you want to take this relationship to the next level.

4. *Intentional Relationship Phase (Courtship)*

It doesn't really matter whether you call it: a relationship, going steady, or courtship. The point is that your goal is now marriage.

This phase of a relationship is not specified anywhere in the scriptures. We can look at the lack of arranged marriage as positive, negative, or morally neutral, an arranged marriage is not typical for most of us. If you live in a culture where you do follow arranged marriages that lead to strong Christian marriages, then by all means, follow the culture.

During this phase, you will have some level of commitment, defined by the users, that will likely include labels, such as girlfriend and boyfriend. For example, I am willing to accept the label of boyfriend if she is aware of and takes responsibility for protecting her own heart. I will likewise protect my own heart. It is not the man's job to protect the woman's heart while dating. Only she can grapple with her thoughts and feelings. Relationships prior to engagement dissolve frequently as we find out more about each other that we cannot deal with or incompatibilities in spiritual matters, personality, or what we want in marriage. Hence, the relationship might end, and someone might be hurt if they don't protect themselves.

Topics of discussion: In this phase of the relationship, you should continue leading in a more defined manner. Specific topics regarding marriage and relationships should be explored more in depth. This is when you can ask some of the deeper theological and personal questions. You want to find out at this stage if this woman wants to be your helpmeet and if you want her to be your helpmeet.

Since this relationship is headed toward marriage, you will want to discuss boundaries and expectations of each other. One of my expectations is that she always tries to look attractive for me, and I will do the same for her. If she is gaining weight, I will let her know that she needs to lose weight as kindly as possible, which is speaking the truth in love. Your masculine traits will really start to shine here. Since these are uncomfortable topics, you can easily brush them under the rug. Do not do that. Address small conflicts as they arise so that they don't build up into volcanoes that can explode later.

At this point, you should begin to discuss more intimate topics regarding children, how to raise your children, divorce, cultural and political issues, and similar subjects. You should also discuss family upbringing. We don't realize how much our family plays a role in shaping our views about the opposite sex and relationships. How you were raised affects your expectations of what you want in a spouse. This is very important, especially if you come from a broken or dysfunctional family or one with many addictions. You might be drawn to someone with these traits, but you must recognize that you need to avoid them.

You should also discuss sex more in depth and inquire about a woman's sexual past as well as disclose your own. Since sex is a large part of marriage, you should not marry a woman who will not discuss her past sexual history and how she views sex regarding God and marriage. In our sexualized culture, you should not ignore this important facet of marriage. God forgives sin, but He might not remove the physical and emotional consequences of sin.

Assertive communication: You need to know how to assertively communicate without being passive, passive-aggressive, or overly aggressive. In this way, you can acknowledge the free will of the other person and let them make their own decisions. They can respond any way that they want to, and you need to be ready for the possibility of responses that you don't like. In fact, she might respond negatively either intentionally or subconsciously so that she can test your assertiveness—to discern whether you are man enough for her.

For example, if I know something is bothering my girlfriend, I will bring it up and ask her to tell me about it. At first, she didn't want to discuss because the topic was uncomfortable for her. Eventually she learned to trust me with that information. How I responded would determine if she was willing to bring up these types of topics the next time. Thus my response on discussing topics that bother her are typically to first thank her for bringing up the issue because I want to communicate effectively with her. Then we talk about the issue.

I never argue. Good leaders never argue. Rather, they facilitate the discussion to bring forth the concerns of those under them so that they feel understood and heard. Then you can assess and evaluate the issue if it needs to be fixed. Sometimes in relating to women, we need to understand that it's not about the problem. They just want you to hold them and tell them it will be okay: to be their emotional rock to weather out their storm.

Assertive communication generally brings your own concerns to the forefront without accusing the other person of anything. This is very difficult to do at first, but as you become stronger and more confident in who you are, you can state your boundaries or concerns just as informational.

For instance, during a conversation, my mother agreed with something my girlfriend said in opposition to my view. My girlfriend made a show of it. Later I communicated that her behavior was disrespectful. I expect her to support me and not publicly disrespect me in front of others. My girlfriend had no idea that she had done anything wrong at the time, and I don't blame her as she has never had to work through that situation before. But if I had let things slide without correcting her, then the situation would probably become worse. In our culture, people easily make fun of or disrespect men without even being aware of it.

If the issue is minor, an easy-going approach of bantering about the disrespect can work, too, as women can pick up on your subtle implications that they did not act appropriately. The goal, though, is to lead and teach your potential wife about how to respect you as we often don't pick up on many cultural scripts and influences until they happen to us.

Your mettle will really be tested in these types of situations. You must be proactive in addressing them. Each opportunity and uncomfortable situation will help you both to learn and grow together. If you do not take advantage of these situations and act on them, you will eventually devolve into a dysfunctional relationship. Refer to the previous section if you need more information.

Church, family and friends: This is the best time to get to know the family and friends and possibly the church of your girlfriend.

When it comes to family or friends, your girlfriend will be spending a lot of time with you, especially if you are attractive. People in general fear what they do not know. Thus they might not like you because they heard rumors about you from the grapevine, or they don't like you taking valuable time away from their own relationships with your girlfriend. Do not get become upset or offended over this. Transcend your circumstances. If you are a masculine man, spend time with them so that they can get to know you and know what you stand for. Even the most stalwart family members will be won over if you continually offer them an olive branch and try to get to know them better and care about their interests.

Bible studies and prayer are healthy for the relationship. I personally like to study the Bible together, but I don't like to pray together as well. But I will pray with her sometimes. Christian culture tells you to have Bible studies and pray with your wife. But this is not in the scriptures. You should resist feeling badly if you don't do these spiritual disciplines together if you are both spiritually healthy. You and your girlfriend should have your own separate walk with Jesus, which means you are going to God to meet the needs that only He can provide. The fact that you are doing it together is healthy, especially when you are married since you are one, but this does not replace your personal spiritual walk. In the same way, the church is not a substitute for your spiritual walk. If you let church become your spiritual walk, then you become a Sunday-only Christian.

You will need to look out for these possible issues, but you are now cultivating the relationship that you started in prior phases and building on it. When you decide to marry her, you should talk to your friends and hopefully to your mentors if you have them about these points so that you can get godly insight as to if they see any blind spots. Then you can ask her father for permission to marry her.

5. Engagement

Engagement rings: The more expensive the engagement ring and wedding, the higher the likelihood of divorce.[1] Perhaps the reason for this is that this emphasizes superficial aspects, such as money and a bridezilla wedding, rather than focusing on the marriage relationship itself. Whatever the case, if a woman is dissatisfied with how much you spend on a ring or a wedding, that can be a yellow or red flag. Your potential wife should want to marry you because she wants to be with you, not because she wants your money or lifestyle. On a related note, buy a ruby—not a diamond—engagement ring. It's biblical according to Proverbs 3:15 and Proverbs 31:10. Feeding the diamond cartel and cultural expectations just leads to more dissatisfaction.

When you enter into engagement, you should have a plan. This means that after you become engaged and celebrate it, you should consider setting a date and start planning for the wedding. The reason for this is that you do not want to stay in the engagement zone for too long with possible increased levels of intimacy. You already know that you want to marry this woman, so you have little reason to wait for long.

Discussing important topics again: While you should have discussed dreams, goals, and most of these important subjects during the prior phase, you can now review them again, especially since your marriage is pending. Some of the most important topics include handling finances, careers and jobs, whether your wife should stay home with the kids, chores, expectations, and all other important topics. The more you discuss and plan, the better off you will be because you won't be blindsided by these major issues. But sometimes life changes, so you might need to make some adjustments with more prayer and agreement on how to handle the situation. You are now reaffirming what you know and confirming the details of your marriage plans.

Family and friends: Family and friends might give advice and suggestions, but you should not allow them to interfere with your decisions and your relationship. This will help set the tone for you two to become one, independent of the influence of others. It's your future marriage and not theirs.

Family and friends are usually very happy for you and want the best for you. But they might think that they can impose their wishes on you instead of you deciding what is best for you. In other words, they think they know better than you do what you should do. Only you can make that decision for yourself. Of course, keep in mind that family and friends often have wise advice. Be thankful for their counsel, and weigh it according to scripture and with wisdom.

6. Marriage

This is not the end but is solely a step on the way.

You should be the same man before marriage who you are after marriage. In other words, the godly masculine man should remain the godly masculine man. This also applies to your wife, and to the children you raise in the future.

Ultimately, the goal is to become one in your marriage, be blessed with a family, and to raise up children in God. Becoming one and having a family requires a lot of work. You can't coast or become complacent. Growth requires that you are challenged or uncomfortable and that you take steps to overcome it.

It is easy for both the husband and the wife to forget this. Marriage and sex is not some magical fantasy where you will always be happy. Once this fantasy about marriage is destroyed, husbands become complacent, get fat and slovenly, sit around, and fail to lead. Likewise, wives, too, become complacent, get fat and slovenly, sit around, and might nag or try to control their husbands. It is easy to fall and give into your sin nature rather than grow in the relationship. Do not let this happen to you.

It is important to not misrepresent yourself prior to the marriage. If you are only trying to do things to impress a woman or your girlfriend, she will expect you to act the same way after marriage. For instance, your girlfriend or wife might have worked out all the time and stayed slim and fit prior to marriage but became lazy and fat after marriage. It is hard not to become angry or bitter in this instance. This is not a reason for divorce, but this often can influence a Christian's emotions so that he or she wants to divorce even though they are not supposed to.

If you have slacked off when it comes to your health, the best time to correct this was years ago, but the second-best time is today. Get off your butt and get back into your relationship with God in the scriptures, prayer, meditation, and fasting. Discipline yourself to work out, eat right, excel in your career, lead by example in the home, be Don Juan with your wife, and be an excellent father.

SECTION FIVE
LEADING A MARRIAGE

Chapter 16
IDENTIFY AND UNDERSTAND YOUR RESPONSIBILITIES

ORIENT YOURSELF TO ALWAYS HONOR GOD FIRST

This goes back to the idea of pursuing holiness and godliness versus success and happiness. If you pursue holiness and godliness, you might have short-term difficulties and suffering, but God's commands are always best for us in the long run despite any obstacles.

The main idea to keep in mind is to always think about honoring God first. The marriage vows you took with your wife were not only with her but before God as He is the center of your marriage. Marriage is not a covenant without God. You made a vow and consented that you would take marriage seriously "'til death do us part."

When keeping all the marital roles and responsibilities, you are doing so because you know God has His best in mind for you. You are going to follow His commands regarding marriage, not because of how your wife treats you, but because He is the most important thing in your life. You want to love God with all your heart, soul, mind, and strength. Ultimately, it's not about us and what we think is right. It's about us orienting our lives toward our mission for God.

This can be very difficult in many different circumstances. Attraction and feelings in marriage often wax and wane. They don't stay the same as when you first married. This can be especially hard if your wife or children have already picked up bad habits: talking back, outbursts, strife, and other negative behaviors. But even though you cannot control what they do, you can control you. And you have the power to ask the Father, Jesus, and the Holy Spirit to help you act in a godly manner instead of in an ungodly manner.

You are a man. Own your behavior. You are tasked to be the leader. Do it with God's power working through you to influence those around you.

TEMPTATIONS (MEN AND WOMEN)

As we discussed in previous chapters, the husband is to be a masculine leader, protector, and provider in accordance with the scriptures. These are the main points to focus on if you have marital issues with a lack of sex or the common expression, "I love you, but I'm not in love with you."

Another way to better learn biblical roles and responsibilities, aside from trial and error, is to learn what not to do. We can use our capacity for rational thought to examine the roles and responsibilities from the scripture to see where we are tempted. If we were naturally good people, we would also naturally adhere to God's commands and prescription. Since the fall, that is far from the case. The scriptures were written because humans are often tempted to do the wrong thing in the situation that they are in.

The temptations are an extension of the scriptural roles and responsibilities listed earlier in the book in Ephesians, Colossians, 1 Peter, Titus, 1 Corinthians, Genesis, and others.

Temptations for Husbands:

- The husband is the head/leader/authority of the wife.

Husbands are tempted to abdicate their role as the head in marriage. This often manifests as a hen-pecked husband with a very nagging and contentious wife. Husbands like this marginalize themselves into the "yes, dear" type and let the wife run the show.

- **Ephesians 5:** A husband is to exhibit sacrificial love toward his wife for the purpose of sanctification (not for other purposes, such as placating her feelings).

This is the sin of Adam. Husbands are tempted to love their wives more than God, as Adam chose eating the fruit that Eve gave him over obeying the command of God. This is the sin of compromise: avoiding conflict for temporary peace or sex. Husbands have the responsibility to point out when a wife is in sin, but they are tempted not to.

This is also one of the most misunderstood responsibilities of husbands in the modern church as it has fallen prey to culture. Love has become such a meaningless word that it is often used from the pulpit to mean that a husband should do whatever his wife wants in order to make her feel better. Her happiness—not sanctification—becomes the goal. Christ's showed His sacrificial love by dying for us, but it was so that we would be sanctified and made holy through repentance from sin and reconciliation to God, not merely to make us happy. The sanctification process is to become holy, and that happens through rooting out sin in the relationship. Husbands are tempted not to point out when their wife is in sin.

- **Ephesians 5:** A husband is to love his wife as his own body/himself. The Bible says this three times in the passage.

Husbands are tempted in one of two directions: to be selfish and think of himself first without understanding that she is part of his one flesh or to be submissive toward his wife, placing her needs above his own so that he idolizes her emotions as his god. But the Bible is saying here that he should neither elevate himself nor her; only God is to be elevated, and the goal is to make sure that both partners are rightly growing in godliness as she follows his lead.

- **Ephesians 5:** A husband is to feed and care his wife. Other translations use the words nourish and cherish.

Husbands are tempted not to address her needs (to feed and nourish her), and they are tempted not to be affectionate (care for and cherish) her. The important needs of marriage have already been discussed: masculine leadership, protection, provision, and sex, which will be discussed later. A husband should also be affectionate with his wife because that is one of the ways that wives are intimate and feel close to their husbands. Also, needs are not wants, so a husband has some discretion if a wife's wants are detrimental to the family.

- **Colossians 3:** A husband is not to be harsh or embittered with his wife.

Husbands can easily become frustrated with wives, especially if they are disrespectful, contentious, or rebellious. Husbands are counselled by the scripture to avoid becoming harsh or bitter toward their wives, especially when they are not acting in a godly manner. This is also similar to the 1 Peter passage where husbands need to understand that their wives are different from them and that these differences should not make them harsh or bitter toward their wives.

- **1 Peter 3:** A husband is to live with the understanding that his wife is weaker.

Husbands might not understand or be tempted to avoid providing wives with physical, emotional, and mental support, especially in difficult times. Women tend to be pushed and pulled by their feelings more than men are. Thus, especially during challenging times or when under a lot of conflict, women tend to need support from their men to be the sturdy tree that weathers the storm. This is not politically correct, but it is true.

Women do not necessarily want men to solve their problems. Understanding and listening to their problems is enough unless she has specifically asked for a solution. A woman who is being pulled here and there by her emotions often simply needs to be hugged and told that everything will be okay.

- **1 Peter 3:** A husband is to honor his wife as a co-heir in the grace of life.

Husbands are tempted to not honor and value their wives as a helpmeet but rather a servant. This goes back to the section on authority. They are one flesh, and they are to tackle the problems of this life together. That is why it was not good for man to be alone and why Eve was created as a helpmeet for Adam. She is with him every step of the journey.

- **1 Corinthians 7:** A husband is not to withhold sex from his wife.

This is a rare scenario, but it does happen. The wife might have a higher sex drive than the husband in a minority of marriages. The husband should not use sex as a weapon, trying to get his wife to act a certain way or manipulate her into doing what he wants.

- **1 Timothy 5:** A husband is to provide for his family.

A husband is to meet the physical needs of his family, such as food, drink, and clothing. This is similar to God's commands in the Old Testament for provision for wives.

The elders and deacons passages are also self-explanatory. Be mature in the faith by exhibiting the fruit of the Spirit in all circumstances. As you can see, many of these are common temptations that husbands struggle with.

Temptations for Wives:

Unfortunately, pastors today might say that a wife's roles and responsibilities are her own. Husbands should not demand them from her. This is false. Christ demands our obedience as Christians. He calls us higher from where we are. This is true of the call to sanctification that Christ has for His church and that husbands should have for their wives. But it needs to be done with a proper attitude of humility and from a place of already working on your own faults, in other words, taking the plank out of your own eye.

To call a wife higher, a husband must also know the roles and responsibilities of a wife as well as the temptations that a wife will face.

- **Genesis 2:** A wife is the helper/helpmeet to her husband.

As Genesis 3:16 states, a wife will be tempted to rebel and usurp her husband's authority. This is echoed in 1 Timothy 2. Wives are tempted to henpeck their husbands so that they are in control of the marriage. But this only leads to significant marital dissatisfaction for both the husband and the wife. Wives initiate most of the divorces today, and they mainly do so because they are unhappy.[1]

- **Ephesians 5:** A wife should submit to her husband as to the Lord.

Wives are tempted to rebel against their husbands when their husbands want them to do something they don't want to do, but they still consider themselves submitting to the Lord. This is a very tough passage because it shows that when a wife obeys her husband, she is also obeying God. If she does not obey her husband, she is not obeying God.

- **Ephesians 5:** A wife should submit in everything as to the Lord.

Wives are tempted to want to pick and choose what they submit to. This is especially difficult if she does not want to do something that her husband wants her to do.

Wives often fall into a trap here because they imagine unlikely scenarios that never occur. If a Christian woman married a Christian man, do you think the Christian man will want her to sin? The common conversation that always comes up with this topic is the exception. It goes like this: "Well, what if my husband wants me to . . . " and then the woman fills in the blank with rob a bank, cheat on taxes, shoplift, or have a threesome. The answer to this is simple. A wife is commanded to submit to her husband as to the Lord. If what a husband asks is a sin according to the scriptures, then she should make her husband aware of it as his helpmeet.

If he continues to insist, she has a choice: disobey God's command to submit to her husband or disobey God's command that as her husband is telling her. In both cases, she offends God's expectations for her life. In the first case, she also offends her husband. Moreover God has made the husband responsible for those placed under his care and leadership, including his wife. As such, the wife should not question her husband's ultimate decision after she has made her concerns known. If he asks her to do something that she believes is sin and he does not, the real choice at that point is whether she's willing to submit to her husband's interpretation of the Bible and the situation. This leads to four possible outcomes:

- If it is sin and she does it, then her sin is on his head as her leader, not hers.
- If it is sin and she does not do it, then she has still sinned by failing to submit to her husband's leadership.
- If it is not sin and she does it, then she has done no wrong, even though she might have thought otherwise.
- If it is not sin and she does not do it, then she has still sinned by failing to submit to her husband's leadership.

If the wife does not do it, she still ends up in sin, whereas in both cases when she does submit to her husband's lead, any possible responsibility for sin is not on her. The two Scriptural examples that are instructive here are in Genesis 12 and Genesis 20 when Abraham lies about Sarah being his wife, saying "She is my sister" to Pharaoh and Abimelech. Sarah goes along with it. First Peter 3 indicates Sarah is one of the premier examples of submission.

Sarah also follows Abraham when God called him out of their homeland of Ur to leave for an unknown land (eventually Canaan). How many wives would be willing to go with their husbands—no questions asked—who said God was calling them to leave the country and wander around until they got where God told them to go? That's a hard sell. Possibly none.

This example is different than Ananias and Sapphira in Acts 5 where they conspired together—"with his wife's full knowledge"—to deceive the disciples. Sapphira, when asked about it later by the disciples, continued to lie, unlike the scenario with Abraham and Sarah. In the scenario above, the wife voiced her dissent, which means the consequences were on the husband's head.

If a husband does not believe that a wife should voice her objection and let it be on her husband's head, then the examples of Esther and Abigail apply. Esther and Abigail show how to respond in a submissive and respectful manner to potentially dangerous situations. They both brought food and gifts. They spoke respectfully and demurely. Abigail spoke to David by saying, "Pardon your servant, my lord . . . " while Esther repeated, "If it pleases the king. . . . " Abigail was even willing to take all her husband's fault upon herself, much like Jesus did for us.

The irony is that these godly women's stories are often twisted by some in the church who say they were the first feminists to object against the tyranny of men and the patriarchy. Not so. They were humble, respectful, and aimed to please to win the hearts of the men in the situation. Abigail speaks to David as "my lord" as Sarah did to Abraham in 1 Peter 3. How many wives will call their husband their lord, especially in a difficult situation?

Most of the time, the crux of the issue is not submission but respect. If the husband asks a wife to do something questionable, the attitude and actions of the wife should be oriented to be respectful, which will manifest in outward behavior consistent with the attitude. For instance, the wife could word her concerns as follows: "Hey, this seems questionable. Are you aware that this might be against the Bible or against the law?" or "This seems like it may be against the Bible. I respect your decision but could we possibly do this another way instead?" The vast majority of the time, even non-Christian husbands will not force their wife to break the law or the Bible, especially if they are treated with respect. Immediate contentiousness is a sign that a wife has little to no respect for her husband.

A Christian wife has very little trust in her husband if she thinks that he will tell them to do something sinful. This is a sign of very subtle but deep rebellion rooted within modern Christianity due to feminist influences and the demonization of men. She thinks the man she chooses to marry is unworthy of her trust. How sad.

- **Ephesians 5:** A wife should respect/revere her husband.

Wives are tempted to disrespect their husbands. This is one of the major themes of modern culture and is almost everywhere, even in the church. The vast majority of movies, TV shows, and other media continually disrespect husbands by making them the butt of jokes, portraying them as a man-child, and so on. Husbands are constantly doing something stupid only to be corrected by their wife, who is always right. Wives need to actively fight against the temptation of this thinking if they are to succeed. 1 Peter 3:1 says, "In the same way, you wives, be submissive to your own husbands so that even if any of them are disobedient to the word, they may be won without a word by the behavior of their wives."

A wife tends to rebel and treat her husband poorly with impure and disrespectful behavior if she thinks her husband is not acting correctly.

Many examples in the church sadly go against this biblical command. We saw the example of Tim Keller's wife and her so-called godly temper tantrum where she threw and broke china when she thought he was paying too much attention to ministry rather than to her. This is the exact opposite of scripture, which counsels wives to be a helpmeet and to win disobedient husbands with chaste and respectful behavior. Still others, such as Joel and Kathy Davisson, say that wives should threaten divorce.[2]

Such manipulative actions should not be condoned or associated with Christianity. The fact that God saves the occasional marriage this way is a testament to the grace of God rather than the effectiveness of this advice because the scriptures counsel the exact opposite: to do good even to our enemies (Matthew 5, Romans 12) and bear with one another in love (Ephesians 4, Colossians 3).

- **1 Peter 3:** A wife's adornment should not be merely external but focused on a gentle and quiet spirit.

Wives are tempted to prioritize vanity over gentle and quiet behavior if there is a conflict between the two. This corresponds to Proverbs 15:1, which says, "A gentle answer turns away wrath, but a harsh word stirs up anger." It also relates to Colossians 3 when husbands are warned about treating their wives harshly.

- **1 Peter 3:** A wife's example of calling her husband lord so that she will not be frightened.

Wives are tempted to disrespect their husbands and disobey them. When Sarah called Abraham lord, this signifies her respect, reverence, and obedience, which led to peace. Disobedience leads to the fear of righteous anger.

- **Titus 2:** A wife is to love (*philandros*) her husbands and children.

A wife is tempted to treat her husband and children with contempt and not affection, especially when she loses her patience or does not like what he is doing.

- **Titus 2:** A wife is to be a sensible, pure, a worker at home, and kind.

A wife is tempted to a lack of self-control, impure words and deeds, laziness, prioritizing obligations outside the home, and unkindness. This corresponds to 1 Timothy 5:9–16, which addresses widows remarrying. Proverbs 31 gives the example of a wife and mother working from her home rather than out in the world.

- **Titus 2:** A wife is to be subject to her own husband.

Wives are tempted to be covetous of other marriages or to use other marriages as examples of how to improve their own. We can see this in the proliferation of so many Christian marriage books and blogs advising the supposed right way to have a successful or spiritual marriage. An example of this is praying with your wife. The scriptures do not tell a husband to pray with his wife. When a wife holds her husband to that standard when he does not want to pray with her, it creates dissatisfaction and disunity, which undermines the marriage.

A wife should ask her husband how he likes things done. Also, a wife needs to be very careful not to allow other marriages to affect her expectations of her own marriage.

- **1 Corinthians 7:** A wife is not to withhold sex from her husband.

This is the more common scenario. Wives usually (but not always) have a lower sex drive then men, so it is tempting for them to "not feel like it" if they do not want to have sex. The wife should not use sex to try to get her husband to act a certain way or to manipulate him into doing anything.

- **Proverbs 21:** A wife should not nag.
- **Proverbs 25 & 27:** A wife should not be contentious or quarrelsome.
- **Proverbs 12:** A wife should have strength of character.
- **Proverbs 11:** A wife/woman should have discretion.
- **Proverbs 14:** A wife should not tear down her own home but rather build it.

Wives are tempted to nag their husbands to do certain things in a certain way or on a certain schedule. A wife is also tempted to be contentious in conflict or to generate conflict. Wives are tempted to gossip and put down their husbands and air their marital baggage, especially to other wives. This is destructive to both parties since other wives see this disrespect and might start to do it in their own marriage. This is why Titus 2 counsels older women to teach younger wives to do what is right. Overall, wives are tempted not to build up their husbands but rather to tear them down.

- **Proverbs 31:** The qualities espoused by a virtuous wife are excellence, trustfulness, diligence, homemaker, charitable, business (if any) out of the home, wisdom, and kindness.

Wives are tempted to the opposite. One of the main ones, especially in our current cultural climate is to be lazy at home, stingy with love, and prioritize working outside of the home as opposed to their own husbands and children.

Wives face many of these temptations throughout the scriptures and in today's culture. The church even espouses much incorrect theology about what scripture says about the roles and responsibilities of husbands and wives. In reviewing the temptations, an apt summary would be that men are tempted to be less manly while women are tempted to be manlier.

Overall, both husbands and wives should know the roles and responsibilities of their spouse. The husband is tasked with sacrificially loving the wife for the purpose of her sanctification. This means he needs to know when a wife is off track so that he can point her back on the right track. Likewise, Christians are to exhort one another to be sound in the faith and virtuous, so it pays for each to know if they are starting to go off track.

LEARN HOW TO LOVE YOURSELF

There's a difference between self-esteem and loving yourself the way God loves you. Notice how the passages mirror each other.

> "Teacher, which is the great commandment in the Law?" And He said to him, "'You shall love the Lord your God with all your heart, and with all your soul, and with all your mind.' This is the great and foremost commandment. The second is like it, 'You shall love your neighbor as yourself' (Matthew 22:36–39).

> For the husband is the head of the wife, as Christ also is the head of the church, He Himself being the Savior of the body. . . . Husbands, love your wives, just as Christ also loved the church and gave Himself up for her, so that He might sanctify her, having cleansed her by the washing of water with the word, that He might present to Himself the church [a]in all her glory, having no spot or wrinkle or any such thing; but that she would be holy and blameless. So husbands ought also to love their own wives as their own bodies. He who loves his own wife loves himself; for no one ever hated his own flesh, but nourishes and cherishes it, just as Christ also does the church, because we are members of His body. For this reason a man shall leave his father and mother and shall be joined to his wife, and the two shall become one flesh. This mystery is great; but I am speaking with reference to Christ and the church. Nevertheless, each

individual among you also is to love his own wife even as himself, and the wife must see to it that she respects her husband. (Ephesians 5:23, 25–33).

The second commandment, which is like the first, according to Jesus, is to "love your neighbor *as yourself*" (emphasis added). This is repeated in the instructions as to how husbands should treat wives. "Husbands are to love their wives *as their own body*" (emphasis added).

What does this mean? How does one take care of his own body? Jesus holds us to a new standard in the new covenant.

A new commandment I give to you, that you love one another, even as I have loved you, that you also love one another. By this all men will know that you are My disciples, if you have love for one another (John 13:34–35).

Our love for God should also mirror Jesus's love for us and our own body. That is the how we love our wives. This means we should be excellent in all that we do. We should give our best every moment, every day, every week, every month, every year, and every decade.

We must also be meeting our own needs in heart, mind, soul, and spirit, especially through the spiritual disciplines. Our wives can certainly influence our mental, emotional, physical, and spiritual well-being, but they are not responsible for it. You are responsible for your own well-being.

How can you fully love someone else if you're running yourself ragged to meet their needs and not taking care of your own? On many occasions, even Jesus took time to Himself without His disciples to go and pray, fast, and destress from the hardships of life.

It might mean waking up earlier to spend time with God or going to bed earlier if you're being run ragged. Maybe you need to cast all your worries on Him so that you can find His peace and joy. Maybe you need to take time in your commute to pray and meditate—with your eyes on the road!—instead of listening to music or talk shows. Maybe you need to plan and carve out time in your daily schedule with your wife and kids so that they can focus on reading their Bible and prayer both together and separately. Jesus went alone to pray, and He also prayed with His disciples. Whatever the case, we need to be making time to focus on our spiritual well-being.

This might also be the case for emotional, mental, and physical well-being. Find time to work out again or plan for your whole family to work out together. Find time to process and address your emotional state so that it does not negatively influence those around you. Look at the areas in your mental state where you have fallen prey to lies from the enemy or chased your own desires instead of obeying the Holy Spirit.

Loving yourself is not what the word thinks: building up your self-esteem and other new age philosophies. It is learning how to take control of your life that has spiralled out of your control due to being run ragged from life, from your wife, or from other stresses and turning it around to center yourself on your relationship with God. You will need to reboot if you have let your previous spiritual disciplines slide into laziness or apathy.

Become the best masculine leader, protector, and provider that you can again. Become attuned to allow the Spirit to properly influence your heart, mind, soul, and strength in your relationship. God will not let you down.

The goal is to love yourself and thereby hold yourself to the standard of Jesus. If your wife is still off track, you can walk in humility and a lack of hypocrisy to help her in the process of her sanctification and show her where she needs to be rid of cultural influence and sin.

Chapter 17
UNDERSTAND DYSFUNCTIONAL PATTERNS

THE FIVE MAIN DYSFUNCTIONAL PATTERNS OF MARRIAGE

In the scripture, a husband and wife each have their own roles and responsibilities in marriage. The husband and wife are each responsible for upholding their end of the covenant of marriage, and by upholding their end of the covenant, they are also positively influencing their spouse to do the same.

To put this another way, keep your eye on the prize. You are responsible for your actions, attitudes, and emotions. She is responsible for her actions, attitudes, and emotions. You can't change your wife, but you can influence her.

Let's look at the five main dysfunctional patterns now.

Ignorance and confusion: These are two different things, but they tend to lead to similar dysfunctional patterns. Therefore, we will discuss them together.

Maybe you're a new Christian or came to Christ after getting married. Maybe you have never thought to study the roles and responsibilities of the husband and wife in the scriptures. Perhaps you followed what the culture, your friends, or your family has told you about how marriage is supposed to be and how it works. You might be a strong Christian who went through pre-marital counseling and had pastors who never went through the marriage roles and responsibilities from the Bible with you.

Whatever the case, ignorance and confusion are big problems in marriage that lead to dysfunction.

In most cases, ignorance tends to default to the natural inclinations of the husband and the wife. This leads to problems because these natural inclinations are not built on godliness but rather are susceptible to temptation and sin. If the husband is naturally more organized than the wife, he might seem more controlling. If the husband is less organized than the wife, the wife can seem controlling. This can lead to the feeling of being controlled from either spouse, which results in resentment and a cycle of negative behavior. Unfortunately the issues tend to become worse and worse because of the ignorance of scriptural roles and responsibilities with no defined expectations.

In most cases with confusion, these dysfunctions tend to arise from a limited knowledge of scriptural roles and responsibilities but mismatched or mismanaged expectations that arise from them. This can often be the case for those in interracial marriages or those from different family structures. What often ends up happening is that a husband and wife have a different set of expectations of what they expect from the other spouse and from themselves in marriage. This leads to confusion and unhappiness because their expectations are not being met.

These issues can be caused by the husband, the wife, or both the husband and the wife. In most cases, it is not one or the other because both individuals have a responsibility to bring up the scriptural roles and responsibilities. This might commonly happen if you marry an unbeliever or if you became a Christian after you marry. These situations will be difficult, but God knows your situation and can use you to influence your wife.

Usually what happens in this scenario is that the husband or wife has changed after marriage. Maybe the husband (or the wife) becomes a bit lazy in his/her role and responsibilities by getting fat or not leading (following). Maybe the expectations were mismatched from the start: most people put their best foot forward in a relationship, and the other person assumes they will do the same in marriage.

Mother and her child: A common dysfunctional pattern involves a mother and her child. It generally consists of two simultaneous components.

- The husband has either become lazy or abdicated his leadership position.
- The wife believes that she needs to fix her husband.

The husband might not have become lazy or abdicated his leadership position, but the wife still believes she needs to fix her husband. The husband might have become lazy and abdicated his leadership position, but the wife does not believe she needs to fix him. This scenario tends to be rarer, though, as the dysfunctions tend to play into each other and become bigger problems.

In this case, the wife becomes her husband's mother. She nags him to do things. She becomes contentious about anything and everything. She becomes critical of what he likes. She is not pleasant or kind to live with. In a family with kids, she might take it out on them as well.

One of the reasons that this dysfunctional pattern can emerge is because of a very outspoken and stubborn mother. Men tend to want to marry women like their mothers, so a single man might unconsciously be drawn to women like this. On the other hand, if a man did not have a mother because she died or was absent in his life, he might try to fill the void left from an absent mother with his wife.

Both manifestations are clearly not healthy marriage relationship patterns, so it would behoove a man to acknowledge and slowly root out this problem through acknowledging that his wife is not his mother and that he has different roles and responsibilities to his wife than to his mother. In some cases, he will need to acknowledge that he might want his wife to fill some things that are not her responsibility. For instance, a husband should not look for unconditional love from his wife but only from God.

Inversion of roles: This is usually—though not always—unintentional in most Christian marriages.

The wife is acting as the head of the relationship, and the husband acts as the wife and is submissive. While this type of relationship might not seem prevalent, this is the most common dysfunctional pattern due to the feminization of the church and much of the church's teaching on marriage. If you subscribe to an egalitarian or even a complementarian marriage, you likely fall into this dysfunctional pattern. Leadership will always default to one person in a two-person relationship, so if the husband eschews responsibility, then it will default to the wife. This plays out in a couple of different ways.

The most common example of this dysfunction is the puppet or figurehead leader. In this scenario, the wife makes the decision, brings it to the husband, and says, "But you're the leader." Through manipulation tactics, he is pressured to adopt her decision as his own. The husband is sadly duping himself into thinking that he made the decision, and the wife is deceiving herself by thinking that she is a submissive wife who follows her husband's lead while still getting everything she wants.

If the wife has done this inadvertently a husband can take up his proper roles and responsibilities in the relationship, thus removing his wife from those positions that she might have unwillingly and/or unwittingly taken. This will reduce her stress level drastically, making her feel more loved in the long term. But it will often cause more stress and contention during the adjustment period.

Christian husbands who are stuck need to mainly focus on being a better masculine leader, protector, and provider. They can do the following: work out, dress well, be clean shaven or keep well-groomed facial hair, be ambitious at work, take the lead at home in the relationship, make clear decisions, and don't waffle. By being a better masculine leader and protector, you are showing her romance because you *desire* to be a good leader and are acting on it. Trying to do the chores or to please her with flowers or gifts is the wrong thing to do because you can't make someone happy by *working* to please them.

If your wife is trying to manipulate you into doing what she wants, you will have to take a stand. Think back to the example of Adam and Eve. Eve encouraged Adam to submit to her choice to eat the fruit of the tree and gave it to him. He could have said, "No, that's not what God told us." Instead, he chose to be complicit. This also means that instead of being passive and reactive, you need to start being proactive about leading your marriage again. This can cause some friction as your wife probably won't like changing what she has been used to. But your goal is to stick to God's Word and structure for marriage, not placate your wife's feelings. Usually she will come around.

One example of an intentional inversion of relationship roles in the Bible is Ahab and Jezebel. Jezebel plotted evil against the prophets of the Lord and murdered people for their land and vineyards. Ahab even knew Elijah was a man of God, but he still went along with Jezebel's evil deeds. Ahab was still held responsible for the leadership of Israel by the Lord even though he handed it over to Jezebel because he was the husband. Both Ahab and Jezebel were ultimately punished for their evil by the Lord.

Rebellion and imposters: The husband is acting as the head of the relationship, and the wife is choosing to rebel instead of submit. She wants to do things her way instead of following his lead.

Generally, a minor but significant chunk of relationships within devoted Christians fall in this category. The husband *is* a responsible husband, fights for his family, provides well for his family with a stable job, and is devoted to his wife and kids. Yet the wife consistently challenges his headship through nagging, constant suggestions on what to do and how her ideas are supposedly better, or she constantly wants her own way.

Jesus had to deal with imposters in His disciple group too. As we know, John 6 shows that many of Jesus's early disciples simply left Him when He started to claim to be the Messiah. Even Judas's relationship with Jesus showed that he was with Jesus for the benefits rather than the relationship. He eventually betrayed Jesus for his own gain. Be very careful of who you marry: a woman might call herself a Christian, but her actions might reflect differently. She is a wolf in sheep's clothing.

This has become much more prevalent since the rise of feminism and the cultural wars. Sometimes churches even enable it, such as churches that preach headship but then tell husbands that the measure of his headship is his wife's happiness or pleasing his wife. This encourages wives to rebel against their husbands because the quality of the marriage is determined by the happiness of the wife. "I'm not happy? My husband must be doing something wrong. He should do it differently instead." We're warring against the culture, which the enemy tries to use against us, but sometimes our spouse can fall prey to the deception just as Eve was deceived and chose to eat the fruit.

There's nothing wrong with striving to please your wife or doing kind things for her. But when these things are done from a dysfunctional relationship by orienting your entire life around it instead of your mission to God, this only leads to further dysfunction. The trap of this dysfunctional relationship pattern is that instead of things being done from desire because you love her, they are instead done from desire to earn her pleasure or sex. This only exacerbates the issues and can ultimately lead to divorce.

There are two different stages of rebellion:

- Total rebellion: Rebellion of attitude and actions.
- Subtle rebellion: Rebellion of attitude while still technically letting her husband lead.
- Marriage: Following her husband's lead.

Total rebellion is obvious. A wife does not follow her husband's lead and decides to make her own decisions. Subtle rebellion is harder to spot. Wives technically obey with their actions but have not quite quashed the temptation to rebel in their hearts. Letting someone lead is an attempt to take control of the situation instead of trusting that the husband has the best in mind. We don't let Christ lead but choose to follow His lead by taking up our cross and following Him. Christ and the church is the model, and the church needs to follow Christ.

Lack of sex: I included this as its own category though I have touched on it in many of the previous categories as well. One of the biggest reasons that men are seeking counseling is that their wives are denying them sex. In a minority of cases, the wife has a higher sex drive.

In many of these cases, a Christian husband has already told his Christian wife about 1 Corinthians 7, which states the husband and wife have a marital debt to each other to not deny each other sex. She obviously disagrees and rebels against the Bible. Perhaps they have already been to marriage counseling.

There are many reasons for this type of behavior. You usually have to do some digging to find figure out the problem in each relationship. The following list includes some of the most common reasons.

- Your wife has a lower sex drive, and she does not want to follow the Bible's commands because her feelings are more important.
- Your wife loves you but is not in love with you anymore. This usually means a lack of sexual attraction or that she is becoming interested in someone else.
- Your wife has a medical condition that makes sex painful.
- Your wife has had sexual trauma or pain in her past that is negatively influencing her ability to be sexually intimate in marriage.
- Your wife has been taught that sex is dirty or has made her virginity into an idol because of her parents' and/or the church's influence, which has put up road blocks to sexual intimacy.
- Pre-marital sex with other men or even the husband himself can negatively influence the marriage bed due to comparisons between the husband and past experiences or due to sin.

- A wife is tempted to potential adultery with other men, has possibly started an emotional or physical affair, or otherwise fantasized about the prospect of either.

OTHER AREAS OF DYSFUNCTION

Although these are the most common reasons, it might be a combination of these in addition to other dysfunctions. For instance, in the case of rebellion or inversion of roles, a wife that is already opposed to or manipulating her husband will often not want to have sex with him. Women are attracted to leaders, and if the wife is not following her husband, that can lead to a loss of respect and attraction. How you approach these can differ, especially when a combination of many factors is in play. We will discuss the solutions to this in the next section as well.

If a wife has pain during sex, had past sexual trauma, or was taught that sex is dirty, she might need to see a professional therapist. In the case of pain, a physical therapist might be necessary for pelvic muscle retraining.

Chapter 18

UNDERSTANDING THE CHRISTIAN APPROACH TO INFLUENCE AND SOLVING MARITAL ISSUES

Christianity is ultimately an inside-out process. We hear the gospel, which convicts us. We accept, believe, and confess that Jesus paid the price for our sin. We repent and turn away from that sin and are baptized. We are then transformed by the Holy Spirit working within us so that we can flee sin, do good works, evangelize others, and disciple them. We are the light that shines on a hill, a lamp on a lampstand, and the salt of the earth. But the process starts because we are transformed to be more like Jesus. Similarly, as your wife is a follower of Jesus and of you, she should also become more like Jesus and you.

The reason the process starts with us is so that we cannot be accused of hypocrisy, according to the words of Jesus Himself.

> "Do not judge so that you will not be judged. For in the way you judge, you will be judged; and by your standard of measure, it will be measured to you. Why do you look at the speck that is in your brother's eye, but do not notice the log that is in your own eye? Or how can you say to your brother, 'Let me take the speck out of your eye,' and behold, the log is in your own eye? You hypocrite, first take the log out of your own eye, and then you will see clearly to take the speck out of your brother's eye" (Matthew 7:1–5).

We remove all the planks from our own eyes first, and only then do we start to lovingly help those around us. This is important in the marriage relationship because, often, those closest to us see all our flaws and mistakes.

It is not wrong to make mistakes, but we should collaborate with the Holy Spirit to change our attitude, behavior, and character first so that we can be a good witness when we influence those around us to change. Whatever we do, we do for the glory of God.

If you recall, God's roles and responsibilities for marriage are unconditional (see Chapter 4). You don't get to ignore them because your spouse is treating you poorly. You are required to do them because your primary goal is to honor God first in what you do. In fact, God can use you when you fulfill your roles and responsibilities while walking with the Holy Spirit to influence and change them. Your wife or your children are not your enemy despite how they act at times. Jesus's (Matthew 15) and Paul's (Romans 14) words ring true when they said, bless your enemies and do good and pray for those who persecute you. That's what the first phase, which takes times, is all about.

Additionally, remember the qualifications for deacons in the church that men should strive for. One of them is to be beyond reproach, and this is why. Almost no one responds well to a perceived hypocrite even one who acts worse than you do. When you fulfill your roles and responsibilities so that they have nothing to accuse you of, you remove the stumbling block of the hypocrite label.

You can use this general outline to exert the most influence to improve your marriage or relationship. We're going to look at improving it in 3 month, 3 month, and 6 month increments, as this gives enough time to see godly positive results and develop good habits in each stage.

THE FIRST THREE MONTHS: LEAD BY EXAMPLE

For the first three months, focus solely on your biblical roles and responsibilities.

- Take the time and effort to be the best masculine leader, protector, and provider that you can possibly be.
- Repeatedly read through and meditate on Ephesians 5, Colossians 3, 1 Peter 3, 1 Corinthians 7, and all the other scriptures on marriage.
- Invite the Holy Spirit to work in your heart and soul.

- Ask for the fruit of the Spirit to be more clearly displayed in your life, particularly God's supernatural peace and joy, especially when your wife and children frustrate you.
- Be patient and self-controlled, slow to anger, and abounding in love.

Don't let this be only a transformative change on the inside. Focus on being excellent on the outside as cultivating the physical body is important as a protector and for your strength.

- If you're overweight or underweight, start to work out to build muscle.
- Change your nutrition habits to a healthy lifestyle.
- Dress well for work and at other times, too.
- Groom and style yourself well.
- Take up or continue a physical hobby or martial arts.

Remember, the goal is to consistently "take off your old self and put on the new self," which is reflected on the inside and outside in Christ. Three months allows you to show a consistent change of attitudes and actions that can slowly be imprinted onto your being as your new character. This also gives your wife and children time to adapt to the new you, which is being transformed into the likeness of Christ.

- If you want to summarize how to think of your attitude and actions, always remind yourself of the following before you do anything stupid: God appointed me as the strong, masculine leader in my marriage. Is what I am doing consistent with being a strong, masculine leader?

If you are holding onto any bitterness, resentment, or frustration due to the fact that your wife or children might not be listening, you might need to walk away or calm yourself down and give it to God. It's not about getting your way or doing it your way; it's about doing it God's way.

Your wife and children and even friends and family will inevitably ask you what is going on. You do not need to give a complicated answer. Simply tell them that you realized that you're not the man who you want to be. You haven't been doing everything you can for the glory of God. You decided that you want to be a better husband and father, so you're making changes in your life.

Make sure that you are reading your Bible and praying in common areas of the house. When you do this, focus on the passages about marriage and the fruit of the Spirit. This is one of the best witnesses you can have since all the positive changes will be visible to your wife and children. You don't have to invite them to participate with you yet. The visible changes you are making are enough for now.

You can then invite them to participate with you in the change. If you're starting to make plans as the leader of the marriage, invite them to help you out and fill in the details. If you're getting back into working out, invite them to join you in making their temple of the Holy Spirit healthy as well. Basically, you can use some of the changes you are making to exert a positive influence on them. If they don't want to join you, don't fret about it.

When you lead, make sure that you continue to act as a leader, even if they aren't buying into what you are doing. If your wife disagrees or is not willing to follow yet, don't be hurt. The measure of the outcome is that you are trying to obey God first. You shouldn't worry about the earthly response that your wife or children give you while you are focusing on God's standards for you. This doesn't come intuitively, so you must be aware that you can easily be hurt or emotional if they don't immediately follow you. This is about re-orienting your heart to God, which makes you a stronger leader in the long run. Your ability to obey God is independent of the earthly outcome.

The hardest areas to change are when you are experiencing negative emotions, such as anger. In these situations, take a deep breath and ask God for wisdom and peace. Try to never make any decisions or statements while you are angry. If you get into an argument, just stop and tell your wife or children that you don't want to argue while you are angry and will come back to the topic later. Anger almost inevitably leads to people saying things they shouldn't say and exacerbates an already poor situation. Ask the Holy Spirit to help increase your kindness, self-control, and patience in these times so that you can respond in a godly manner.

You do not have to mention that your goal is to influence your wife and children. You do not have to mention that you're unhappy with how things have been in the family, even when it comes to sensitive issues, such as the lack of sex. These areas will change with time.

Changes are best made from a pro-active position rather than a reactive. Those of you who have been to marriage counseling before might know that it doesn't work. This is because the counselor acts as a mediator of problems, telling each spouse to do something they don't want to do to fix the problems. This is the desire-and-works mentality that we talked about in prior chapters. If you're doing it because you have to make your marriage better, then you're in a works mentality. The pro-active way is the desire mentality. You're doing it because you *want to* not because you *have to*.

The dysfunctional patterns of a wife with low sex drive and a wife that loves you but is not in love with you can be solved simultaneously with counsel in this section. This is because you are working on God's roles and responsibilities for husbands in marriage, which are attractive to women.

In this instance, a husband has typically either become a bit complacent in the marriage in key areas, such as acting in a feminine manner rather than a masculine one, gaining weight, not living a healthy lifestyle, not leading in his marriage, losing his job, and related issues. This leads to a loss of attraction on the wife's part. She is turned off and does not want to have sex with her husband. A wife might also gain substantial significant amount of weight in the marriage and thus become unattractive to her husband. The concept is the same.

When it comes to other sexual dysfunctions, never deny sex. Christian husbands don't like duty sex because it feels bad or wrong. Always be grateful and thankful to your wife when she does the right thing, such as duty sex, even if she's not enthusiastic about it. Duty sex does not necessarily have to be duty sex. Wives tend to pick up on the emotional state of the husband, so if you're disappointed or frustrated with duty sex, she will likely end up frustrated as well. Instead, have fun with her and tease her. You can probably draw your wife out of a bad mood, but you can't let her negative emotions drag you down. Be her rock when her emotions are bad, and weather the storm to pull her out of it.

THE NEXT THREE MONTHS: START TO ADDRESS SCRIPTURAL ISSUES

At this point, hopefully your wife and children are accepting of and getting used to the changes. Perhaps they have already begun to be influenced by your changes. Unfortunately, the longer that the marriage has been a certain way, the longer it will take for your change and influence to turn it around. You can usually start to see some change and influence take effect in three months in a two- or three-year marriage or relationship. Those in a five-year or even a ten-year marriage, might need to wait several months or even years to see change or watch your influence take effect. A decent rule of thumb is about one month for every year of the marriage. So if the marriage was dysfunctional for twenty to thirty years, it might take two to three years of consistent godly behavioral change to see any significant effects.

Don't be disheartened by a lack of progress in your wife or children. Remember the ultimate goal is to please God by fulfilling and excelling in the scriptural roles and responsibilities of marriage. Pleasing God is the most important thing, and even if there are little to no earthly results, you are storing up treasure in heaven by choosing to do what is right.

This is where a knowledge of the different dysfunctional patterns comes into play.

Ignorance and confusion are usually simple to resolve. If you've been doing Bible studies regularly and publicly in your home, you can invite your wife and children to study some of the various scriptures on marriage roles and responsibilities. You can ask thought-provoking questions, such as, Why do you think God designed marriage this way? You can end the studies with questions, such as How do you think I can be a better husband and father? You can also address relevant topics, such as how your wife can be a better helper to you and how your kids can learn, grow, and help around the house.

One of the hardest things to do after these types of conversations is to help keep the momentum on track. Your family might change, but if they start to fall back into old habits, approach it as kindly and gently as possible: "Hey, you might not have meant to come off like this, but I noticed that (insert action here)." You can also give her gentle reminders about how she hasn't followed through in certain areas as applicable. You can then demonstrate God's love in marriage by helping her with the sanctification process. You're supposed to help your wife and kids become more Christlike, and these are very simple ways to do it.

The dysfunctional pattern of a mother and her child can be more difficult. One way to approach this is to frame it in a way that she can understand.

For instance, this type of situation can be best diffused with banter first rather than serious conversation. For example, if she continually nags you about doing things, you can reply "I'm sorry, Mommy, I'll get to it right away. Can you warm up a bottle for me?" This type of diffusion works well because you're responding to her treatment of you as an infant with a similar response, which makes her realize that she should not treat you like this.

If her nagging becomes worse or she doesn't take the hint, you can move to a serious conversation, such as "When you continually tell me to do something (nag), I feel frustrated because I already know what I am supposed to do. Please try to encourage me instead as that makes me more receptive to your requests." This often works because you are communicating how nagging makes you feel, and women tend to empathize and don't want to make others feel badly (unless they're being snarky). Try to approach this when both of you are calm and not angry instead of when it happens unless you can maintain your patience and calmness while it's happening.

Alternatively, if she likes lists and organization, you should give her a list as the leader rather than have her give you a list.

If you haven't gone over marital roles and responsibilities and communicated your various expectations to each other, this is the right time to do it. Hashing out these things will help prevent some—but not all—of the misunderstandings from cropping up. You can demonstrate your leadership capabilities by delegating various responsibilities equitably. Don't be afraid to help if your wife feels overwhelmed, and don't be afraid to ask her for help if you feel overwhelmed. Invite your children to helping with household chores to learn responsibility as well.

If roles are inverted, you can resolve this dysfunction easily if it is inadvertent. When a husband reassumes the mantle of leadership, this will significantly decrease the wife's stress and responsibility. As he becomes a leader again, he will be more attractive to her. As such, the relationship tends to fall back into alignment.

Intentional inversions of roles and rebellion are the most difficult problems to address. If your marriage has struggled with these for a long time and your wife is adamantly opposed to the scriptures about leadership and submission, you will face serious issues. As you step into who God has called you to be in the marriage as a stronger and more masculine leader, you will often butt heads with your wife on various topics. In these situations, remember the commands from Ephesians 5, Colossians 3, 1 Peter 3, and 1 Corinthians 13.

- Continue to nurture and nourish your wife as much as possible.
- Don't become embittered against her.
- Continue to honor her as a co-heir in Christ.
- Love her via 1 Corinthians 13.

What you say will not win her to Christ, but your consistent loving behavior will bring change. Your goal is to keep on leading to the best of your ability and consistently invite her to follow. This is what Jesus does for us though we often go astray and follow our own ways.

As to the lack of sex, this might have already improved as you step back into your role as a strong, masculine leader. This will usually increase your attractiveness to your wife again. Leading in the marital bed will also help. Most men are more concerned about her pleasure but do not neglect yours either. The more fun you have by leading in sex the better—different positions, teasing, going hard and rough or soft and slow, butt slaps, light biting, tying each other up, or whatever you think is fun. These can all help bring your wife out of her shell.

Many Christian women have been told all their lives to avoid having sex with men, so even in marriage they don't know how to let go and experience the fullness of joy and intimacy. Draw her into that place by leading her in the marital bed.

Along with the mindset that sex is dirty, another terrible analogies the church uses is the "slow cooker" analogy. This is the concept that women take a long time to get in the mood for sex and that you need to do chores throughout the day or compliment her to get her in the mood. This is false. It always takes two to tango. Women love having sex, too, but usually only with attractive men. Hook-up culture only works because the women want to go out and have sex. The key is to find out what turns your wife on the most to break down her sexual barriers. Usually this is making her feel sexy or desired. Compliments don't generally work because they focus on her instead of on your desire and passion for her.

You can do this in multiple ways, such as playful touching, giving her a long, deep kiss, and similar gestures that you both enjoy. You can also tell her to put on that sexy lingerie and be ready by 9:00 p.m. for a night of fun or tell her that you've been thinking all day about how sexy she is and what you explicitly want to do later that night. The goal is to show genuine desire and leave her in anticipation. This can be done throughout the day but does not necessarily have to be. Women and wives are turned on by passionate desire and by men who take charge of the situation.

Note: If you try these things, and your wife is not attracted to you, she might react negatively. Remember the unattractive creep versus the attractive hunk showing romantic gestures. In this case, continue to work on being more attractive through fulfilling God's roles and responsibilities for you in the marriage. If she doesn't respond with outright rejection but responds less than enthusiastically, file it away for later as you continue to change your circumstances. Don't be hurt by rejection, just move on with your life. If your wife sees that she can manipulate you through rejection, she might start to use it against you.

A YEAR AND BEYOND: CONTINUE TO BE PERSISTENT AND KIND AND STAND STRONG

By this time, your wife and children might start to come around if you have been consistent and persistent with being a better strong, masculine leader, protector, and provider and in your fulfillment of your marital roles and responsibilities. If you have been less consistent, your wife and children might still be in the same or a similar spot. If that's you, you're still at step one. Take it seriously.

If you have been consistent with this stage, your behavior will be slowly influencing your wife and children. If you have been stuck in that five- to ten-year or longer rut, it can take even longer than this, but you should still see some signs of melting the freeze. The issue with melting a freeze or standoff is that it can result in a positive or negative reaction. The positive will be good, but the negative needs to be considered.

Some people are extremely resistant to change, even positive godly change, which might result in backlash. This is especially true in the dysfunctional patterns of mothering, inversion of roles, and rebellion. Wives can become very uncomfortable and angry with how they perceive the relationship to be changing because they feel like they are losing control of the situation. They previously had you under their thumb and could basically tell you what to do. This is not negative but positive if you didn't try to implement too much too quickly.

If you do too much too soon, you are charging around like a bull in a china shop. Gradual, consistent changes are typically better than a type-A personality who is all gung-ho about immediate changes. Even if you are making internal changes to align with God's principles, you don't have to do all of it right away. Let it come out with time as your character changes.

Think of the bandage analogy regarding overall change. It will hurt to rip off the bandage, but you don't want the bandage to heal on your skin. You must be willing to destroy the dysfunctional aspects of the relationship, which will be painful for both sides as you remove the bandage. You will probably become angry at each other, but the key is to not let the anger fester into bitterness or resentment. Stand on God's Word and cultivate the fruit of the Spirit during this period. God will give you His peace and joy if you continue to cling to Him and His Word to weather the difficult season of confronting the dysfunctional relationship patterns.

If the dysfunctional pattern was so ingrained that your wife now leans toward separation or divorce, then stay the course. It is much better to have obeyed God and His standards for marriage than to obey your wife and continue to live in a dysfunctional marriage pattern. This is the Adam dilemma in your own marriage: Do you obey God and His plan for marriage, or do you obey your wife and eat from the fruit of the tree that God told you not to eat from? The answer should be clear to any Christian, but it is hard in the moment because it means consistently standing firm on God's Word even in the face of confrontation with your wife. How does Jesus treat the church when she is disobedient to Him? He absolutely chastises her and calls her to repent (Revelation 2 and 3).

Many husbands will give into their wives to keep the peace, but this is only temporary peace because when you give into sin, it is never satisfied. You will be constantly presented with more opportunities to sin and give in until you become entrapped in a pattern of sin with no way of escape. Do the hard but right thing so that you don't go down a road that you might not be able to walk back from.

In some cases, you will be faced with threats, even of divorce. This is a common but extreme phenomenon when some women feel as if they're losing control of the situation. Threats are particularly effective against most men because we don't like to be painted as the bad guy. But giving into threats and manipulative behavior is often the worst thing you can do. Once a wife or child sees that they can manipulate you with threats, they will use every opportunity to get what they want. You can see this constantly in popular culture with parents and children. Parents who spoil their kids or give into their temper tantrums are ruled by the emotions of their children. This is another way in which husbands and fathers can become a slave to the emotional whims of their wives and children.

Threats should not be taken seriously; we don't negotiate with emotional or manipulative terrorism. Usually the best way to handle threats is to just calmly ignore them and don't react or to take it to the literal end game. An example of the end game would be if a wife threatens divorce, then you offer to help her pack up her things to move out or simply hand her divorce papers and tell her to fill them out. If she's going to do it anyway, then you can't stop her, and you have nothing to fear. But if it was simply a threat because of an emotional reaction, your refusal to be manipulated will stop it right in its tracks. In most cases of an emotional outburst of threats, your wife probably does not want to divorce you. Usually once wives and children see that they can no longer manipulate you with threats or emotional reactions, they will stop.

In these cases, you can help your wife become more holy and call her to repentance. If she does feel guilty about threatening you and apologizes, thank her for her apology and give her a big hug and a kiss. The goal is always reconciliation and strengthening of the marriage bond. Even if she doesn't apologize, you can likewise comfort her but reinforce that threats aren't the answer with a big hug and a kiss.

Your overarching goal is to influence your wife and children to change through God working in their lives. Do not lose sight of this goal. Any time you can reinforce reconciliation and strengthening of the marital bond, you are making progress.

Let's look at some additional topics that relate to difficult marriage situations.

DIVORCE AND SEPARATION

Sometimes there's nothing you can do that will satisfy your wife. Perhaps she was already thinking of divorcing you, and you taking on becoming a godlier husband only pushed her over the edge. It's certainly possible a wife that calls herself Christian who has given into temptation to rebel or invert roles repeatedly will choose to divorce rather than submit to a godly example of a leader.

God does not guarantee us that He will change our spouse in the scriptures. This is a difficult word for most husbands and even wives to understand. We try everything in our power to change them, but at the end of the day it's the other person's decision whether or not to respond. First Corinthians 7:10–11 tells us, "But to the married I give instructions, not I, but the Lord, that the wife should not leave her husband (but if she does leave, she must remain unmarried, or else be reconciled to her husband), and that the husband should not put away his wife."

In these cases, God is your refuge. Stand on the scriptures and stay single. Pray to God for reconciliation.

Although God does not cause bad things to happen to His children, He always uses our difficult situations to draw us closer to Him. How can we better run to Him when we are distressed and in need of help? How can we draw closer to Him? It might be helpful to look at the various stories of the saints of God in the Bible and throughout church history.

One thing you can do is read the Psalms, which are basically David's prayers to God. You'll notice that at times, he's joyful. But his emotions run the gamut: depression, anger, sadness, vengefulness, grief, celebration, and everything in between. No matter what, David always came back to God, even when he royally screwed up on multiple occasions, such as when he committed adultery and murder. That's why God calls him a man after His own heart.

Most of the time, we, as Christians, only talk to God and thank Him when we're happy and everything is going right. But when things go wrong, we stop going to church, stop praying, and are scared to go to Him. That's not what He wants for us, especially when we need him most.

Beware the temptation to run away from God or blame Him in troubled times. Take this time to grow stronger in the faith and pray that God changes and reaches the heart of your spouse.

DO NOT ENABLE AND AVOID MANIPULATION

One of the most difficult scenarios is a situation that seems to be lose-lose. For instance, consider a situation when a wife is destroying the family finances with overspending.

Your biblical obligation to the family as the provider is to oversee the family finances though this responsibility can be delegated to the wife if she can do it. But if the wife is engaged in destructive financial behavior, such as overspending that is putting the family into deep debt, can a husband do anything about it? Since this is widely considered destructive behavior and your first loyalty is to God as the responsible provider, you should cut up credit cards, freeze your credit, and remove avenues that encourage the temptation to overspend.

One of the problems you might encounter is that many in the world and even other Christians would consider cutting up the credit cards and freezing the credit as so-called abuse. But what you are really doing is refusing to enable destructive behavior. This destructive behavior, if allowed to continue, means possibly losing the house, the car, savings, other assets, and ultimately bankruptcy. This is a very difficult situation to walk through because you will feel besieged from both sides. You don't want to be labeled as abusing your wife, but you know that you have the responsibility to oversee the well-being of your entire family.

If that means cutting up credit cards, freezing your credit, and finding other ways to stop her destructive behavior, then you should do it. It's actually a win-win situation. You are first showing your loyalty to God as responsible for the family finances, and you are stopping and not enabling the destructive behavior of your wife. She might be angry and bitter toward you in the moment, but over the long-term, she needs to be prevented from engaging in this behavior. If you have self-control issues, get yourself the right counseling from God and from others: the church, mentors, or psychologists. To operate effectively, you need a sound mind and discipline. Don't be afraid to ask for help.

Compare this to enabling any other addiction. If you removed the financial ability of an alcoholic or smoking addict to buy more alcohol or cigarettes, would you be labeled an abuser or a hero? You'd be labeled a hero for refusing to enable the destructive behavior.

What about some other destructive situations? What if your wife is addicted to romance novels? Will you rip them up and throw them away? What if you struggle with an addiction, such as a secret pornography habit? Can you remove the computer or phone from your house so that you don't keep doing it?

Be aware. You, your wife, or your children can be caught in destructive behavior. Stick with God's standards and remove the ability to potentially engage in destructive behavior. This might be unpopular in certain situations, especially according to the world and even in the church, but the goal was never to please other people. It is to be responsible to God and to not allow poor behavior to spiral out of control for the addicted and those surrounding them.

This is a very difficult topic, so continue to read the Bible and pray extensively before making any hard decisions about these matters. Consult mature Christians in the faith about the situation and seek godly counsel.

DUTY SEX

I talked about duty sex before, but it needs its own section.

The concept of duty sex is already a compromise and a worldly state of mind rather than a biblical framework. Denial of sex is unbiblical (1 Corinthians 7), but most Christians have a hard time discerning why duty sex is negative. If the denial of sex is a total compromise of feelings over obedience to scripture, duty sex is the lukewarm compromise. The person is saying, "I'll have sex because God tells me to do it, but I'm going to have a bad attitude and just lay there."

In general, most husbands and wives don't want to force their husbands or wives to have sex with them when they don't feel like it. After all, we want our spouse to be excited and enthusiastic about sex. This can often lead to a situation where a husband or wife wants to have sex, the other spouse feels unenthusiastic but willing, and then the initiator becomes depressed and turned off, so sex doesn't happen. Then the other spouse also becomes depressed or angry because they were willing, but the initiator stopped it.

My stance on this is simple: almost *never* deny duty sex and don't acknowledge any sex as duty sex.

While it is true that holding out over bad sex can sometimes improve your sex life, this is not an either/or question. I always recommend sex despite feelings because of the power of sex; the intimacy and bonding is like nothing that God has created. First Corinthians 7 describes how the husband and wife have authority over each other's bodies when it comes to sex. It's never wrong to do the right thing. Freezing out your spouse because of a bad attitude shows self-control, which is also attractive, but it doesn't increase intimacy.

Some in the church have described this authority over the other spouse's body to not have sex, which is false. The authority is to the marital debt, which means the authority is to have sex and not to refuse sex.

In looking at anecdotal experiences from various marital challenges, such as wives who have done a challenge to never deny their husbands for a certain length of time, the wives inevitably reported increased intimacy and satisfaction in marriage even if they keep doing it when they don't feel like it.[1] This helps both the husband and the wife continue to strengthen their bond so that a negative attitude comes less and less into play. Indeed, your spouse can become much more enthusiastic during foreplay or sex itself with a positive attitude by having fun and leading the sexual encounter. The only way it turns into a so-called dead fish experience is if you let it.

If you are not mentally strong enough to overcome the so-called dead fish experience, and it negatively affects you so that sex is a hollow experience, tempting you to pornography, this might be one of the few reasons to avoid perceived duty sex.

Don't fall into her frame of mind by begrudgingly having sex. Stay within yours, and center it on the Holy Spirit. Our job is not necessarily to police wrong attitudes or emotions. Our job is to follow God's commands. As we follow God's Word and stand on His commands, attitudes will inevitably improve as time goes on. Why? Because the fruit of His Spirit is joy and peace. Denying sex is like denying the Spirit to work through the marital act of intimacy.

Now that you know this, always bring your excitement and enthusiasm to sex even if your spouse isn't always feeling it. If you're having a hard time, ask the Holy Spirit to help you to be enthusiastic even if your spouse is not into it at first. You will almost always be surprised at how God can work through your obedience.

Chapter 19
COMMON PITFALLS TO MARITAL HEADSHIP

MASTER YOURSELF SO THAT YOU AREN'T MANIPULATED

If you're married and you've read this whole book so far, you know that marriage is a process that builds on itself. Somewhere along the way, many Christian men do end up getting married without many different key points that we have covered. These can range from the following to others that aren't even listed.

- Don't know their identity and purpose
- Don't know what the Bible says about marriage
- Don't know how to lead effectively
- Don't have a mentor
- Haven't been discipled effectively by the church
- Became lazy along the way

The preceding chapters outline many of the various steps you can take, but the reason for taking all these steps might not be clear. Take a look at the following list:

- You want to walk in what God has called you to do
- Christianity is an inside-out faith
- You can only change yourself, not others
- You don't want to be a hypocrite to your wife or children

One of the most important reason is that men without knowledge and purpose are very easily manipulated.

> My people are destroyed for lack of knowledge. Because you have rejected knowledge, I also will reject you from being My priest. Since you have forgotten the law of your God, I also will forget your children (Hosea 4:6).

If you don't know what you're doing, you're very easily swayed to and fro by whatever everyone is saying around you: the culture, the church, family, or friends. Most of these groups often do not have wise knowledge or advice for your particular situation. This is especially true when it seems like the marriage is spiraling out of control.

If you ever come to the point where you're feeling as if you're walking on eggshells, whipped, on a dog leash, or any of the similar idioms, you are most certainly far along the path of being so manipulated that you are now cowed like a beaten animal. Maybe you have dealt with role reversal or rebellion or dysfunctional patterns, but the fact of the matter is that you're a manipulated man.

This is not what God wants. He wants you to be the leader of the marriage, but it starts with you. This is important in understanding God's mission for you and your purpose. You're grounded on the solid foundation of Jesus so that you cannot be manipulated to and fro by the storm with its wind and the waves—whether that's your wife and children, the culture, the church, your family, or your friends.

You are first and foremost responsible for you. That's where you start even if the circumstances surrounding your situation are crazy and overwhelming.

SOME NEEDS CAN ONLY BE MET BY GOD

This was briefly addressed in the prior chapter but deserves its own section.

Some Christians have a testimony of engaging in a sinful lifestyle—alcohol, drugs, sex, and other morally deficient behaviors—prior to coming to Christ. Once they heard the gospel, it all made sense. Prior to hearing the gospel, they threw themselves into all those sinful activities to fill the God-sized hole in their heart. But nothing could fill it except Jesus.

Unfortunately we sometimes lose sight of the gospel and allow this to happen again in our lives. For instance, many single and even married individuals feel very lonely and socially isolated in our current culture. Many Christian singles believe that a relationship with the opposite sex will improve their lives, and many married Christians believe that if only they could connect and communicate with their spouse on a more intimate level, their lives would turn around.

While it is true that "man is not meant to be alone" (Genesis 2), we need to make sure that our needs are being met in the right places. Part of our loneliness can be in our identity and purpose. We don't feel like we are children of God or have a purpose from God. Maybe we also neglect the many verses in the scriptures that refer to one another, where the church is supposed to disciple, advise, and live with one another in community. When your needs are being met in the right places, you usually find you didn't need them met in the places you thought. If you're growing in your relationship with God and His church, you won't feel that you *need* a relationship with the opposite sex because you are not alone anymore.

This is true in some of the dysfunctional marital patterns, especially the mother and her son. You shouldn't be asking your wife to meet any of the needs that your mother or even God should have met when you were a child. This is why you need to understand the scriptures on the entirety of the Christian walk and on marital roles and responsibilities. We might incorrectly seek our needs from places that we shouldn't have them met, which can ruin our other relationships because our wife will never be able to meet the needs that only God or our earthly mother could meet.

Ask yourself these questions:

- What needs should God be meeting?
- What needs should the church, community, family, and friends be meeting?
- What needs should a mentor or a mentored person be meeting?
- What needs should your wife be meeting?

When you look at a dysfunctional relationship, you're often burdening your wife or your family and friends with expectations that God or other people (mentors) should be meeting. The same can be true of a wife with her husband.

You might need to sit down and evaluate each of these points one by one and lead your wife through the same process. This is activity will help you develop great stewardship for yourself and leadership with your wife.

ATTRACTION AND SEX IN MARRIAGE

Attraction, or a lack thereof, is not always a magical problem solver in marriage. In some marriages with dysfunctional patterns, the husband and wife have lots of sex. In some marriages with healthy patterns, the couple has no sex. But we know that when husbands improve attraction in the areas of masculine leadership, protector, and provider qualities as well as when wives improve their physical appearance, this generally increases attraction and sex with each other.

The statistics regarding a low frequency of sex in marriage are telling.[1] Additional research from the Kinsey Institute agrees with these estimates.[2]

- More than seven times a week: 3 percent
- Seven times a week: 1 percent
- Six times a week: 3 percent
- Five times a week: 9 percent
- Four times a week: 11 percent
- Three times a week: 13 percent
- Two times a week: 21 percent
- Once a week: 25 percent
- Once a month: 8 percent
- Less than once a month: 9 percent

Roughly 17 percent of marriages are sexless, and if you consider a frequency of once a week low, that number jumps up to 42 percent. Although marriages with a higher frequency of sex encounter divorce, too, this number is nearly equal to the approximate rate of 40 percent of first marriages dissolving although this number has been slightly declining over time.[3]

This roughly coincides with the marriages that appear to trend toward headship or away from it.

- Husband leads/in control: 22 percent
- Equal, but husband is more equal: 33 percent
- Egalitarian: 27 percent
- Equal, but wife is more equal: 13 percent
- Wife leads/in control: 4 percent

Fifty-five percent of marriages are husband-led or under the assumption that they are husband-led, while 44 percent of relationships are wife-led. Yes, egalitarian marriages are wife-led as someone always takes up the reins of leadership. Inversion of roles and rebellion dysfunctional patterns often result in decreased sex, so this is an interesting correlation to note.

One other common cultural assumption is that when men do more housework, this results in more sex as wives have more time free to want to have sex. This is false.

Our results do not support the notion that more egalitarian divisions of labor are associated with higher sexual frequency. Instead, we find that households in which men do more traditionally male labor and women do more traditionally female labor report higher sexual frequency. This suggests that among heterosexual couples, the relationship between housework and a couple's sex life is governed by a gendered set of sexual scripts.[4]

Husbands doing traditionally masculine chores, such as fixing up the house, yard work, and taking out the trash, as opposed to doing the dishes, laundry, and other cleaning were associated with higher sexual frequency. You need to be gracious to each other if you or your wife is overworked—you can help out with each other's chores. However, excessively adding to your burdens with so-called "choreplay"—a combination of chores and foreplay—won't bring about a sexually positive result. The reason for this should be obvious to you: you can't work hard enough to placate your wife or make her want to have more sex with you. It's not borne from genuine desire.

The church's slow cooker analogy of sex is faulty as we saw when debunking the paradigm of godliness is sexy. In fact, when the husband leads the sexual interaction with the wife with more *gusto*, sex tends to be more enjoyable for both the husband and the wife.[5]

Type of sex (most preferred)	Male		Female
Gentle (slow, rhythmic)	35%	>	17%
Not-so-gentle (faster, harder)	62%	<	70%
Rough (spanking, hair-pulling)	3%	<	13%

This makes sense—given that husband-led marriages are God's design—for both the non-sexual and sexual parts of the marriage. It should not be surprising that wives tend to prefer faster and harder sex, either. It is important to understand where each gender is coming from in relationship to sexual behavior.

- A husband's sexual passion is heightened when he wants to possess his wife.
- A wife's sexual passion is heightened when she is possessed by her husband.

Faster and harder sex as opposed to slower and rhythmic sex shows a husband's heightened passion to sexually possess his wife while her husband's passion for her inflames her own passion to be possessed. Many husbands who have fallen into dysfunctional relationship patterns and have seen decreases in sex will default to slow and rhythmic sex, thinking that this is the style that their wife prefers, not realizing that they are only sabotaging themselves further.

Christian women are not immune to pornography though their preferred form of pornography is romance novels. Is it any wonder that these bodice-ripper novels often have a muscular, sexy, famous, rich man on the cover and in the story? Is it any wonder that this man who has it all can't help but try to aggressively possess the woman he is seducing—while the female reader imagines herself as the heroine? Look no further than the popularity of *50 Shades of Grey* even among Christian women. A novel that has been universally acknowledged with terrible writing is the fastest-selling novel of all time and has sold more than 125 million copies worldwide.

Yes, Christians can ironically learn from pornography, but this should also come as no surprise. One of the ways the Bible teaches us concepts is by doing things a certain way, but it also teaches us the pitfalls of what not to do and what temptations to avoid. The one important concept we can learn from pornography is that men and women are tempted by certain things—bodice rippers, in the case of women. This might be exacerbated if they are not being properly fulfilled within marriage.

> The husband must fulfill his duty to his wife, and likewise also the wife to her husband. The wife does not have authority over her own

body, but the husband does; and likewise also the husband does not have authority over his own body, but the wife does. Stop depriving one another, except by agreement for a time, so that you may devote yourselves to prayer, and come together again so that Satan will not tempt you because of your lack of self-control (1 Corinthians 7:3–5).

Though the scriptures do not speak to the type of sex that husbands and wives prefer, this gives us freedom of choice. A husband who is fulfilling his duty to his wife, no matter the type of sex—slow and rhythmic, fast and hard, or hair-pulling—will influence her to be less tempted by romance novels and other explicit material. A wife who is fulfilling her duty to her husband with her own enthusiasm for sex will influence her husband to be less tempted toward pornography. This doesn't excuse a husband or wife from making choices to look at or read pornography or step outside the marriage, but they might be complicit in influencing their spouse to be tempted.

All of this is to say that husbands need to take up the mantle of leadership within both the non-sexual and the sexual aspect of marriage as this is important to a godly marriage. The process usually ends up as follows:

1. The husband starts to put God and His marital roles and responsibilities first.
2. As the husband asserts himself as the head of marriage—for the first time or again—by leading in the non-sexual parts of the marriage, he is now more attractive to his wife.
3. His improved attraction leads to less rejections from his wife when it comes to sex.
4. Fewer rejections from his wife over sex empower him to be more confident and lead sex faster and harder, which increases his wife's passion.
5. Both the husband and the wife are now more fulfilled and happier with their marriage and sex life.

This is a general pattern that we see in how dysfunctional marriages can become functional again.

Remember, it's not wrong to want to please your wife outside or inside the bedroom, but you should be doing it from the perspective of leading with passion. This is especially true in the bedroom. When you don't care about her pleasure and passionately do what you want, you can actually meet her needs.

REPENTANCE IS IMPORTANT FOR SANCTIFICATION

The husband as the head of the marriage rightly bears more responsibility as he is in a position of authority, but that does not mean that the wife doesn't have her own responsibilities. For example, remember the earlier section about God and Jesus leading perfectly. You might lead perfectly, but a wife can still choose to rebel or walk away. Of course, husbands are not perfect like God or Jesus, so there is usually enough blame to go around to both parties.

As we saw in the previous section, dysfunctional patterns, such as the inversion of roles and sexless marriages, tend to improve with obedience to God and following God's marital roles and responsibilities. One of the things you will realize as you become a godly, strong leader is that your wife might become increasingly attracted to you in the bedroom and start to follow your lead. This is wonderful, yet it is not the end goal.

What if—God forbid—you suddenly became disabled or came down with cancer? When it rains it pours, so this resulted in the loss of your job. That would certainly affect your ability to be a masculine leader, protector, and provider. In this case, since you are not able to operate at your best, does your marriage fall back into similar dysfunction with an inversion of roles and a lack of sex? No, it shouldn't. From worst-case scenarios like this, we can see that fixing the problems of the marriage might not be as easy as you thought.

Stepping back for a moment, in many cases, a Christian husband knows the Bible verses about sex, such as 1 Corinthians 7. Yet, even if he brings up these passages to his wife, she will still deny him sex. In these situations, the wife is choosing her own feelings over the Bible, God, and her husband. When the husband starts to lead by example through putting God first and working on the marital roles and responsibilities, this starts to turn around. He becomes more attractive. His wife starts to want to have more sex with him. From this, we understand that modeling behavior through leading by example is more effective than brow-beating someone with Bible verses even though telling them these scriptures should motivate them to change, especially if they call themselves a Christian.

After the husband becomes a better masculine leader, protector, and provider, his wife is also more receptive to the scriptures on sex. Funny how that works. Yet if the husband were to become disabled and lose his job, he will become less attractive and will not be able to perform his roles and responsibilities as well. The marriage will be strained and might start to default back into those similar dysfunctional patterns, even heading toward divorce.

This is where the sanctification process comes in. It is not enough to simply be the leader in your marriage and have a healthy sex life. The husband needs to be actively teaching his wife to put God first rather than her feelings. For instance, if she's angry or disagrees with a decision, how can she approach her husband respectfully and submissively? If her husband isn't treating her correctly for whatever reason, will she respond graciously or kindly and not with snark or contentiousness?

- A wife that naturally starts to follow her husband's lead again has not repented of her past sinful actions. The marriage might have improved, but her disposition has not fundamentally changed without her repentance.
- The goal is to teach your wife all the marital roles and responsibilities and help her become a mature Christian in the faith.

You need to call your wife to repentance for her past sinful behavior against you and help her on the road to sanctification to be more holy after her repentance. That way, if some horrible calamity befalls your marriage, she has the spiritual and practical maturity to weather the difficult circumstances with you instead of giving into her human nature and defaulting back to dysfunctional relationship patterns and possibly even divorce.

DEMAND OBEDIENCE BUT ACCEPT THE PROCESS

One of the hardest things for husbands in today's culture and even in the church to do is to demand and expect obedience from his wife. Remember Jesus's words to His disciples and the church: If you love me, obey my commandments (John 13 and 15).

This flies directly in the face of the culture. The majority of the church has taken a lukewarm position on this, trying to marry headship with feminist teachings. Some in the church say that the wife is responsible to submit and that her husband can't tell her to do that. Jesus said differently, and Christ and the church is the model for husbands and wives. The husband is responsible for helping to sanctify his wife, which means that he needs to help her obey him.

The hard part of demanding obedience is doing it in love while not coming off as authoritarian. For instance, if you make a decision, always expect her to obey even if she disagrees. Even if she has a poor attitude, don't worry about that. As she develops the habit of submission and obedience, her attitude will gradually start to change. Though attitudes affect actions, actions turned into habits will affect attitudes.

If she disagrees and rebels, you will need to lead by example instead of trying to browbeat her with the Bible. But you must also make a note to come back to and address the issue later after emotions have calmed down and/or she has a change of heart. Addressing disobedience during rebellion doesn't work as she is already rebelling. Repentance can only be had when she acknowledges wrong and changes her heart.

The sanctification process in the light of dysfunctional marriage patterns takes time. Your wife will need to transcend her emotions and other circumstances to do what you say, even if it is hard and if both of your emotions are running high.

Be persistent and never give up on God's expectations for your marriage. You should expect that your wife will become godlier and more obedient. Make sure that she is aware that you are grateful when she is obedient yet displeased and not overbearing when she isn't. All the same, you still love her. The constant expectation to do what is godly is a powerful motivating force both for you as the godly leader of the marriage and for her to cast off her rebellion, especially as you continue to lead by example.

Chapter 20
COMMON PITFALLS TO MARITAL INTERACTIONS

YOU'RE NOT RESPONSIBLE FOR YOUR WIFE'S EMOTIONS

Any words or actions that a husband takes regarding his wife are not about making her happy but rather to draw her closer to Christ. Husbands and men must realize that women's feelings will fluctuate as will the feelings of men.

Feelings are neither wrong nor right. But we are responsible for how we act despite our emotions.

One example of this is when the husband and wife disagree on a subject, but the husband makes the final decision to do it his way. The wife might be upset or unhappy about it. Do not attempt to try to fix her or reason with her emotions. You can't reason emotions away. The right thing to do is to thank her for her input on the decision. You will be responsible for any consequences. Give her a hug and move on.

Husbands tend to have a difficult time leading effectively when their wife has negative emotions. Again, our job is not necessarily to police our spouse's emotions. The scriptures don't tell you to make her feel differently, but as the head, you must facilitate her on the right path toward God. She will need to make a decision about what to do with her feelings though your words and actions can facilitate her away from focusing on them in many cases. The scriptures rarely emphasize our feelings but focus on our conduct in love.

When men attempt to fix a woman's emotional state, they are confirming that her emotions are her husband's responsibility, which usually makes her dwell on how she's feeling and makes matters worse. This is very difficult for men, especially husbands, to learn, because men are doers. If we see a problem, we like to do something to fix it. Unfortunately, that is the wrong approach. You can no more fix a woman's emotional state than you can control how they act. Attempting to do so will set you up for failure.

Think of it this way: if you were angry or sad and someone tried to come and make you feel differently, wouldn't that frustrate you further? Sometimes the best thing to do is let it be and give her time to process through her emotions on her own. In some cases, you might even have to remind her that you can't fix her emotions, and she needs to take responsibility for them. You can help her if needed, but each person is responsible for their own emotions and their own behavior.

Happiness is not the be-all end-all of marriage. We certainly want to be happy and want our spouse to be happy, but it is not always possible all the time. Avoid making the mistake of focusing on making your wife happy all the time. Emotions come and go like the wind. You can't grasp them or change them, so don't even attempt to do so. Otherwise you fall prey to the cultural mantra, happy wife, happy life, which is ungodly and destructive to marriage.

WOMEN THINK AND FEEL DIFFERENTLY THAN MEN AND HAVE DIFFERENT NEEDS THAN MEN DO

We went over all the gender differences in prior chapters, but a reminder and new insight is helpful, especially if you are married. In the world today, Christians implicitly buy into the secular lie that men and women are the same except for the anatomy between their legs.

The scriptures emphasize these differences.

- Nourish and cherish your wife (Ephesians 5).
- Don't become bitter toward your wife (Colossians 3).
- Live with her in an understanding way as the weaker vessel (1 Peter 3).
- Give her honor as a fellow co-heir in Christ (1 Peter 3).

Likewise, the scriptures are clear that you will need different responses, depending on the attitudes or actions.

> We urge you, brethren, admonish the unruly, encourage the fainthearted, help the weak, be patient with everyone. See that no one

repays another with evil for evil, but always seek after that which is good for one another and for all people (1 Thessalonians 5:14–15).

What wives need from their husbands aren't answers and solutions but a strong man to comfort, support, and hold her when she is buffeted by the storms of life and her emotions. Men tend to internally process motions while women want to talk about and externally process them. This is not to say that you need to be at the beck and call of her emotions every time they go crazy but take them into consideration.

We looked at some of the aspects of the Big Five Personality test (scientifically reliable unlike the more popular Myers-Briggs Type Indicator), which shows that women tend to score higher on neuroticism, agreeableness, and different aspects of extraversion.

Neuroticism describes the tendency to experience negative emotion and related processes in response to perceived threat and punishment; these include anxiety, depression, anger, self-consciousness, and emotional lability. Women have been found to score higher than men on Neuroticism as measured at the Big Five trait level, as well as on most facets of Neuroticism included in a common measure of the Big Five, the NEO-PI-R.

Agreeableness comprises traits relating to altruism, such as empathy and kindness. Agreeableness involves the tendency toward cooperation, maintenance of social harmony, and consideration of the concerns of others (as opposed to exploitation or victimization of others). Women consistently score higher than men on Agreeableness and related measures, such as tender-mindedness.

Women tend to score higher than men on Warmth, Gregariousness, and Positive Emotions, whereas men score higher than women on Assertiveness and Excitement Seeking.[1]

Keep these areas in mind as it takes practice to understand and determine when your wife needs:

- A Listening Ear
- Comfort
- Support

- A Big Hug
- Affection
- Her Other Needs Met

If your wife is more neurotic (experiences negative emotions) than other women, you must minimize or eliminate your anger and frustration when you are discussing difficult topics or correcting her. She'll pick up more on the negative emotions and perceive them as threatening or punishing when that might not even be the case. Likewise, husbands tend to be more justice-and-righteousness oriented while wives tend to be more gracious-and-mercy oriented. This justice-and-righteousness approach can come off as mean and insensitive to women at times. When approaching her about difficult topics, kindness and gentleness will go a long way. Children need both their father and mother as their understanding of the gospel and the Christian walk is influenced by both.

Though all women have these needs, each one expresses them differently. It can be helpful to sit down with your wife and talk with her about better communication in these different situations. Men are not mind readers even though women assume we sometimes are.

Another way to consider this topic is through the expression, "women need flavor with food."

In this analogy, reason and logic are like food, and emotions are like flavor. In the context of Christians, scripture is the foundation of our reason and logic. This is how we properly align our values, our morals, and our consciences to see and understand how to live a godly life.

Men tend to do a bit better compartmentalizing issues because of how our brains are wired, but a dish doesn't exist to women if it is separated into individual ingredients. In fact, individual ingredients are simply distasteful. Blunt truth without perceived kindness is mean and might not communicate a point well. However, genuine concern with kindness, even in difficult topics, will help convey your meaning.

Therefore, it is important to engage in conflict (and at all times) with the fruit of the Spirit.

MARRIAGE COUNSELING CAN WORK BUT CAN FAIL

Marriage counseling can work in some very specific cases but will not always bring consistent, godly, positive results.

Marriage counseling works when a husband is busy with his life at church, work, and involvement with others. He might not have much time for his wife. He might rarely express his love for her for whatever reason. This archetype is of the loving husband who is already set on his mission but who needs to become more invested in the relationship. The wife doesn't know how she fits into her husband's leadership and doesn't feel valued. She wants reassurance that she is a priority to her husband. This seems to be the case with most pastors when the wife feels neglected. One of the problems is that when pastors are asked to counsel members of their congregation, they only have this limited perspective, which does not work for other marital problems.

Marriage counseling also works when it comes to misplaced responsibilities. An example of this is when a marriage counselor knows scripture and can tell a wife to stop focusing on other distractions and listen to her husband. A wife might learn about what a wife should do via marriage counseling, marriage books, the church, or even the culture. But this is not what her husband wants her to do. In this case, he wants to lead her in a certain way, but she is taking leadership cues from other sources. He might need to sit her down and explain how he wants to lead the marriage and tell her to ignore these outside sources of information that are not helping their marriage.

Another reason that marriage counseling might fail is the inadvertent one-upmanship that can happen in marriage counseling. For example, if a marriage counselor tells a husband to work on X, Y, and Z in front of the wife, the wife can develop the attitude of "I told you so," which is extremely counterproductive to developing respect for her husband. In other words, the wife is now submitting to the counselor and what the counselor says instead of submitting to her own husband.

In other cases, marriage counseling does not work because it does not address the root issues. The issue of a lack of sex is often due to a lack of attraction or both sexes eschewing their marital roles and responsibilities. Marital counseling can fall into a works-based mindset rather than a desire-based mindset or the attitude of continually working and doing things to fix the marriage.

Marital counseling can fail if it uses a works-based approach to marriage. This approach uses books, such as *The 5 Love Languages*. The counselor and

~~your wife expect you to learn her love language and demonstrate it so that she feels more loved. But you're basically being told what to do, which reinforces the dysfunctional pattern of inverted roles and makes you a slave to how your wife is feeling. You have to continue to work, work, work to earn your wife's favor.~~

~~Good Christian counseling should focus squarely on the Christian walk.~~ The Holy Spirit's transformation in our lives is from the inside out. We must be willing to actively participate with the Holy Spirit to assume our proper roles and responsibilities in the marriage—first to honor God, which will lead toward behavior that reflects this inner change.

AVOID COVERT CONTRACTS

Robert Glover has a popular book, *No More Mr. Nice Guy*, which elaborates on the existence of covert contracts.

- A Nice Guy's primary goal is to make other people happy.
- Nice Guys are dependent on external validation and avoid conflict like the plague.

Nice Guys are guided by the following three covert contracts:

- If I am a good guy, then everyone [should] love me and like me (and people I desire will desire me).
- If I meet other people's needs without them having to ask, then they [should also] meet my needs without me having to ask.
- If I do everything right, then I will have a smooth, problem-free life.

These covert contracts operate at an unconscious level. They don't work for a number of reasons, but Nice Guys are convinced they should.

Because most Nice Guys believe they have kept their side of the contract, they often feel helpless and resentful when other people (and the world) don't keep their side of the contract.[2]

You might recognize the errors of nice guys right away as we have already discussed some of them.

How does this apply to us? We are not concerned about being nice but about being holy. Unfortunately, people can easily slip into a pattern of covert contracts as a Christian, especially with the scriptures.

For instance, a husband who is following his roles and responsibilities in marriage as a masculine leader, protector, and provider will become more objectively attractive to his wife. Usually—not always—this will result in more sex. If it doesn't, the husband might feel helpless and resentful.

Can you see the covert contract?

The unmet covert contract is an expectation that the other person will do something in return, in this case, more sex. When that expectation is not met, the result is anger, hurt, and bitterness. We can only influence others through our actions. We can't change them, make them change, or fix them.

Covert contracts are always based on a works mindset rather than on desire. You think that doing something for another person will make them do something for you. The key is to operate from a desire mindset instead. You need to let go of the expectation that the other person *owes* you anything. A husband who falls prey to covert contracts is sabotaging his own efforts. If he gets angry, resentful, or depressed, this will negatively influence his wife away from the very thing that he is trying to accomplish.

The key thing to remember is that we are primarily following God's roles and responsibilities for marriage to honor Him. He's at the center of what we are doing. God can use our behavior and influence to change hearts but it might not happen right away if at all. We need to be ready and prepared to honor God even if our situations never change. He is giving us the grace to walk through these situations with His Spirit, which leads us to contentment, peace, and joy despite whether those around us are influenced to become more like Him. It's ultimately not about us; it's about Him.

SHOULD WIVES/MOTHERS WORK OUTSIDE THE HOME?

Many different, strong opinions exist about this even in the Christian community.

The scriptures do not discuss this extensively, which does mean there is considerable freedom. Titus 2 counsels younger wives (with children) to be workers at home though the passage does not specify what it means to be a worker at home. Those in first-world countries might interpret this as a stay-at-home mother, but this has not traditionally been the case in most cultures. The women and wives helped in many family businesses and trades. Thus workers from home can indicate childcare as well as part-time work from home. The virtuous wife in Proverbs 31 seems to have some sort of business that she runs out of her house.

The husband should marry a wife who will follow what he determines to be the best course of action. Not all families have the luxury of the husband and father earning enough money for the wife to stay at home. This was true even in Bible times. One could argue that working outside the home is an extenuating circumstance, but it underscores the need for leadership and provision.

It might be best to think of this in terms of priorities:

- It is preferable if your wife stays at home with the kids and possibly works part-time.
- If not, it is preferable if she has a job that works well with the kids' school schedules, such as a grade-school teaching job or nursing with flexible shift schedules or other part-time employment.
- If not, your wife might have to work full-time as a last resort.

Keep some general things in mind. Of course, you as the man should be working full-time and possibly picking up extra jobs here and there. As we have discussed previously, a correlation exists toward increased divorce when women earn more than men or when they are tasked with the provision for the marriage. Circumstances, such as losing a job or a call to a specific ministry, might be out of your control, so there are exceptions.

Today's world is very technologically advanced but very socially isolated. If your wife can stay at home and work from home with the children, make sure she can be involved with family, friends, church, and other social interaction. Social isolation can negatively influence both men and women, so you need to ensure that this doesn't happen to your wife if she stays home.

DO YOUR JOB AND GO ABOVE AND BEYOND

The most successful NFL coach of all time, Bill Belichick, is famous for the phrase, "Do your job."[3] This is important in team sports, especially in the NFL where eleven players on offense, defense, and special teams all need to work in unison. If one person is not doing what they are supposed to do, the team might lose opportunities to score or give up points to their opponents.

The Bible is very much like this when it comes to marital roles and responsibilities. Ultimately you need to focus on "doing your job." Jesus talks in a similar way in the parable of the talents (Matthew 25) and the parable of the minas (Luke 19). Each servant was entrusted with talents or minas by the master who eventually settled accounts with them. The ones that did well heard, "Well done, good and faithful servant" while those who did not had their talents/minas taken away and were punished.

We have been given stewardship of biblical marital roles and responsibilities. A wife's stewardship is measured through her role and responsibility as a wife. A husband's stewardship is measured through his role and responsibility as a husband. Each of these is different in the scriptures. A wife gains nothing through usurping her husband's role and responsibility. Indeed, it can be said that by usurping her husband's role and responsibility, she neglects her own. Thus, she is being irresponsible with what she has been given in addition to being rebellious.

A wife gains nothing by loving her husband. But she will gain much from respecting her husband. A husband gains nothing by respecting his wife. Rather he gains much by loving his wife. A wife gains nothing by allowing her husband to lead. But she gains much from following his lead and submitting to him. A husband gains nothing by letting his wife be the head or by being passive. Yet he gains much by being the head of his wife and his family.

We are often so desperate to rebel against the simplicity of God's marital roles and responsibilities for the husband and the wife that we miss the bigger picture. Paul, inspired by the Holy Spirit, had to write these commands to the church because they were going off track and following secular culture. These are simply the minimum requirements for godly living in marriage.

Jesus came to give us life and life abundantly, and true abundance in Christ is about doing so much more than just these basics. If only we could get over ourselves and be humble enough to walk in the ways of our God rather than choose to rebel against His design.

As we begin to walk into what He calls us to in scripture, we will then partner with the Holy Spirit and experience His peace and joy. That peace and joy will multiply despite our circumstances, our successes, and our failures. God will truly be able to shine a light with our lives.

CONCLUSION

This book was written to help guide you in understanding the importance of the scriptures and how walking into manhood by following them will help you learn to grow in discipleship in Christ.

Whether you are single, in a relationship, or married, you can always continue to grow deeper in becoming a more mature Christian who can live out the roles and responsibilities that God has given us with the fruit of the Spirit. God has given us grace and mercy so that we can become salt and light to those around us. Yet we often become caught up in our own feelings and circumstances and walk away from Him instead of toward Him. First Timothy 6:12 says, "Fight the good fight for the true faith. Hold tightly to the eternal life to which God has called you, which you have confessed so well before many witnesses."

Let us continue to stand upon His Word, even when it isn't popular according to culture or even in the church. Be wary of the enemy's lies and deceptions that tend to creep in through the culture and sometimes even the church. It is never wrong to do the right thing and trust that God is faithful with what He says in His Word.

NOTES

Chapter 1

1. Frank Newport, "Percentage of Christians in U.S. Drifting Down, but Still High" *Gallup*, December 24, 2015, http://www.gallup.com/poll/187955/percentage-christians-drifting-down-high.aspx

Chapter 2

1. Andrea Veltman and Mark Piper, eds., *Autonomy, Oppression, and Gender (Studies in Feminist Philosophy)* (Cambridge: Oxford University Press, 2014).
2. Katie Drummond, "Are You a 'Benevolent' Sexist?", *Prevention*, December 6, 2012, http://www.prevention.com/mind-body/emotional-health/both-women-and-men-display-attitudes-benevolent-sexism
3. Mona Chalabi, "Dear Mona, How Many Flight Attendants Are Men?", *FiveThirtyEight*, October 12, 2014, http://fivethirtyeight.com/datalab/dear-mona-how-many-flight-attendants-are-men
4. Rowan Scarborough, "Army May Train Women for Rigor of Front Lines," *The Washington Times*, July 30, 2012, http://www.washingtontimes.com/news/2012/jul/30/army-may-train-women-for-rigor-of-front-lines/#ixzz3HHni04o
5. *Oxford Dictionary online*, s.v., "feminism (n.)," accessed October 16, 2018, http://en.oxforddictionaries.com/definition/feminism
6. Betsy Hart, "Hart: Men Are Meant to Protect Women and Children," *The Daily Republic*, February 25, 2011, http://dailyrepublic.com/archives/hart-men-are-meant-to-protect-women-and-children
7. Fareed Zakaria, "To Hell in a Handbasket," *The New York Times*, April 19, 1998, http://www.nytimes.com/1998/04/19/books/to-hell-in-a-handbasket.html
8. Unknown, "Topics of the Times," *The New York Times*, April 19, 1912, http://query.nytimes.com/gst/abstract.html?res=F20611FE3E5813738DDDA00994DC405B828DF1D3
9. A N Wilson, "Whatever Happened to Women and Children First?", *The Daily Mail*, January 17, 2012, http://www.dailymail.co.uk/debate/article-2087585/Cruise-ship-Costa-Concordia-sinking-Whatever-happened-women-children-first.html
10. Betty Friedan, *The Feminine Mystique* (New York: W.W. Norton and Co., 1963).
11. Jenna Goudreau, "20 Surprising Jobs Women Are Taking Over," *Forbes*, March 7, 2011, http://www.forbes.com/sites/jennagoudreau/2011/03/07/20-surprising-jobs-women-are-taking-over

12. Mona Chalabi, "Dear Mona, How Many Flight Attendants Are Men?", *FiveThirtyEight*, October 3, 2014, http://fivethirtyeight.com/features/dear-mona-how-many-flight-attendants-are-men
13. Belinda Luscombe, "Workplace Salaries. At Last, Women on Top," *Time*, September 1, 2010, http://www.time.com/time/business/article/0,8599,2015274,00.html
14. Olinka Koster, "Women Are More Unhappy Despite 40 Years of Feminism, Claims Study," *Daily Mail*, June 1, 2009, http://www.dailymail.co.uk/femail/article-1189894/Women-happy-years-ago-.html
15. Meghan Casserly, "Is 'Opting Out' The New American Dream For Working Women?", *Forbes*, September 12, 2012, http://www.forbes.com/sites/meghancasserly/2012/09/12/is-opting-out-the-new-american-dream-for-working-women
16. Dana Hamplová, "Does Work Make Mothers Happy?", *Journal of Happiness Studies*, January 12, 2018, https://link.springer.com/article/10.1007/s10902-018-9958-2. p. 1-27.
17. Carrie L. Lukas, The Politically Incorrect Guide to Women, Sex and Feminism (Washington, D.C.: Regnery Publishing, 2006).
18. Rod Dreher, "Sex After Christianity," *The American Conservative*, April 11, 2013, http://www.theamericanconservative.com/articles/sex-after-christianity
19. Hanna Rosin, "Boys on the Side," *The Atlantic*, September 2012, http://www.theatlantic.com/magazine/archive/2012/09/boys-on-the-side/309062
20. Kate Bolick, "All the Single Ladies," *The Atlantic* November 2011, http://www.theatlantic.com/magazine/archive/2011/11/all-the-single-ladies/308654/11
21. Helen Smith, "8 Reasons Straight Men Don't Want To Get Married," *Huffington Post*, June 20, 2013, http://www.huffingtonpost.com/helen-smith/8-reasons-men-dont-want-t_b_3467778.html
22. Penny Young Nance, "Why Does America Have So Many 'Peter Pan' Men?", *Fox News Live*, October 7, 2011, http://www.foxnews.com/opinion/2011/10/07/why-does-america-have-so-many-peter-pan-men
23. Jordan Peterson, "The Tragic Story of the Man-Child," *YouTube*, July 27, 2017, http://www.youtube.com/watch?v=JjfClL6nogo
24. Richard Stim, "Breach of Contract: Material Breach," *Nolo*, accessed October 15, 2018, http://www.nolo.com/legal-encyclopedia/breach-of-contract-material-breach-32655.html
25. Jane Anderson, "The Impact of Family Structure on the Health of Children: Effects of Divorce," *US National Library of Medicine National Institutes of Health*, November, 2014, http://www.ncbi.nlm.nih.gov/pmc/articles/PMC4240051
26. ibid.
27. George A. Akerlof, Janet L. Yellen, "An Analysis of Out-of-Wedlock Births in the United States," *Brookings*, August 1, 1996, http://www.brookings.edu/research/an-analysis-of-out-of-wedlock-births-in-the-united-states
28. Sheri Stritof, "Estimated Median Age of First Marriage by Gender: 1890 to 2015," *The Spruce*, August 4, 2018, http://www.thespruce.com/estimated-median-age-marriage-2303878
29. "Induced Abortion in the United States," *Guttmacher Institute*, January 2018, http://www.guttmacher.org/fact-sheet/induced-abortion-united-states

30. "Statistics," *The Fatherless Generation*, April 2010, accessed October 15, 2018, http://thefatherlessgeneration.wordpress.com/statistics/
31. Jeanine Martin, "What Do ALL the Mass Shooters Have in Common? No Father in the Home," *The Bull Elephant*, February 14, 2018, http://thebullelephant.com/what-do-all-the-mass-shooters-have-in-common-no-father-in-the-home

Chapter 3

1. David Murrow, *Why Men Hate Going to Church* (Nashville: Thomas Nelson, 2011).
2. ibid.
3. ibid.
4. John Gray, *Men Are from Mars, Women Are from Venus: Practical Guide for Improving Communication and Getting What You Want in Your Relationships* (New York City: HarperCollins, 1992).
5. Leon J. Podles, "The Church Impotent: The Feminization of Christianity," Leon J. Podles (website), 2010, accessed October 15, 2018, http://podles.org/church-impotent.htm
6. ibid.
7. Holly Pivec, "The Feminization of the Church Why Its Music, Messages and Ministries Are Driving Men Away," *Biola magazine*, Spring 2006, http://magazine.biola.edu/article/06-spring/the-feminization-of-the-church
8. Charles Taylor, *A Secular Age* (Cambridge, MA: The Belknap Press of Harvard University Press, 2007).
9. Callum G. Brown, *The Death of Christian Britain: Understanding Secularisation, 1800-2000 (Christianity and Society in the Modern World)* (Abingdon: Routledge, 2007).
10. ibid.
11. ibid.
12. Carolyn Curtis James, *Malestrom: Manhood Swept into the Currents of a Changing World* (Grand Rapids: Zondervan, 2015).
13. Glenn T. Stanton, "Why Man and Woman Are Not Equal," *First Things* (blog), August 26, 2016, accessed October 15, 2018, http://www.firstthings.com/blogs/firstthoughts/2016/08/why-man-and-woman-are-not-equal
14. Matt Chandler, "Woman's Hurdles," *TVC Resources.net*, November 2, 2014, http://www.tvcresources.net/resource-library/sermons/womans-hurdles
15. Matt Chandler, "Jesus Wants the Rose," *YouTube*, February 3, 2009, http://www.youtube.com/watch?v=bLgIecL1IdY
16. Henry Allen, "The Messiah of Masculinity," *The Wall Street Journal*, November 4, 2016, http://www.wsj.com/articles/the-messiah-of-masculinity-1478280156
17. "The Art of Manliness," *The Art of Manliness* (blog), accessed October 15, 2018, http://www.artofmanliness.com/tag/christianity
18. Brett and Kate Mckay, "When Christianity was Muscular," *The Art of Manliness* (blog), accessed October 15, 2018, http://www.artofmanliness.com/articles/when-christianity-was-muscular

19. ibid.
20. Joy Tibbs, "The Rise and Fall of Mark Driscoll," *Premier Christianity*, December 2014, http://www.premierchristianity.com/Past-Issues/2014/December-2014/The-rise-and-fall-of-Mark-Driscoll

Chapter 4

1. Blue Letter Bible, online, http://www.blueletterbible.org/lang/lexicon/lexicon.cfm?t=kjv&strongs=h8669, *tĕshuwqah* = desire.
2. Leslie McFall, PhD, "Good Order in the Church," (blog), accessed October 30, 2018, http://lmf12.wordpress.com/good-order-in-the-church
3. "With Great Power Comes Great Responsibility," *Quote Investigator*, accessed October 15, 2018, http://quoteinvestigator.com/2015/07/23/great-power
4. Wayne Grudem, "Personal Reflections on the History of the CBMW and the State of the Gender Debate," *The Journal for Biblical Manhood & Womanhood*, Spring 2009, http://cbmw.org/wp-content/uploads/2013/05/14-1.pdf

Chapter 6

1. Adapted from Busby, Carroll, and Willoughby (2010). "Compatibility or restraint? The effects of sexual timing on marriage relationships," *Journal of Family Psychology*, 24, 766 – 774.
2. ibid; . . . Andrew Francis-Tan and Hugo M. Mialon, "'A Diamond Is Forever' and Other Fairy Tales: The Relationship Between Wedding Expenses and Marriage Duration," *Wiley Online Library*, March 10, 2015, http://onlinelibrary.wiley.com/doi/abs/10.1111/j.1741-3737.2012.00996.x
3. Strong's Concordance, online edition, http://www.biblestudytools.com/concordances/strongs-exhaustive-concordance, G1937/G1939 for *epithumia/epithumeo*; G1135 for *gune*.

Chapter 8

1. Wayne Grudem, *Countering the Claims of Evangelical Feminism: Biblical Responses to the Key Questions* (Colorado Springs: Multnomah Publishers, 2006), 26.
2. These two articles reveal Myers-Briggs is not scientifically valid: Adam Grant, "Goodbye to MBTI, the Fad that Won't Die," *Psychology Today*, September 18, 2013, http://www.psychologytoday.com/us/blog/give-and-take/201309/goodbye-mbti-the-fad-won-t-die; . . . Roman Krznaric, "Have We All Been Duped by the Myers-Briggs Test?", *Fortune*, May 15, 2013, http://fortune.com/2013/05/15/have-we-all-been-duped-by-the-myers-briggs-test; . . . This article makes a case for the Big Five method: Maggie Koerth-Baker, "Most Personality Quizzes are Junk Science. I Found One That Isn't," *FiveThirtyEight*, January 2, 2018, http://fivethirtyeight.com/features/most-personality-quizzes-are-junk-science-i-found-one-that-isnt
3. Patti Breitman & Connie Hatch, *How to Say No Without Feeling Guilty* (New York: Broadway Books, 2000).

Chapter 9

1. Statistics taken from http://thefatherlessgeneration.wordpress.com/statistics (individual sources are cited on this website).

Chapter 10

1. Donal Graeme, "Going Ape—What Attributes do Women Find Attractive in Men? Looks, Athleticism, Money, Power and Status (LAMPS)," *Donal Graeme* (blog), July 21, 2013, accessed October 15, 2018, http://donalgraeme.wordpress.com/2013/07/21/going-ape-what-attributes-do-women-find-attractive-in-men-looks-athleticism-money-power-and-status-lamps
2. Aaron M. Renn, "The Masculinist #17: The Basis of Attraction," *Urbanophile*, January 12, 2018, http://www.urbanophile.com/wp-content/uploads/2018/03/The-Masculinist-17-The-Basis-of-Attraction.pdf
3. "How To Be More Attractive (Regardless Of Your Height)," *The Modest Man*, April 4, 2017, http://www.themodestman.com/how-to-be-attractive
4. There have been several studies performed on waist-to-hip ratios. Here are a few I drew from: http://ncbi.nlm.nih.gov/pmc/articles/PMC4050298, http://ncbi.nlm.nih.gov/pmc/articles/PMC4401783, http://ncbi.nlm.nih.gov/pubmed/17160976, http://ncbi.nlm.nih.gov/pmc/articles/PMC2918777
5. "Hypergamy," *Wikipedia* entry, http://en.wikipedia.org/wiki/Hypergamy
6. Elizabeth Cashdan, "Women's Mating Strategies," *Evolutionary Anthropology*, 1996, 5(4), 134-143.
7. Gary Chapman, *The 5 Love Languages: The Secret to Love that Lasts* (Chicago: Northfield Publishing, 1995).

Chapter 11

1. Wikipedia, s.v., "Chivalry," accessed October 15, 2018, http://en.wikipedia.org/wiki/Chivalry.
2. Stephen Arterburn, *Every Man's Marriage: An Every Man's Guide to Winning the Heart of a Woman* (Colorado Springs: WaterBrook, 2010), 57.
3. ibid, 107-108.
4. Douglas Wilson, *Reforming Marriage* (Moscow, ID: Canon Press, 2009), 9-10.
5. R. Albert Mohler, "The Seduction of Pornography and the Integrity of Christian Marriage, Part 2," *The Christian Post*, June 2, 2012, http://www.christianpost.com/news/the-seduction-of-pornography-and-the-integrity-of-christian-marriage-part-2-75949
6. Timothy Keller, *The Meaning of Marriage: Facing the Complexities of Commitment with the Wisdom of God* (New York: Timothy Keller, 2013), 160-161.
7. "Lowering the Boom," *Dalrock* (blog), December 31, 2012, accessed October 15, 2018, http://dalrock.wordpress.com/2012/12/31/lowering-the-boom.
8. Dave and Ann Wilson, "The Mystery of Intimacy in Marriage," *Family Life Today*, May 2018, http://familylifetoday.com/series/the-mystery-of-intimacy-in-marriage
9. Film description for *Fireproof* (2008) taken from the *Internet Movie Database (IMDb)*, accessed October 15, 2018 http://imdb.com/title/tt1129423
10. Matt Chandler, "10 Questions on Dating with Matt Chandler," *Desiring God*, February 14, 2015, http://www.desiringgod.org/articles/10-questions-on-dating-with-matt-chandler.

11. Dennis Rainey, "The Irresistible Man (Part 1)," *Men Stepping Up* (blog), January 2, 2014, http://mensteppingupblog.com/2014/01/02/irresistible-man-1; . . . Rainey, "The Irresistible Man (Part 2)," January 5, 2014, http://mensteppingupblog.com/2014/01/05/irresistible-man-2
12. C. S. Lewis, *The Allegory of Love* (New York: Oxford University Press, 1958), 36-37.
13. Statistics taken from the *National Institute of Diabetes and Digestive and Kidney Diseases*, Overweight & Obesity Statistics, http://niddk.nih.gov/health-information/health-statistics/overweight-obesity
14. Patricia K. Smith, *Obesity among Poor Americans: Is Public Assistance the Problem?* (Nashville: Vanderbilt University Press, 2009); . . . Tianji Cai, "Obesity and the Timing of Cohabitation and Marriage," (master's thesis, University of NC at Chapel Hill, 2007) http://cdr.lib.unc.edu/indexablecontent/uuid:6cc11cee-eb34-45f0-8ec5-61b78347e48c; . . . Malin Kark and Nina Karnehed, "Weight Status at Age 18 Influences Marriage Prospects. A Population-Based Study of Swedish Men," *US National Library of Medicine National Institute of Health*, September 28, 2012, http://www.ncbi.nlm.nih.gov/pmc/articles/PMC3505734

Chapter 12

1. Wayne Grudem, *Countering the Claims of Evangelical Feminism: Biblical Responses to the Key Questions* (New York: The Doubleday Religious Publishing Co., 2006).

Chapter 13

1. Sheri Stritof, "Estimated Median Age of First Marriage by Gender: 1890 to 2015," *The Spruce*, updated August 4, 2018, http://www.thespruce.com/estimated-median-age-marriage-2303878
2. "The Nations of Europe by the Average Age at First Marriage," accessed January 15, 2019, http://www.worldatlas.com/articles/the-nations-of-europe-by-the-average-age-at-first-marriage.html

Chapter 14

1. Bella DePaulo, Ph.D., "What Is the Divorce Rate, Really?," *Psychology Today*, February 2, 2017, http://www.psychologytoday.com/us/blog/living-single/201702/what-is-the-divorce-rate-really
2. Kirk Johnson, Shannan Martin, Lauren Noyes, and Robert Rector, "Harmful Effects of Early Sexual Activity and Multiple Sexual Partners Among Women: A Book of Charts," *The Heritage Foundation*, June 26, 2003, http://heritage.org/research/reports/2003/06/harmful-effects-of-early-sexual-activity-and-multiple-sexual-partners-among-women-a-book-of-charts
3. "Sexual Partner Divorce Risk," *The Social Pathologist*, September 16, 2010, http://socialpathology.blogspot.com/2010/09/sexual-partner-divorce-risk.html.
4. Steph Cockroft, "Women who Don't Sleep around before their Wedding Have Happier Marriages—but Men Can Play the Field without Worry, Study Finds," *The Daily Mail*, August 24, 2014, http://www.dailymail.co.uk/news/article-2733220/Women-don-t-sleep-wedding-happier-marriages.

5. "Fertility, Family Planning, and Women's Health: New Data From the 1995 National Survey of Family Growth," *U.S. Department of Health and Human Services*, Series 23, No. 19, May 1997, http://cdc.gov/nchs/data/series/sr_23/sr23_019.pdf.
6. "Sexonomics: Odds of Divorce," *Free Northerner*, accessed October 16, 2018, http://free northerner.com/2013/06/21/sexonomics-odds-of-divorce.
7. "Cohabitation, Marriage, Divorce, and Remarriage in the United States," *U.S. Department of Health and Human Services Centers for Disease Control and Prevention National Center for Health Statistics*, Series 23, Number 22, July 2002, http://cdc.gov/nchs/data/series/sr_23/sr23_022.pdf.
8. "Marriage and Cohabitation in the United States: A Statistical Portrait Based on Cycle 6 (2002) of the National Survey of Family Growth," *U.S. Department of Health and Human Services Centers for Disease Control and Prevention National Center for Health Statistics*, Series 23, Number 28, (PHS) 2010-1980, February 2010 http://cdc.gov/nchs/data/series/sr_23/sr23_028.pdf.
9. Anneli Rufus, "Divorce Stats that Can Predict Your Marriage's Success," *The Daily Beast*, May 19, 2010, http://thedailybeast.com/divorce-stats-that-can-predict-your-marriages-success.
10. Rich Morin, "Is Divorce Contagious?", *Pew Research Center*, October 21, 2013, http://pewresearch.org/fact-tank/2013/10/21/is-divorce-contagious
11. American Sociological Association, "Women More Likely than Men to Initiate Divorces, but not Non-Marital Breakups," *American Sociological Association*, August 22, 2015, accessed October 15, 2018, http://asanet.org/press-center/press-releases/women-more-likely-men-initiate-divorces-not-non-marital-breakups
12. Douglas LaBier, "Women Initiate Divorce Much More than Men, Here's Why," *Psychology Today*, August 28, 2015, accessed October 15, 2018, http://psychologytoday.com/us/blog/the-new-resilience/201508/women-initiate-divorce-much-more-men-heres-why

Chapter 15

1. Francis-Tan and Mialon, "A Diamond Is Forever" and "Other Fairy Tales: The Relationship Between Wedding Expenses and Marriage Duration."

Chapter 16

1. "Women More Likely than Men to Initiate Divorces, but not Non-Marital Breakups," . . . "Women Initiate Divorce Much More than Men, Here's Why."
2. "Lowering the Boom."

Chapter 18

1. Brittany Gibbons, "My Husband and I Had Sex Every Day for a Year—Here's How We're Doing Now," *Good Housekeeping*, August 29, 2016, accessed October 16, 2018, http://www.goodhousekeeping.com/life/relationships/a40163/sex-with-my-husband-every-day-for-a-year

Chapter 19

1. Jay Dee, "Some 'Rough' Sex Statistics," *Uncovering Intimacy*, Sex Within Marriage (website), July 19, 2013, accessed October 16, 2018, http://sexwithinmarriage.com/some-rough-sex-statistics
2. "FAQs & Sex Information," *Kinsey Institute University of Indiana*, 2018, accessed October 16, 2018, http://kinseyinstitute.org/research/faq.php
3. "Marriage and Divorce: Patterns by Gender, Race, and Educational Attainment," *United States Department of Labor Bureau of Labor Statistics*, October 2013, accessed October 16, 2018, http://www.bls.gov/opub/mlr/2013/article/marriage-and-divorce-patterns-by-gender-race-and-educational-attainment.htm
4. Sabino Kornrich, Julie Brines, and Katrina Leupp, "Egalitarianism, Housework, and Sexual Frequency in Marriage," *American Sociological Review*, January 30, 2013, http://journals.sagepub.com/doi/abs/10.1177/0003122412472340?journalCode=asra
5. Dee, "Some 'Rough' Sex Statistics."

Chapter 20

1. Yanna J. Weisberg, Colin G. DeYoung, and Jacob B. Hirsh, "Gender Differences in Personality across the Ten Aspects of the Big Five," *Frontiers in Psychology*, 2011; 2: 178. August 1, 2011, http://www.ncbi.nlm.nih.gov/pmc/articles/PMC3149680
2. Dr. Robert Glover, Taken from "The Nice Guy Syndrome," *Dr. Glover* (website), 2018, accessed October 16, 2018, http://www.drglover.com/no-more-mr-nice-guy.html
3. Luke Kerr-Dineen, "17 of the Most Bill Belichick Quotes of All Time: 'We're onto Cincinnati,'" *USA Today*, July 31, 2017, http://ftw.usatoday.com/2017/07/bill-belichick-funny-press-conderence-quotes

ABOUT THE AUTHOR

Stephen Casper lives in the Pacific Northwest, after having traveled all over the country for his education. He currently serves as a leader in the men's ministry at his church and is involved in discipling young men.

He was inspired to write *The Biblical Masculinity Blueprint* after having seen many different churches across the country that had a lack of quality men's ministry, resulting in floundering young adults in a culture that is progressively becoming more hostile toward Christians. Stephen also noticed that many churches avoid addressing difficult topics like attraction, relationships, and marriage from a biblical perspective out of fear of offending others. This has led to incomplete discipleship for both single and married Christian men.

Stephen works as a consultant for a healthcare company and enjoys spending time with his wife, Meghan, and their children.

Made in the USA
Las Vegas, NV
09 May 2021

22556016R00164